SOUTH AFRICAN WAR MACHINE

SOUTH AFRICAN WAR MACHINE

Helmoed-Römer Heitman

R 27104

Published in United states by
Presidio Press
31 Pamaron Way
Novato, CA 94947
USA

Produced by Bison Books Corp.
17 Sherwood Place,
Greenwich, CT. 06830
USA

ISBN 0−89141−240−9

Printed in Hong Kong

Reprinted 1985.

AUTHOR'S NOTE: Statistics and equipment
performance figures are taken from generally-
available published sources.

Page 1: A patrol pictured during counterinsurgency
training in the northern Cape.
Page 2-3: Ratel-20 infantry fighting vehicle.
Below: An Alouette helicopter moves into a guarded
landing zone.

CONTENTS

PUBLISHER'S PREFACE

The purpose of this book is to present the facts of the South African defence establishment to a Western audience who have not had much opportunity to appreciate the strengths and weaknesses of this formidable force. Little is known about the specific policies of South Africa, particularly with respect to its military machine. Some argue that its principal purpose is, more often than not, to contain its own black citizens. Others believe it maintains a defence force to protect its borders against aggressive neighbours, including those backed by the Soviets. Still others would argue that South Africa secretly harbours expansionist ambitions toward these neighbours and is building up its military might, perhaps the strongest on the African continent, to accomplish these ends. Critics might advance a case for a combination of all these factors. Whatever the reasons, South Africa has a powerful air force, a small but well-organised naval force, and a dynamic though idiosyncratic land army. Details on the composition of these forces are known only to experts on the subject and are often highly classified.

Right: Two of the strike craft flotilla cruising off the Natal coast.
Below: A Buccaneer of 24 Squadron makes a high-speed low-level pass.

The author, for the first time, presents the facts on South Africa's war machine to a wider public. Helmoed-Römer Heitman is well informed on the subject, having served for 15 years in the South African Army, and has taken many of the photographs in this book.

In order to obtain other excellent photographs, and to publish the book in the Republic of South Africa, the manuscript had to be cleared by the Government in Pretoria. Readers should be aware of this fact. This does not mean that the book is a propaganda piece or an apologia; it is not. *The South African War Machine* presents the facts and illuminates areas not covered as succinctly or openly in any reasonably available publication. The publishers believe that these facts should be known. Although South African Defence Force officials read the manuscript, they made very few changes, all of them related to items perceived as affecting national security.

When he was commissioned by the publishers, the author was asked to eschew any discussion of political matters, particularly the subject of racial discrimination. He has followed his brief in explaining how the South African war machine works. He does not explain fully its motivations. The publishers feel that

some mention of this point must be made in this preface. The author shows that South Africa, while it was a self-governing Dominion within the British Commonwealth, played a substantial role as an ally of the Western Powers during both World Wars and thereafter. The erosion of the Simonstown Agreement, South Africa's gradual withdrawal from the Commonwealth, and the country's subsequent isolation were caused principally by changing attitudes in the West toward the Government's *apartheid* policy and its posture of white racial supremacy. This fundamental fact is alluded to, but not openly discussed, in the book. Similarly, unconfirmed rumours of the presence and development of lethal gas in South Africa are not discussed, and the possibility of South African possession of nuclear weapons is touched upon only briefly. The author confines himself almost entirely to areas of substantiated fact. These facts indicate that the policy of isolation undertaken by the United States and its NATO allies have made very little difference in the overall policies of the country.

Therefore, the publishers welcome Mr. Heitman's manuscript and its circulation throughout the world. In the African context, the South African war machine is formidable and complex, incorporating black as well as white soldiers, employing weapons from many countries as well as those produced locally, showing both great strengths and significant weaknesses. It is in the interest of presenting these facts that the publishers see fit to produce and distribute this unique work.

S L Mayer
Publisher, Bison Books

INTRODUCTION

Militarily the most powerful nation in southern Africa, the Republic of South Africa has often been cast in the role of regional bully in recent years. Major accusations have revolved around the Angolan intervention of 1975/6, the 'illegal occupation' of South-West Africa and, most recently, the supposed 'destabilisation' of her neighbours. To these is added the spice of possible RSA possession of nuclear weapons, and the whole is then used to substantiate the older claim that South Africa is a threat to world peace because of her internal policies.

The South African Defence Force (SADF) today is indeed disproportionately more powerful than the forces of any neighbouring state. The reasons for this, however, are readily apparent. First, the primary current threat to South Africa is one of cross-border insurgency, which by its very nature makes heavy manpower demands on the defender and requires a good measure of conventional power if the insurgents are to be hit in their bases rather than allowed to take the initiative. Second, the SADF is faced with long open

Right: Troops being transported in a C-160 Transall.
Below: Preparing for a sortie in an Impala I trainer.

borders and the additional problem of a second front in northern South-West Africa (SWA). Third, the events in Angola and Ethiopia have amply demonstrated the rapidity with which the military situation can be changed by intervention from outside.

From another viewpoint, South Africa is seen as an essential ally of the West. Initially, this argument was predicated chiefly on her importance as protector of a key choke point on the vital shipping route around the Cape of Good Hope. In more recent times, some strategists have taken to discounting the importance of this role, arguing that the Soviets do not have any demonstrable intention to interfere with Western shipping in the southern oceans. While this may be open to debate, the risk inherent in this assumption is great – fully 60% of Europe's and more than 20% of America's oil imports pass around the Cape, as do some 25% of Europe's food supplies. Given the realities of war, the limited Soviet bases in parts of Africa might also prove less easy to neutralise than is now envisaged – if only because Western forces may be too heavily engaged elsewhere. Even small numbers of submarines and long-range aircraft operating from such bases could prove to have a disproportionately dangerous effect.

Other aspects of South Africa's potential importance to the West have also been recognised in recent years and accorded their true relevance. South Africa is a major or even primary source of many minerals essential to Western technology, and is also the industrial base on which much of the exploitation of similar minerals elsewhere in the region depends. This aspect has been all-too-clearly recognised by the Soviets – with typical frankness, Brezhnev stated in 1977 that it was their aim to gain control of 'the two great treasure houses of the world, the fuel treasure house of the Middle East and the minerals treasure house of southern Africa'. An even more recent realisation revolves around the sad fact that South Africa is also virtually the only nation on the continent still able to produce a food surplus. With population growth almost everywhere outstripping the growth in food supplies, this is fast becoming a factor of critical importance in long-term planning.

Whatever the particular view of South Africa, the question of her defence potential is a matter of considerable relevance to the region and – in longer-term consideration – beyond. An understanding of the capabilities of this regionally very powerful force and of the policy governing its possible employment is, therefore, important.

The basic philosophy of South African defence policy and the core of its strategic and operational doctrine can be traced to just after the arrival of the first European settlers at the Cape in 1652. Intended merely as a refreshment station for ships of the Dutch East India Company, this early settlement comprised only company officials and their families defended by a small detachment of mercenaries. Within a few years, however, some of those officials and soldiers whose service had expired chose to stay on at the Cape as 'free burghers', most of whom settled down to farm on the fringes of the settlement. Inevitably, they soon came into conflict with the migrant Hottentot cattle farmers.

The small detachment at the Company's fort quickly proved too weak and too immobile to offer any real protection beyond its immediate environs. Faced with this problem and increasing difficulties with Hottentot raids, the outlying free burghers formed themselves into small volunteer mounted defence units. As the station changed into a colony and expanded into the interior, these mounted Commandos, as they had become known, increasingly formed the backbone of the settlers' defence. One of the cornerstones of South African defence policy had been laid – the almost complete reliance on a citizen army.

The British period in southern Africa began with the seizure of the Cape by an expeditionary force in September 1795. The colony was formally ceded to Great Britain by the Batavian Republic in 1814 after the defeat of Napoleon. For the next century and a half, South Africa was to remain solidly within the British sphere of influence and could hardly be said to have an independent defence policy. The only real exception to British domination of South Africa were the Boer republics, formed by Afrikaners migrating northward from 1834 to escape British influence. They finally gained their independence in the Orange Free State and the Transvaal early in the 1850s, when Britain briefly lost interest in the region. This period saw a major resurgence of the Commando system, which the British had

Above: Former Chief of the Army and current Chief of the SADF, General Constand Viljoen.

phased out. The need for fast-moving, wide-ranging operations conducted with élan became particularly clear, as relatively small Commandos were often pitted against much larger raiding forces and responsible for long stretches of frontier. The key to Commando success was largely in mobility coupled with flexible and sometimes innovative tactics. This approach to the conduct of war has remained one of the cornerstones of South African defence ever since and is reflected in Army doctrine.

Once the Boers had settled down, they attempted to live in peace with their neighbours if at all possible. But if hostili-

Below: Part of the Republic Day parade in Durban on 31 May 1980.

Above: A mounty rides up to refill his water bottles from the capacious water tanks of a Buffel. All SA Army vehicles are designed with water supplies in mind.

ties were inevitable, they seized the initiative, if only to the extent of demonstrating to the errant neighbour that hostility was unprofitable. Another cornerstone of South African defence policy had been laid.

As soon as it became clear that the Boers' territory was worth having – first diamonds and then gold having been discovered – Britain quickly regained her interest in the region as a whole and especially in the two Republics. The Transvaal was reannexed in 1877, only to be released again after its Commandos had inflicted a painful military setback on British forces. Not to be put off, Britain was soon back in the game, seizing territory around the Republics and striving to isolate them. A small-scale invasion of the Transvaal followed in 1895 – the notorious Jameson Raid, which it had been hoped would spark off a revolt of the non-Afrikaners in the Transvaal and lead to the fall of the Kruger Government. This having failed, and neither Republic showing any signs of succumbing, full-scale war came

in 1899, as described in chapter 2. As a result, all of South Africa remained part of the British Empire until 1962, albeit as a self-governing entity after 1910. The two British colonies of the Cape and Natal were joined by the former Transvaal and Orange Free State Republics in the Union of South Africa in 1910, and a national defence force was established two years later. The Union Defence Force (UDF) incorporated elements of both the British and Boer defence systems. The final cornerstone of the South African approach to defence had been laid – a blend of the freewheeling warfare of the Boer Commandos and the more systematic approach required in modern war. By and large, this spirit has been maintained and fostered in the South African forces ever since.

Another milestone in the development of defence policy – and of the South African Defence Force (SADF) – came in 1961 when South Africa opted to become a republic; she left the Commonwealth in the following year. While basic defence policy did not change appreciably at that stage – remaining essentially an extension of British and Western defence interests – the SADF itself began to evolve from a

virtual appendage of British forces into a defence force in its own right, with its own doctrines, policies, intelligence system, senior training programmes and strategic forecasting ability. At service level, a distinct South African character also began to emerge which, in turn, affected the development of doctrines and policy. This coincided with a limited modernisation of the SADF resulting from a 1960 defence appreciation of the increasingly unstable international situation and the then poor state of the SADF.

Turmoil in Africa during the early 1960s, as exemplified by the events in the Congo and the outbreak of terrorism in Angola and Mozambique, confirmed the possibility of a southern African problem unrelated to an actual East-West armed clash. Despite this, no serious local threat was foreseen – any insurgency problems that might crop up would be left largely to the police. Much of the existing danger would, in any event, be absorbed by the Portuguese provinces and Rhodesia, as there was no direct access to South Africa herself. Even the insurgency beginning in northern SWA with the South-West Africa People's Organzation, or SWAPO, did not evoke a major re-evaluation of the situ-

Above: DC-4s are used for shuttle duties within South Africa as well as for transport tasks within the Operational Area.

ation. A conventional threat was regarded as so obviously unfeasible that it hardly merited consideration. As late as the early 1970s, many held that it would be 'logistically impossible' for any major conventional force to be deployed to and operated in Africa south of the Sahara.

To some extent, this sense of security was fostered by police successes in putting a virtual end to the sabotage efforts of the 'military wings' of the African National Congress (ANC) and the Pan African Congress (PAC) which had been active from the early 1950s until 1963. The ANC had been founded in 1912 to promote black interests, but had been gradually taken over by the SA Communist Party; a communist became secretary-general of the ANC as early as 1936. Banned in 1950, the South African Communist Party created the 'Congress of Democrats' through which it exercised a good measure of control over the various organisations it had infiltrated. The PAC was created in 1959 by a breakaway faction that found the ANC too moderate. A 'military wing' of the PAC – Poqo – was soon established, with the ANC creating its 'Spear of the Nation' in 1961. Both organisations resorted increasingly to sabotage and were finally banned in 1963, after which sabotage died down almost completely.

The importance of the Cape Sea Route was underlined after the 1967 war in the Middle East, which resulted in closing of the Suez Canal until after the 1973 war in the same region. This period saw a massive increase in shipping movements around the Cape, an increase which would recur should the Canal be closed again for any reason. The rapidly increasing naval potential of the Soviets – not least the growth in their 'blue water' capability and their submarine fleet – served as a further pointer to the importance of protecting the Sea Lines of Communication. Against this background, the protection of the Cape of Good Hope 'choke point' on the Cape sea route, and of its strategic hinterland in the form of the South African industrial base and ports, continued to be seen by many as the major function of the SADF acting in effect as a component of Western defence. Even the early efforts at imposing an arms embargo on the RSA during the mid-1960s initially did little to change the Republic's self-image as an outlying bastion of the West.

By the late 1960s, South Africa had come to accept that she could not fully rely on support from her erstwhile allies, although the idea did linger that the West would come to her aid in the event of a major Soviet-sponsored attack. While this did not bring with it any major reorientation of defence policy, it did result in efforts to

Below: A Super Frelon transport helicopter moves in to land with a reaction force during a counter-insurgency exercise.

Above: Map of South Africa, her neighbours and the homelands.
Below: Jan Smuts and Louis Botha in 1919.

make her less dependent on foreign support and arms. The basis for an expanded defence force was also created by the introduction in 1968 of universal national service for white males. Arguably the most important result of this realisation was the considerable upgrading of local armaments production capability. This investment was shown to be a wise one when the Western Powers let the mandatory arms embargo be imposed against South Africa. By then South Africa was well on the way toward meeting many of her defence requirements from internal production and had provided for the immediate future in other fields by means of judicious purchases such as the Mirage F-1s and the navy's strike craft.

Another development of the late 1960s and through the 1970s was the evolution of what has since became known as a 'total defence' policy. This grew out of the realisation that South Africa was not faced merely with low-level insurgency and perhaps a somewhat nebulous conventional threat, but was, in fact, being subjected to a well-orchestrated campaign in several fields. In addition to the military threat, a series of both external and internal measures were being effected via the strategic indirect approach, fitting in neatly with the Marxist preference for achieving gains without war whenever possible. Fortunately, this aspect of the Marxist approach to the conduct of both war and peace had been frankly discussed by its originators and practitioners on many occasions and had also been exemplified in the recent past. Thus there was little difficulty in grasping first its essentials and then its application to the question of South Africa.

Designed to isolate South Africa from her former Western allies, the external component of this attack covers trade, scientific, cultural and even sporting matters, as well as the more obvious areas of arms supplies and military contacts. Internally, there are renewed and continuing efforts at aggravating existing problems, alienating elements of the population from each other and from the government and subverting specific groups – not least the intellectual element of white youth. In combination, these two components are intended to weaken South Africa sufficiently to allow successful development of insurgency. Should insurgency alone not succeed, South Africa would by then be sufficiently isolated from possible allies to allow the necessary military intervention without fear of seriously complicating the East-West situation.

The most effective counter seemed to be a properly co-ordinated and fully integrated national security policy addressing much the same spectrum as the attacks. The basic mechanism for devising, co-ordinating and controlling such a policy was created in 1977 in the form of the State Security Council, which groups those ministries most concerned with national security matters – Defence, Foreign Affairs, Police and Justice. Its brief is to formulate a co-ordinated and fully interdepartmental national security policy for the cabinet and thereafter to monitor its execution and modification as necessary. The new integrated national security system began to operate by the end of the 1970s. The result has been the formulation of a 'total' strategy to counter what was termed a 'total onslaught'. 'Total' in each case refers not to the extent to which measures are taken, but to the fact that the entire spectrum of possible activities is taken into account and addressed.

Meanwhile, a coup in Portugal in 1974 led to her withdrawal from her African provinces. Almost overnight, the situation had changed from one of the insurgencies in South Africa's neighbours facing certain and relatively early defeat, to one where hostile Marxist governments would soon be in power on her borders. A major rethink of South African defence policy was now urgently required, although the problem was not entirely unforeseen and the first steps toward upgrading the army and air force had already been taken. In 1973 the Army had also assumed responsibility for operations in northern SWA. The real turning point in South African defence thinking and policy then came with the arrival of the Cuban expeditionary force in Angola. This proved once and for all what some had been warning of for many years – that a major military force could be inserted into southern Africa at very short notice. The events in the Ogaden served only to highlight this fact.

The combination of these developments –the end of the Simonstown era, the collapse of the Portuguese, the arrival of the Cubans and the imposition of a mandatory arms embargo – finally cleared South Africa's vision to the fact that she was essentially on her own. This was emphasised by the unhappy experience of Operation Savannah, which saw SA forces enter Angola. The Angolan civil war also left South Africa with the legacy of the large Cuban force that had been inserted by the Soviets. Hanging over SWA as an ever-present baleful hint of what could well happen should SWAPO be rejected at the polls, this force has also further complicated the issue.

Other factors have influenced South Africa's view of her defence position, including Western inability to deal with the 1973 crisis in the Middle East, the termination of the US-Chinese (Taipei) defence treaty and the handling of Rhodesia's transition to majority rule, none of which gave any cause for confidence in the West. Even then, however, defence expenditure remained relatively low. Over the ten years from 1975 to 1984, defence expenditure averaged just over 16 percent of government spending and only once exceeded 5 percent of GNP. By contrast, neutral Switzerland and Yugoslavia both devote over 20 percent of government expenditure to defence, as do Germany (28.2 percent in 1982), Greece (25.7), Turkey (21.6) and the USA (27), and France spends around 18 percent. Many of the Latin American and Asian countries spend well over 16 per-

Above: Churchill and Smuts meeting during World War II. Despite his background as a Boer leader Smuts became one of the most-respected statesmen within the British Empire.

Below: Minister of Defence Magnus Malan is particularly experienced for his post having been both Chief of the Army and of the SADF.

cent and the figures for Middle Eastern countries such as Israel, Oman and Saudi Arabia are much higher.

The upshot of these developments was that South Africa found herself in a position not dissimilar to that of the old Boer republics: dependent on a militia-based defence force, cut off from ready sources of new equipment and faced with hostile neighbours. Not surprisingly, she took recourse to the traditional South African approach to defence forged in the early frontier wars and clashes. The first clear sign of a change in policy since the shift to a local rather than a Western outlook came in 1978, when a number of PLAN bases in southern Angola were attacked by SA forces. The message was clear: the insurgents could not expect to carry out their campaign of terrorism in northern SWA from the cosy security of inviolate sanctuaries in neighbouring Angola.

The Angolan Government initially misread the situation and reacted by allowing PLAN elements to 'hug' FAPLA bases, in the belief that South Africa would not risk the escalation inherent in a clash with a neighbouring country's forces. While they were correct in that this was something South Africa has strenuously sought to avoid, they were incorrect in thinking that it would end security-force raids on PLAN bases and camps. Limited intervention by FAPLA followed, including demonstrations by their air force. These did not produce the desired result either, as FAPLA – equipped largely with second-hand and often obsolescent Soviet equipment, and under trained – proved unable seriously to hinder the raiding forces.

Finally, in 1983, the Angolan Government – faced with increasing Unita pressure and successes – accepted the situation as it was and entered into a disengagement agreement with South Africa. In terms of this agreement, a wide strip of southern Angola will be cleared of

and closed to PLAN. In return, the security forces will cease their operations into this region. This move will prove seriously embarassing to SWAPO, as its 'military' wing will be unable to sustain the present level of operations for long without access through Angola. An attempt in early 1984 to infiltrate through Botswana failed when the group was picked up and destroyed on entering SWA. It has also done little to endear SWAPO to the Botswana Government, which has no desire to become involved in this way.

A major aspect of this agreement for the Angolan Government is that it will free FAPLA to concentrate entirely on its operations against Unita. Another hope will be that whatever assistance that movement may still be getting from South Africa via SWA will now cease. While it has frequently been alleged that South Africa is Unita's chief backer, there is doubt as to just how much of Unita's support does in fact still come from South Africa. Certainly there are several other African states, and also strong interests in the West, that favour Unita. In any event, it seems most unlikely that no alternatives have been prepared for the possible termination of South African aid. Thus while this agreement will prove a setback for Unita, that movement is probably too well established to be readily defeated by any means short of a major increase in the foreign forces in Angola. This, in turn, would bring forth a South African reaction, as it would be seen as materially affecting both the security and the political situation in SWA.

On South Africa's eastern border, meanwhile, the installation of a Marxist government in Mozambique had come to the ANC and PAC like a gift from the gods,

Bottom right: Stopping for a quick brew of tea is still a regular occurrence in the South African Army – a legacy of former days that seems unlikely to die out.
Below: Buffels crossing a dry river bed while following a tracker team. The trackers are ahead out of earshot while a relief team rests on the vehicles.

Left: A Puma refuels from a fuel bladder on a 10 tonne Kwevoel at a company base in northern Owambo.
Right: An Eland-60 being rearmed and reloaded after a regular maintenance check at a battalion base in central Owambo.

finally providing them with direct access to their targets in South Africa. Acts of sabotage and terrorism within the RSA increased quite markedly in the years after 1975, including a number of such 'spectaculars' as the blasting of a part of the SASOL oil-from-coal plant and the rocketing of the Voortrekkerhoogte military township outside Pretoria. Other attacks were launched by a revitalised ANC operation from Lesotho, which now had a home base nearby, while other groups operated through Swaziland. The situation was further complicated by the operations of insurgents in both Lesotho and Mozambique.

The former country has been suffering the predations of the Lesotho Liberation Army since the late 1970s. The LLA is the 'military' wing of the Basotho Congress Party, which was banned and exiled by Prime Minister Leabua Jonathan after it defeated him in the 1970 elections. Its activities increased markedly from 1979, leading to repeated allegations that it is armed and fostered by South Africa. Certainly the LLA has operated through South Africa in the past – 20 Libyan-

trained LLA personnel were arrested by the SAP in late 1979 en route to Lesotho, for instance, and smaller groups have been encountered from time to time since. Whether South Africa has actively supported the LLA is another question. It does seem quite likely, however, that South Africa has not been particularly concerned with preventing LLA operations against Lesotho while she has to guard against ANC raids from that country. Indeed, the Lesotho Government has gone so far as to claim that the former Commissioner of Police said as much to them in discussion.

Mozambique, in turn, has long been suffering the attentions of the Mozambique National Resistance Movement, which has recently taken to calling itself Renamo. Initially fostered and probably started by the Rhodesian Central Intelligence Organisation in an effort to hinder Frelimo support for the insurgents of Robert Mugabe, the MNR appears to have taken on a life of its own. Again, South African backing is regularly alleged, although this may often be done chiefly to save face – it cannot, after all, be easy for a 'Liberation Movement' like Frelimo to admit that a few years after coming to power it finds itself facing an insurgency: far better that the problems be ascribed to a powerful capitalist neighbour. Similar reasoning is applied by Afghanistan and the Soviets *vis à vis* the Mujahiddin. According to the allegations, South Africa took over the operation from the CIO after Rhodesia became Zimbabwe in 1980 and has been running it ever since. South Africa has consistently denied this and, given her record in keeping secrets, it seems likely that any major involvement would have leaked long ago.

Whether or not South Africa was indeed involved in backing either of these insurgent groups, she did give warning in February 1983 that she might consider doing so. Declaring her intention of fighting her enemies by all possible means, Minister of Defence Magnus Malan went on to say: 'Even if it means we will have to support anti-communist movements ... and allow them to operate from our territory'. This clear warning that South Africa might choose to interpret the succouring of insurgents as an act of covert war and respond accordingly was reinforced by repeated warnings that she would certainly hit at insurgent targets in neighbouring states if their governments did nothing

Left: An Eland-90 on patrol in central Owambo. The Eland-90 is said to be particularly feared by insurgents.
Right: Alouette III on the ground after a contact with the dead insurgents lying in the foreground.

to stop the launching of terrorism from their territory. All of these warnings went unheeded in the neighbouring capitals.

Finally, two-and-a-half years after the first raid into Angola, South Africa also stopped turning the other cheek on her eastern frontier with the raids on Matola and Maseru described below. The final clincher was the raid on ANC offices in Maputo city itself in October 1983.

The message now finally registered with the Mozambique Government, and earlier talks with South Africa were quickly followed up. The two countries signed a treaty of non-aggression and good neighbourliness on 16 March 1984, which provided – among other points – for

the prevention of insurgent operations from the territory of either against the other. The Swazi Government had already taken steps to expel armed ANC elements after the Maseru raid, preferring to learn from others' unhappy experiences rather than at first hand. The government of Lesotho took similar steps soon after. The net result is that, for the time being at least, the ANC and PAC will face considerable difficulties in infiltrating the Republic. Much as in an earlier era, the policy of uncompromising reaction to violence, coupled with an offer of good neighbourliness as an alternative to escalating military action, has brought a respite from conflict. How long this will last will depend, as always, on the degree to which the respective governments can learn to live with each other.

Below: Eland-90s in supporting positions as infantry cast around for traces of a spoor that has become difficult to follow.

Above: An Albatross P166S in flight near Cape Town.
Right: Trackers in the Owambo bush following a group of about ten insurgents who were later caught and attacked by another unit.

R 723 35

SOUTH AFRICAN DEFENCE TODAY

It should be noted at the outset that the South African Defence Force has a policy of not giving information concerning equipment holdings or purchases. It also does not, as a rule, give technical information concerning locally produced or modified equipment, making an exception here only with regard to items offered for export. All figures quoted in this book have, therefore, been compiled from reputable public sources such as the Jane's series of handbooks and *The Military Balance* of the International Institute for Strategic Studies.

The South African defence family consists essentially of the South African Defence Force (SADF) and the Armaments Corporation of South Africa (Armscor), both of which fall directly under the Minister of Defence. Armscor is also responsible directly to the SADF in matters of armaments procurement. The SADF itself presently comprises a Defence Headquarters (DHQ) in Pretoria, four combat services (Army, Air Force, Navy and Medical) and two supporting services (Quartermaster General and Chaplain General). Fellow members of the wider security family are the National Intelligence Service (NIS) under the Prime Minister, and the South African Police (SAP) which has specific counterinsurgency and anti-terrorist elements.

National defence policy is generated by the State Security Council (SSC) for the Cabinet as a part of National Security Policy. Chaired by the Prime Minister, the SSC comprises the Ministers of Defence, Foreign Affairs, Interior, Police and Justice and the longest-serving minister (if

Previous page: Mirage F-1CZs of 3 Squadron in formation.
Below: Radio-control model aircraft are used as training aids and as targets for air defence units.

he is not one of the above), the Chief of the SADF, the Commissioner of Police, the head of the NIS and the Directors General of Foreign Affairs, Interior and Justice. These top officials also form the SSC Work Committee, which is responsible for national strategic planning and for co-ordinating the work of the 14 interdepartmental committees which process SSC directives into interdepartmental strategies. The executive function is with the individual departments.

Planning within the SADF has three basic elements. The first is Force Design, which encompasses the determination of SADF strategy in accordance with national strategy, threat analyses, national and SADF capabilities. From this basic SADF strategy are derived missions, tasks and requirements and their order of priority. Force Development then seeks to provide the manpower, materiel and funds in the optimum mix and order. Finally, Force Application concerns itself with the concrete planning required to execute SADF strategy to satisfy the requirements of national strategy.

The chief planning organs of the SADF are the Defence Command Council (DCC), the Defence Planning Committee (DPC) and the Defence Staff Council (DSC), all chaired by the Chief of the SADF. They are supported by the Defence Staff, which carries out preliminary and detail work, provides most of the necessary information and translates decisions into action at SADF level. The DCC is the highest command authority within the SADF and conforms SADF policy and strategy to national strategy and SSC guidelines, subject to Ministerial approval. It is also responsible for the conduct of strategic planning and the operational application of the SADF. Its members are the Chiefs of the services, the Inspector General of the SADF, the Chief of Staff, Operations and the Chiefs of the other staff divisions.

The DPC provides SADF/Armscor liaison and is responsible for ensuring that the budget, five-year plan and procurement plan are in accordance with the policy formulated by the Defence Command Council and remain within the financial limits set by the Cabinet. It also exercises control over joint SADF/Armscor project teams and project definition committees. Its members are the Chiefs of the combat services, the Inspector General of the SADF, the Chiefs of Staff, Operations, Logistics and Finance, the Chairman and the Chief Executive of Armscor and an industry representative.

The DSC is the highest co-ordinating level within the SADF. Its members are the Chief of Staff, Operations (Deputy Chairman), the Chiefs of the other staff divisions (Intelligence, Logistics, Personnel and Finance), the Chaplain General and the Inspector General of the SADF.

One other top-level body is the Defence Manpower Liaison Committee. This comprises the Chief of Staff, Personnel; the Chiefs of Staff, Personnel of the combat services; and representatives of 21 employer organisations. Its primary role is to ensure communication and understanding between the SADF and the private sector concerning the common manpower base. It confines its work to the policy level, leaving the practical aspects to regional committees under the chairmanship of the officers commanding the territorial commands.

Actual command is exercised by the Chief of the SADF through the Chiefs of the Army, Air Force, Navy and Medical Service and through Joint Forces Commanders who are appointed when major elements of different services are to

operate together for extended periods or in an important operation. Joint Air Force/ Navy operations are largely planned and controlled by the Maritime HQ at Silvermine near Cape Town. Operations in northern South-West Africa fall under the General Officer Commanding the SWA Territory Force. General directives, missions and specific tasks are assigned by the DCC.

The available force consists of two components. First, there is a small full-

Right: Army earth boring equipment reflects the South African Forces' concern to support their operations in dry areas.
Below: An Olifant main battle tank and transporter on parade. The Olifant is based on the elderly British Centurion design.

time force of Permanent Force (PF) personnel and National Servicemen (NSM) rendering their initial period of continuous service. Second, there is the part-time force consisting of the Citizen Force (CF) and the Commandos, comprising some 80% of total SADF strength and available en bloc only upon mobilisation. Elements are called up on a cyclic basis for 90-day periods of operational duty, but these represent only a fraction of the total force. Both the Air Force and the Navy man the greater part of their combat elements from the full-time force and rely on their CF component mainly for supportive tasks. The Army, on the other hand, relies on the part-time force for most of its combat strength.

This manpower shortage is a serious constraint on SADF strategic thinking and planning. With the bulk of the Army available only upon mobilisation, it is essential that the SADF not be surprised by any major attack. An attacker with the advantage of surprise could hope to inflict a defeat in detail by forcing the SADF to accept combat piecemeal. At the speed of conventional operations today, it would simply not be feasible for the SADF to allow an enemy to roam unhindered while it mobilises and groups for battle. At the same time, it cannot guard against this danger by means of a preventive mobilisation, as this would draw off many workers from the economy, possibly causing irreparable harm if maintained for any length of time.

This manpower base situation mandates that the SADF adopts a policy of pre-empting any serious threat that cannot be deterred. Only in this way can the demands of defence be reconciled with minimal economic disruption. This policy applies equally to a conventional threat and to one of cross-border insurgency. The latter may not bring with it the danger of immediate catastrophe, but it could impose such manpower demands as to impair economic activity seriously. Quite apart from this, both the government and the SADF feel very strongly that they have a moral duty to protect their citizens by the most effective means available. As a result, trans-border sanctuaries for insurgents are not a concept enjoying their support.

Pre-emption is a task falling chiefly to

Main picture: Mirage F-1CZ of 3 Squadron on a training flight from the squadron's base at Waterkloof near Pretoria.
Below right: A formation of Alouette III helicopters. Alouettes serve in a number of utility roles including search and rescue and casualty evacuation.
Below: Mounting a V3B air-to-air missile on a Mirage F-1. The V3B's seeker head is linked to a sighting system on the pilot's helmet, giving a very effective performance.

the SAAF and to the small full-time element of the Army. Even so, both economic and manpower costs are involved, in addition to political problems. Then too, a major operation of this nature will require mobilising at least part of the Citizen Force – the Parachute Brigade, for example, is largely CF. Pre-emption, then, is not the whole answer but a complement to the deterrent effect of a fully mobilised SADF. The bulk of this deterrent lies in the Army's conventional force of two largely CF-manned divisions. Here lies the true role of the CF: in providing the defence potential that raises an attacker's risk to an unattrative level. The hope is that those too powerful to be deterred will be at least dissuaded. Pre-emption is the last resort.

The same considerations that govern

Right: Infantry prepare to set out on patrol in their Buffel in the central Owambo district of SWA.

Above: A casualty being evacuated to a waiting Puma helicopter.

the SADF's adoption of this policy make it nearly incapable of invading or occupying a neighbour. The necessary mobilisation would rob it of any real measure of surprise, and the economic damage attendant on a lengthy operation would be unacceptable in all but the gravest circumstances. Thus the basic policy of deterrence cum pre-emption is expressed in a 'short-sharp' war strategy for conventional war and semi-conventional operations in counterinsurgency. This, in turn, is expressed in a doctrine of fast-moving, flexible, wide-ranging and violent joint operations.

In spite of the inherent difficulties and limitations, there is no likelihood that the SADF will change its nature, which is essentially that of a militia. This is partly a matter of tradition, but more a result of the dual economy that combines a small, highly developed industrial sector with a rather larger, less developed one. As such, the economy is systemically short of skilled manpower – the most pressing need of a modern defence system. The situation is further complicated by the very rapid growth of the black population; job-creation, therefore, forms a critical element of government policy, placing more strain on available skilled manpower. Thus requests for an enlarged full-time force will not be well received for the time being.

What the SADF may seek to do in the future, however, is to push for extension of national service to the Coloured and Indian groups. This, it is hoped, will enlarge the full-time force sufficiently to eliminate, or at least greatly reduce, the need to call up CF personnel for extended service. What it will not do is address the serious shortfall in the PF. This is due largely to the intense competition by industry for the available technical and managerial manpower, which has long caused the SADF a grave retention problem. To some extent, this is being addressed by a new differentiated pay structure, but this has yet to prove itself. For now, the SADF remains excessively dependent on university-qualified NSM to fill important posts.

If national service is, in fact, extended to the Coloured and Indian groups, this could have one major effect on policy in that it would allow the SADF to absorb a higher level of insurgency before resorting to cross-border strikes. It would not, however, affect the general principle and would have no real effect on the reaction to a conventional threat, as both long-term mobilisation and lengthy operations would remain impractical options except in dire circumstances. The SADF of the

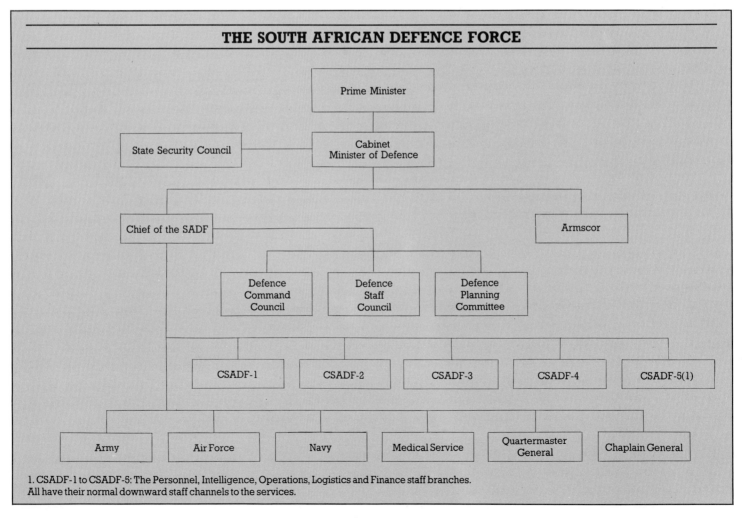

THE SOUTH AFRICAN DEFENCE FORCE

Prime Minister

State Security Council

Cabinet
Minister of Defence

Chief of the SADF

Armscor

Defence Command Council

Defence Staff Council

Defence Planning Committee

CSADF-1

CSADF-2

CSADF-3

CSADF-4

CSADF-5(1)

Army

Air Force

Navy

Medical Service

Quartermaster General

Chaplain General

1. CSADF-1 to CSADF-5: The Personnel, Intelligence, Operations, Logistics and Finance staff branches. All have their normal downward staff channels to the services.

medium-term future will remain, therefore, a force that is compelled to pre-empt any serious threat simply as a byproduct of its essentially defensive structure and posture.

The National Service System

The SADF is manned primarily by personnel rendering some phase of their national service. PF personnel and civilians in the employ of the SADF make up only some 10% of total strength. NSM make up another 10%, while the rest comprises the CF and the Commandos and is essentially a militia.

The national service system presently provides for white male South Africans to be liable for service from the year in which they turn 18 to that in which they turn 55. Women and members of other groups are not liable for compulsory service but are free to render voluntary service or to join the PF if they wish. National Service itself is divided into four basic periods.

1. Two years of full-time initial service, during which the NSM are trained for their specific duties and roles and experience some routine or operational service. Some are trained as junior leaders during the first year, then serve the rest of this period as second lieutenants or corporals.

2. Twelve years in a CF unit or 20 years in a Commando for those declared 'area bound' because they are unable to leave their work or dependents for lengthy periods.

3. Five years in the Active CF Reserve, during which personnel will not be called up except in emergency. There is no equivalent period for the Commandos.

4. Nineteen years (CF) or 16 years (Commando) service in a Commando with a maximum liability of 12 days a year. Again, personnel will only be called on to serve these days if actually needed.

Those serving in CF units are required to serve a maximum of 720 days during this period. This is theoretically divided into two-year cycles of one 30-day training camp or promotion course and one 90-day period of operational service. In practice, personnel are only called up when they are actually needed, so many will not serve the full term. Those who receive any deferment of their service will have to stay in this phase until they have completed the requisite number of days. Commando personnel are required to serve a maximum of 50 days per year during this period and are not employed outside the area of their territorial Command.

The South African Medical Service

The SA Medical Service (SAMS) can trace its origin to the formation of the Transvaal Ambulance Corps – all of 100 strong with 500 pounds worth of equipment and stores – in 1893. Renamed the Transvaal Red Cross when the Transvaal Republic

signed the Geneva Convention in 1896, this service was disbanded by the British after the Boer War. A South African military medical service reappeared in 1912 with the formation of the SA Medical Corps (SAMC) as a part of the newly created UDF. Members of the SAMC saw considerable service during both World Wars. In July 1979 the SAMC was reorganised as a fourth service of the SADF, becoming the SAMS.

The SAMS is organised along essentially the same lines as the other services, with its headquarters in Pretoria and its operations decentralised to Regional Medical Commands. These control the three Military Hospitals – Pretoria, Cape Town and Bloemfontein – as well as the sick bays which are to be found in all but the smallest camps. Other responsibilities include the examination of NSM prior to their induction, the provision of medical and welfare services to dependents and the medical aspects of disaster relief operations. A Training Command controls the SAMS Training Centre and the SAMS College, which between them provide all of the SADF internal SAMS-specific training.

Another major aspect of SAMS work involves providing medical support to the local population in the Operational Area and also in the poorer rural areas of South Africa itself. In some areas the SAMS personnel are the only medical staff available. One programme in the Operational Area sees civilian specialist volunteers being taken to the various hospitals and clinics of the area by SAMS teams which also provide the necessary supporting staff and equipment. Finally, the SAMS is also responsible for the provision of veterinary support, both to the SADF's four-legged members and to the livestock-farming side of civic action programmes.

Above: A universal image – a tired recruit takes a well earned rest during training.

The hostilities along the Angola/South-West Africa border have resulted in the SAMS maintaining a high proficiency in the treatment of battle casualties. One aspect has been the streamlining of the evacuation procedures which are able to whisk a casualty from the Operational Area to 1 Military Hospital outside Pretoria within five or six hours of having been wounded. Less serious casualties are, naturally, first treated locally and only then moved to Pretoria for further treatment, recuperation or rehabilitation if required. Casevac within the Operational Area is generally by Puma, with a doctor and a medical orderly on board to provide immediate treatment to follow on to the initial work of the trained medic who accompanies every patrol.

These casevac missions have their frightening moments, not a few having been flown under fire. Ondangwa Hospital, too, has had its little excitements. In one case the casualty brought in was a 32 Bn trooper with a live rifle grenade embedded in his chest. Brought into the hospital after what must have been a very unhappy helicopter flight for all concerned, he faced the staff with quite a dilemma. The solution finally adopted was to rig a lifting tackle through an eye screwed into the theatre roof in just the right location to allow the grenade to be extracted without causing further damage. A wire was then fastened to the tail of the grenade and run through the eye to a sandbagged corner of the theatre from where this phase of the operation was carried out. Against this sort of background, it is not surprising that SAMS members hold three of the fewer than 100 *Honoris Crux* decorations awarded thus far.

THE SOUTH AFRICAN ARMY

The Army, largest and most important of the services, has been able in recent years to make up for much of the neglect it suffered after World War II. Initial attempts to undo the damage were made in the 1960s, but the most important impetus came from the 1975/6 incursion into Angola. This proved beyond doubt what some had argued for years – that the Army was woefully ill-equipped for anything but small-scale counterinsurgency operations. This was most obvious in the artillery field, where the World War II equipment still in general service as the only items of their kind were totally outranged by the enemy guns and rocket launchers.

The reaction was swifter than might have been expected after such long neglect. Existing programmes were accelerated and new ones were initiated to provide modern equipment. At the same time, a start was made toward overhauling both the doctrines and the organisation of conventional forces. This process continues today, with the Army adapting itself to its growing capabilities as more new equipment enters service and operational experience pays dividends. The result has been a quantum leap from the status of a true 'third world' army in equipment terms to that of a peer among the best-equipped armies outside the major power blocs.

The Army has also been engaged in a long-drawn-out counterinsurgency campaign in northern SWA. While this has absorbed scarce funds and entailed all the usual problems of a low-intensity campaign, it has also brought some benefits. For one, it has allowed the Army to

Previous page: Olifant at speed on the practice range.
Below: General Beyers, one of the leading Boer commando generals.

Above: The future Prime Minister, General Louis Botha, pictured with his son during his service in the Anglo-Boer War c. 1900.
Right: Members of a commando pose for the camera after the Battle of Spion Kop in 1900. Note the absence of any uniform and the several types of rifle carried.

introduce both personnel and equipment to operational conditions, which could serve to balance out many of the attendant problems. Rather more importantly, cross-border operations against insurgent bases have given a measure of semi-conventional experience – which has proved invaluable in refining doctrine, equipment, organisation and training. These missions have also demonstrated the Army's ability to execute its doctrine of fast-moving, deep and wide-ranging operations.

Not formally founded until the Defence Act of 1912, the Army can, in fact, trace its history back to around 1658. The original Dutch East India Company refreshment station at the Cape was founded in 1652 and provided with a small garrison for local security. Over the next decade, this force varied in strength between 70 and 170. Not surprisingly, it soon proved too weak, and a burgher militia was formed in 1658 or '59 to supplement it. By the 1670s this had grown into the commando system, with mixed forces of burghers and

regular soldiers operating against hostile tribes. The first true burgher commando under burgher officers was authorised in 1715, a system that remained in force until Britain took permanent control of the Cape.

The British occupied the Cape for the first time in 1795 to forestall any French attempt to do so. Unpopular with the settlers, the British soon saw the need for a regular force of mounted troops to keep them in line. In 1796 this force was supplemented by a Hottentot Corps, again with the dual purpose of defending against external attack and 'intimidating' the colonists. After the British withdrew, however, the commando system soon re-established itself, as the Dutch Government found regular forces too expensive to maintain. When the British returned in

1806 they retained the basic system.

By this time, however, the strain of border wars was beginning to tell and commando members were serving two months in every six. This was, naturally, harming the economy and by 1812 plans were afoot to raise regular Hottentot regiments to take the load off the burghers. The burgher commandos were then abolished in 1834. Cape defence was now largely in the hands of British regular troops reinforced by local volunteers and the Hottentot troops. By the 1880s this structure was being supplemented by a number of volunteer units which have since become the CF (Citizen Force) element of the Army.

The commando system did not, in the event, die with its abolition by the British. Dissatisfied with British rule, many of the Dutch settlers began to move into the interior of the country from around 1836 onward. They took with them the commando system and proved its worth in clashes with hostile tribes and also against British forces in the first Boer War. By the time of the 1899-1902 war, the commandos had been augmented by regular artillery units and, in the Transvaal, the police.

The outbreak of war in 1899 had brought the Boers' militia armies into direct conflict with regular British forces. While they did acquit themselves very well in the early stages of the war, the outcome was a foregone conclusion once Britain could bring the might of her Empire to bear. Nevertheless, the Boers' innovative approach both to mobile

operations and the use of well-camouflaged and dug-in defensive positions had a considerable impact on many armies. The commando system was such that the Boer forces were able to conduct effective guerrilla warfare for another two years after their defeat as conventional armies. The best evidence of their ability is the fact that some 20,000 mounted riflemen with minimal support kept 250,000 British troops fully occupied for three years.

With British rule established in the former Boer Republics, the commando system was abolished there too. In its

Above: South African troops outside the former Italian fortress of Mega in East Africa shortly after its fall to the Allied advance in 1941.

stead, volunteer units along British lines were established in the Transvaal from those Uitlander units that had served with the British forces after 1900. In Natal the volunteer units were converted into a militia that was backed by a reserve from which reinforcements would be selected by ballot as needed. The Cape Colony reverted again to a purely regular force of mounted riflemen.

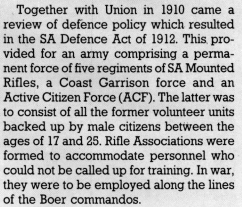

Together with Union in 1910 came a review of defence policy which resulted in the SA Defence Act of 1912. This provided for an army comprising a permanent force of five regiments of SA Mounted Rifles, a Coast Garrison force and an Active Citizen Force (ACF). The latter was to consist of all the former volunteer units backed up by male citizens between the ages of 17 and 25. Rifle Associations were formed to accommodate personnel who could not be called up for training. In war, they were to be employed along the lines of the Boer commandos.

This reorganisation was not nearly complete when World War I broke out in 1914. South Africa was automatically involved as a part of the Empire: Britain asked her to enter German South-West Africa to seize the powerful radio transmitters there and to deny the ports to German raiders. South-West Africa was duly invaded, both across the border with SA and by means of landings at Lüderitz

Left: Troops of 1 SA Brigade parade at Gilgil in East Africa early in World War II.
Main picture: The devastated remains of Delville Wood after the Somme fighting in 1916.
Bottom: South African troops with captured Italian guns at Mega in 1941.

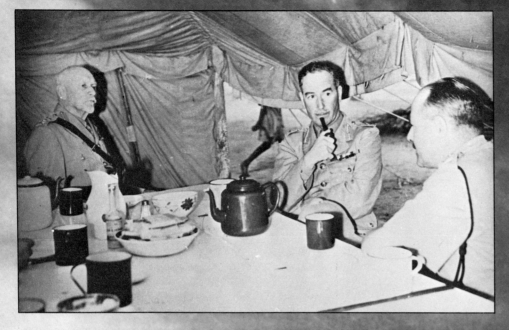

Above: General Smuts conferring with General Sir Alan Cunningham, comander of the British and Allied forces fighting the Italians in East Africa.

and, later, at Walvis Bay. The campaign that followed was characterised by many hard marches under gruelling conditions, as the invaders strove to come to grips with the smaller German force, which borrowed time by evading decisive contact. An idea of the hardship involved can be gained from the 1st Infanty Brigade's march of 390km in 16 days – the last 72km were covered in 36 hours. The remaining German forces finally surrendered in July 1915.

The next step saw a brigade of volunteers leave for East Africa to aid British forces against the small German garrison there. But the very able German Commander von Lettow-Vorbeck was to lead the Allies a merry dance: he was still in the field and a potent force some two weeks after the 1918 armistice. Originally it had been estimated that some 8000 troops would suffice for this campaign. By 1918 the force had grown to over 111,000! It is particularly ironical that von Lettow-Vorbeck was using mobile guerrilla tactics against his enemies, who were commanded for much of the campaign by the successful former Boer General Jan Smuts. In all, two SA divisions served in East Africa with Empire forces, conducting another campaign of endless moves and countermoves over considerable distances, often in heavy bush and under poor climatic conditions.

Meanwhile, another volunteer brigade had been formed under Brigadier General Lukin and sent to England to be trained for employment on the Western Front. Instead, it found itself back in Africa operating against the Senussi tribes, who were posing a threat to the canal region. This campaign ended in February 1916 and the brigade was posted back to Europe, arriving in time for the Somme Offensive. It was to serve on the Western Front for the rest of the war, being virtually destroyed several times in heavy fighting. Its best-known action was at Delville Wood and Longueval in 1916. Acting in support of the 26th Division, the brigade became involved in heavy fighting for the village and in Delville Wood itself. When it was finally relieved after holding the wood for six days, it had all of 750 men. Worse was to come. Covering the retreat of the V Corps of the Third Army in 1918, it was written down to a composite battalion of some 450 men. Nevertheless, it was reconstituted again and saw further action, forming the advance guard of the Fourth Army when the armistice became effective on 11 November 1918.

With the war over, the question of Army reorganisation was raised again. The basic system dating from 1912 was retained, but financial constraints forced reduction of the SA Mounted Rifles to one regiment in 1923 and also restricted ACF training. On the other hand, Army organisation was improved by establishing several new branches including a Staff Corps, Engineers, Field Artillery and a Corps of Instructors. Interestingly, an Infantry Corps was not formed, as all of the infantry units fell under the ACF. In

1926 further cuts in defence funds forced the disbandment of the SA Mounted Rifles. The early 1930s saw training curtailed still further: even ammunition supplies to the Rifle Associations were cut by half.

By 1934 the situation had improved somewhat, and the Minister of Defence could announce the goal of a 56,000-man trained force with a 100,000-man reserve. Organisationally, this force was to comprise nine CF infantry brigades supported by three field artillery brigades and some independent artillery batteries. Nevertheless, the outbreak of war in 1939 caught

Above: A South African Marmon Herrington armoured car pictured near Derna during the North African campaign in World War II.

the SA Army totally unprepared again, only part way into its reorganisation programme. Permanent Force (PF) strength stood at 3500 and the CF units were all grossly under strength. While there were over 120,000 men in the Commandos, only some 18,000 were properly armed and many lacked training. To make matters worse, there were only 104 trained instructors available to help make up the initial shortfall.

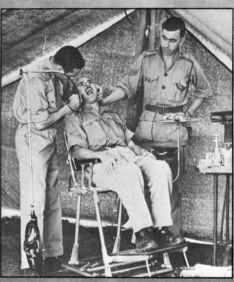

Above: South African Army dentist at work in Kenya early in World War II.
Left: Marmon Herrington armoured cars in the desert. The Marmon Herrington was built in South Africa in a wide variety of versions.

Above: A 25-pounder artillery unit of the 6th South African Armoured Division in Italy during World War II. The 25-pounder remained in South African service until the 1980s.

Despite this unhappy start, 1st SA Brigade arrived in East Africa in July 1940, soon followed by the remainder of 1st SA Infantry Division. Once it had settled in, the Division was given responsibility for a 400km sector stretching from the Sudan border eastward to Moyale. In February 1941 British and SA forces began to move against the Italians. Progress was rapid, hindered more by demolitions than by combat, and the 1st SA Brigade entered Addis Ababa on 6 April. After some fur-

Below: 105mm self-propelled guns of the 6th SA Armoured Division ready to move up to join the front-line fighting in Italy in 1944-45.

ther fighting the Duke of Aosta surrendered (16 May) and the Brigade moved to Egypt, where the division HQ and 5th Brigade had already arrived. The 2nd SA Brigade, meanwhile, had been engaged in clearing up eastern Somaliland, and elements were involved in operations against Italian forces south of the capital before their own departure for Egypt.

Operations in the new theatre began disastrously when the 5th SA Brigade was overrun and destroyed by more than 100 German tanks on 23 November in the Sidi Rezegh area. An attempt by 1st Brigade to assist came to nothing when it was withdrawn to cover 30 Corps' line of communication, beating off several heavy attacks on the 25th. The 2nd SA Division and 1st Division's 2nd Brigade had now entered the battle, and 2nd Division took Bardia on

2 January 1942. Sollum and Halfaya followed on the 12th and the 17th. These operations cost some 500 casualties but gained more than 14,000 prisoners, including 4000 Germans. On 27 January 1st SA Division took up positions in the Gazala area to stem the renewed enemy advance. In March 2nd SA Division moved to Tobruk, having detached 3rd SA Brigade to 1st SA Division.

British armour suffered several heavy defeats in June, which finally led to a general withdrawal; 1st SA Division was ordered to evacuate the Gazala Line on the 14th. By the 17th the Germans had isolated Tobruk, which was held by 2nd SA Division – less 3rd Brigade, 201 Guards Brigade and 11 Indian Brigade. Short of transport and ammunition, with the Guards Brigade diminished by heavy casualties and the minefields seriously depleted, Tobruk's defence was not as strong as it might have appeared on paper. On 20 June the Germans overran the Indian Brigade and then destroyed the Guards Brigade and what armour there was, reaching the town by 1600 hours and overrunning the fortress HQ. In all, they took more than 25,000 prisoners, including 10,722 South Africans.

The 1st SA Division was now ordered to El Alamein, where 2nd SA Division had spent its first weeks in the theatre preparing a position. The last of the Allied rearguard passed through the position around midday on 30 June, and 3rd SA Brigade found itself under heavy attack soon after. Attacks and heavy shelling continued until 3 July, which brought a lull. Another heavy attack followed on the 13th; then Rommel made his final unsuccessful bid on 30 August. The Second Battle of El Alamein opened with a massive artillery barrage on 23 October, when SA gunners fired some 62,000

Above: Sherman tanks of the 6th SA Armoured Division at the Victory Parade in Italy in 1945. The Sherman had by this time become the standard Allied tank.

rounds. The 1st SA Division was one of four attacking. The 4th and 6th SA Armoured Car Regiments were instrumental in disrupting the enemy's rear areas and were the first Eighth Army troops to enter Tobruk on 12 November. Early in 1943 1st SA Division then returned home to South Africa.

Meanwhile, 7th SA Brigade had joined in the invasion and occupation of Madagascar between June and December 1942. The next major participation by SA ground forces came with the arrival of the 6th SA Armoured Division in Italy (20 April 1944). Formed in February 1943, the Division had been in training at Khatatba, Egypt, since May of that year. Comprising 11th Armoured and 12th Motorised Brigades with various supporting units, this was the most powerful SA formation of the war. The 12th Motorised Brigade operated first under the New Zealand Division, but 6th SA Armoured Division was concentrated by the end of May 1944 and also received 24 Guards Brigade Group under command.

Its first divisional action came on 3 June when it took Piglio and Paliano. Passing through Rome on 6 June, the Division went on to fight through the Trasimeno and Hilde Lines, reaching the outposts of the Gothic Line in September. Grim mountain fighting followed until winter put a stop to all major action. In the interim the Guards Brigade was replaced by the 13th SA Brigade. In April 1945 the Division reassumed its sector of the Appenine Front and took part in the heavy fighting that finally drove the Germans out of the mountains into the plains of the Po Valley. Resistance began to crumble, ending in the surrender of German forces in May.

The war over, the Army was quickly run down to a small Land Force. The only real balancing factor was the provision of an armoured division for service in the Middle East in the event of hostilities there. To this end, 200 Centurion main battle tanks (MBT) were ordered, the first

Right: General view of the Allied Victory Parade in Italy in 1945.

Above: Lieutenant General J. J. Geldenhuys, current Chief of the Army, photographed during his time as GOC South-West Africa.

two arriving in July 1952. This was the only major equipment purchase for the Army until the 1960s. In 1956 the Army conducted Exercise Oranje, which simulated brigade operations in a nuclear environment. But that same year, half of the Centurions were sold to Switzerland

effectively reducing the Army to an infantry force. Ironically, the SADF has had to go to extraordinary lengths to obtain more Centurions in recent years, while those sold to Switzerland are still rendering sterling service in the Swiss Army.

The 1960s brought the first results of a defence review; thus some bright spots emerged, notably the beginning of Panhard AML-60 and -90 armoured car production under licence in 1961. A parachute battalion was established in the same year. In 1962 six infantry training battalions (1 to 6 SAI) were established to handle the expansion resulting from introduction of universal military service for white males to replace the earlier ballot system. Three armoured squadrons were created for the same purpose. A dog centre was started in 1964 to train both handlers and dogs for the SADF and also to breed suitable dogs. The first locally manufactured FN-FAL rifle – known as the R-1 – was handed over to the Prime Minister on the same occasion. In 1968 the Danie Theron Combat School was established at Kimberley to train NSM drafted to the Commandos.

The early 1970s saw the Army still leading a quiet existence with only some organisational changes to disturb its even tenor. One was the establishment in 1971 of a civil defence college for women volunteers at George. Another was the beginning of a voluntary national service

system for coloureds in 1973, training being conducted at the SA Cape Corps Service Battalion base near Cape Town. Then things began to accelerate for the Army and, indeed, for the entire SADF. The Army took over responsibility for counterinsurgency operations in northern SWA from the Police (1973) and in 1974 came the Portuguese collapse that brought civil war in Angola and a hostile government in Mozambique. The deplorable situation in Angola finally resulted in Operation Savannah – the SA incursion into Angola – launched late in 1975. Though not unsuccessful militarily, this intervention was terminated for a variety of reasons before the desired result could be achieved – but not before the Army had been granted an extremely valuable insight into its own capabilities and shortcomings.

Developments now came thick and fast, not least as a result of the Savannah experience, which had demonstrated just how fast a large conventional force could be set up in southern Africa. In 1976 the Army unveiled its Ratel IFV; 1977 brought 24 months' national service in place of the earlier 12; the first formation-level exercise in conventional warfare for almost ten years followed in 1978, when a parachute brigade was also established and the

Below: Troops practicing debussing drills from a Samil-20 truck. The troops will gradually learn to dismount from a fairly fast-moving vehicle.

Right: Training under tough field conditions. Bayonet exercises are now little seen, however, since the new R-4 rifle is not equipped with a bayonet fitting.

Army Battle School created in the northern Cape. A 155mm gun of exceptional performance and a 127mm multiple rocket launcher were revealed in 1979 and 1980 respectively, followed by the Ratel-90 and -60 derivatives of the IFV, the Ratel 'Log' and the upgraded Centurion (Olifant) in 1981. Other developments included a family of long-range ammunition for the 140mm (5.5 inch) gun, various mine-protected vehicles, a truck family and a new assault rifle.

The Army's major preoccupation for much of this period was with absorbing the additional manpower and the new equipment – the latter in terms of both quantity and enhanced capabilities. Among other things, this has led to a reorganisation of the conventional forces and the formulation of new tactical doctrines. Apart from this, the Army was also deeply involved in reassessing the strategic situation and preparing plans to meet likely eventualities. Concurrently with this new and, to some, strange, emphasis on conventional operations, the Army still had to conduct the counterinsurgency campaign in northern SWA.

At this writing the Army is organised into a Territorial Force and a Conventional Force plus the independent 44 Parachute Brigade. In addition, there are the elements stationed in SWA and the SWA Territory Force (SWATF) itself, which consists chiefly of army elements and remains part of the SADF until SWA independence. The Army Battle School and Army College both fall directly under the Chief of the Army. Corps Schools and training units are responsible to their Corps Directors at Army HQ in matters of doctrine and training, but the relevant territorial commands oversee their operation and support. Army HQ itself is located in Pretoria and comprises the usual five staff departments and an Inspector General. Each of the Army's Corps is represented by a Director who is responsible for developing doctrines, organisation, equipment tables and tactics for the units of his Corps in accordance with overall Army doctrine.

The bulk of the Army's strength consists of NSM and CF personnel. The NSM generally receive some six to eight months of basic, advanced individual and sub-unit level training at one of the training units before being posted to operational duties. Infantry and commandos are trained at one of the eight SAI battalions, while most of the other corps handle all of their training at their respective schools.

Right: The 81mm mortar is the standard infantry fire support weapon. Normally moved by vehicle, it is shown here split into manpack loads of base, tube and bipod. Each soldier retains his personal weapon, however.

Above: Members of a Junior Leader course at Infantry School. Such courses are designed to test candidates' suitability to become officers or NCOs. *Left:* A Catering Corps member learning to bake bread in an improvised oven in the field. Soldiers in the support services also receive the standard basic infantry training.

Combat arms personnel then generally also stay with their units, which post entire companies to the operational area for tours of around four months' duration. Supporting and services personnel are posted to various units and HQs for the greater part of their initial service. Once the initial two years are over, the NSM are posted to CF units or commandos for the remainder of their service commitment.

Potential NCOs and officers are selected in the course of the basic training phase and then undergo some twelve months of junior leader training at their corps school prior to being appointed as corporals or second lieutenants. Further promotion generally follows only during their CF career and is dependent on successfully completing the relevant courses. Most such courses are offered by the corps schools, but some of the more generally applicable are offered elsewhere. Thus the Army College offers staff duties courses at all levels, the Defence College offers various joint warfare courses and the Intelligence School offers several intelligence courses including those for unit intelligence officers and clerks. PF personnel, excluding specialists in certain fields, are generally accepted as such only after completion of their initial two years' national service. Their promotion path is similar, but involves more and longer courses.

Unit training is handled in two ways. One is for the unit to conduct a thirty-day training camp, addressing those aspects of its mission that demand greatest attention and also honing individual skills. Such camps often end with a short field exercise, and the unit's officers and NCOs are usually assisted by PF personnel from the corps school, a training battalion or the local command HQ. Some training is also conducted in the evenings and over weekends. Training camps involving the

Right: Engineering units in training for bridging operations. South African engineers, unlike those in many other armies, emphasise provision of water supplies in their training rather than the crossing of water obstacles.
Below right: A Vickers machine gun team prepares to open fire.
Below: A recruit at work on the assault course. .

Above: One of the most impressive items in the South African armoury, the G-6 155mm self-propelled gun. The vehicle can carry some 44 rounds of ready-use ammunition.

Above: General Viljoen, chief of the SADF, demonstrates a tactical point during a farm protection exercise. Looking on, third from left, is General Geldenhuys, Chief of the Army.

whole unit are usually held only in alternate years, leaving the other year free for personnel to attend courses.

The other main approach – generally restricted to conventional units – has the unit go to the Army Battle School at Lohatla in the northern Cape – usually as a part of its brigade. Here a similar programme is conducted under the eagle eye of the training staff, who are carefully selected not only for their experience and competence in their fields, but for their ability to pass this on tactfully to CF personnel, who are often older and in very senior civilian posts. These training periods generally end with a brigade exercise, which is often expanded to allow participation by division staff members. Simultaneously, training tests and refines doctrinal and organisational changes.

The Territorial Force is organised into ten regional commands, the Walvis Bay Military Area and Army Logistics Command. The regional commands are of roughly divisional level and are headed by Brigadiers. They are responsible first for the security of their regions; other tasks include logistic, administrative and service support to other units or formations stationed or operating in their area of responsibility. In the event of war, the conventional forces would 'plug in' to the Commands for logistic support, to streamline the resupply effort and narrow the gap created by a relatively thin road and rail net over great distances. The Far North and Eastern Transvaal Commands are different in that they also have a primary conventional role in planning and conduct of operations in their areas. Both also differ from the others in being headed by Major Generals. Disaster relief operations also fall within the ambit of the regional commands.

The Territorial Force's 'teeth' comprise commando and CF units. Most training units also have some combat capability and can be called upon when necessary. The CF units assigned to the regional commands are mostly light infantry battalions optimised for the counterinsurgency (COIN) role. They are equipped with the usual light infantry weapons including, for rural operations, 81mm mortars and the old Vickers machine gun. Rural units use mine-protected Armored Personnel Carriers (APCs) for transport, whereas urban units generally rely on trucks. Some of the commands also dispose of an armoured car regiment with Eland-60s and a light artillery regiment with old 25pdr guns. All have CF services and support units and also have CF personnel in their HQ staffs.

The commandos are essentially area-bound light infantry units, readily mobilised and responsible for local internal security. They take their name from the old Boer commandos and are, in fact, similar in that they draw their personnel from a particular area for its defence. Based on a set structure similar to that of the CF COIN battalions, their actual organisation, equipment and strength varies according to their location and its terrain, their specific mission and the personnel available in the area. Thus some rural commandos include trackers and mounted infantry while urban units may include motorcycle troops. Considerable importance is attached to their local knowledge and their close contact with area populations. Many commandos include women and older or semi-fit personnel, generally in administrative tasks. Most are grouped into Commando Groups of five or more commandos under a small brigade-level HQ.

Those commandos with a specific protection task are an offshoot of the system. They generally draw their personnel from the staff of strategic industries or government departments and are responsible for the protection of vital installations. These units vary widely in strength, organisation and equipment, each being specifically

tailored to its task. Unlike regular commando personnel, who generally first complete their full two-year period of national service and receive their initial training at infantry training battalions, the 'industrials' are usually volunteers who receive their basic training locally on a non-continuous basis. Advanced training then follows the normal course for those who desire promotion. Initially, however, most of the leadership and specialist posts will be filled with personnel of the unit who have, in fact, completed their national service. Most commando promotion courses are offered by the Danie Theron Combat School at Kimberley.

Counterinsurgency doctrine is generally similar to that accepted in most armies. Thus the primary military tasks

Below: The Valkiri 127mm multiple-launch rocket system firing. The Valkiri rockets can range out to 22,000 meters and the equipment can be reloaded in roughly ten minutes.

are those of preventing infiltration and protecting population and infrastructure. To this end a combination of semi-static protective elements and highly mobile patrols and reaction forces is employed. Mobility is provided by mine-protected vehicles, helicopters, motorcycles and horses, while armoured cars are also employed in the convoy escort, road patrol and area patrol roles. As far as possible, the protective tasks are left to the police in order to free available Army elements for more aggressive operations. Where feasible, these will include strikes on the insurgents' bases and staging areas. Concurrent civic action is aimed at bettering the lot of the local population in every way possible and at replacing those other government services that may have been displaced by the hostilities.

The current conventional force comprises two divisions of near-identical organisation. Each has one armoured and two semi-mechanised brigades. This

Above: The elderly 3.5-inch rocket launcher is still in service in the anti-armour role, though it is likely that captured Soviet-made RPG-7s are also used.

force is backed by the Parachute Brigade, which is directly under the Chief of the SADF for operational purposes, and by a small standing element manned by NSM from various training units. The divisions are even more dependent on the CF than is the Territorial Force. In fact, only the formation commanders, their principal staff officers and a small administrative skeleton are supplied by the PF and NSM. Almost all units are entirely CF manned and led; CF personnel also fill most of the staff and HQ posts.

Two other aspects of the conventional organisation are worthy of mention, both resulting from the unfavourable force: space ratio that will inevitably pertain. One is the strong reconnaissance element, the other is that most of the units tend to be larger than their European equivalents without fielding more combat power. This is due simply to the fact that they will often be operating widely separated and far from supporting elements and must therefore incorporate more of an internal supporting and service structure. While this is unavoidable, it does not go well with the relatively thin road net of southern Africa, which presents problems that are still to be effectively addressed.

Doctrinally, the Army intends to fight as mobile a war as possible – which is, in fact, necessitated by the geographic factors. Accordingly, the emphasis is very much on gaining and retaining the initiative, keeping the enemy off balance by means of manoeuvre and offensive action until he can be destroyed. Within this basic doctrine, the mechanised brigades are expected to conduct the manoeuvre battle with the aim of presenting the enemy to the armoured brigades for destruction at a suitable time and place. The value of armoured cars and mobile, long-range

ARMY EQUIPMENT

Olifant

Type: Main Battle Tank
Crew: 4
Armament: *Main* 1×105mm
Secondary 1×7.62mm co-axial; 1×7.62mm anti-aircraft; smoke dischargers
Weight: 56 tonnes
Dimensions: Length 7.56m; width 3.39m; height 2.94m; ground clearance 45.7cm
Engine: 12-cylinder turbo-charged diesel
Performance: Speed 44km/h; range 500km; gradient 60%; step 91.4cm; trench 3.35m; ford 1.45m; 2.74m after preparation
Comments: Developed as an interim MBT on the basis of original Centurion MBT bought for the SA Army in the 1950s and reportedly supplemented by various purchases since. The basic modification includes the installation of a diesel engine and a new transmission and the replacement of the 20pdr (87mm) gun with a 105mm gun and a modern fire control system. While few details have been released, it can be assumed that the Olifant has been brought to a similar standard to the Centurions that have been refitted in other countries such as Israel and Switzerland.

Eland-90

Type: Armoured car
Crew: 3
Armament: *Main* 1×90mm low-recoil gun in a two-man turret
Secondary 1×7.62mm co-axial machine gun; 1×7.62mm anti-aircraft machine gun on turret roof; smoke dischargers
Weight: 5.5 tonnes
Dimensions: Length: 3.79m; width 1.97m; height 2.07m; ground clearance 33cm
Engine: 4 cylinder water-cooled petrol
Performance: Speed 90km/h; range 600km; gradient 60%; side slope 30%; step 30cm; trench 80cm with 1 channel; ford 1.1m
Comments: The original Panhard AML-90 was developed as a fire-support vehicle for light reconnaissance units. The Eland-90 is the South-African-built version incorporating many changes and improvements designed to optimise it for local requirements. It is the basic vehicle of the armoured car regiments, with both a reconnaissance and a secondary anti-tank role. Operations have shown the Eland-90 in the hands of a good crew to be a fair match for T-54/55 series tanks. The technical data given here is for the AML-90 but is essentially similar to that of the Eland.

Eland-60

Type: Armoured car
Crew: 3
Armament: *Main* 1×60mm breech-loading mortar in a two-man turret
Secondary 1×7.62mm co-axial machine gun; 1×7.62mm anti-aircraft machine gun on turret roof; smoke dischargers
Comments: The original version of the Panhard AML, designed for reconnaissance and patrol missions in counterinsurgency operations. The Eland-60 has been modified similarly to the Eland-90 to suit local requirements and is used chiefly in the counterinsurgency role, equipping the armoured car regiments of the Commands.

Right: An Eland 90 armoured car at a company base in Owambo. Armoured cars have been surprisingly successful in the counter-insurgency role.

Ratel-20

Type: Infantry Fighting Vehicle; wheeled, 6×6
Crew: 4+7 infantry
Armament: *Main* 1×20mm semi-automatic cannon in two-man turret
Secondary 1×7.62mm co-axial machine gun; 1×7.62mm machine gun on ring at rear of vehicle for close-in and anti-aircraft defence; smoke dischargers; firing ports in hull sides
Weight: 18 tonnes, combat loaded
Dimensions: Length 7.21m; width 2.7m; height 3.11m; ground clearance 35cm
Engine: 230kW six-cylinder water-cooled diesel
Performance: Speed 90km/h, 50km/h (off road); range 1200km; gradient 70%; step 35cm; ford 1.2m; side slope 30%; trench 1.2m
Comments: Basic IFV of the mechanised infantry battalions. Developed for the SA Army taking local conditions and requirements into account. The first wheeled IFV in service and also the first IFV to mount a commander's cupola. Armour protection is given against small-arms fire and shell fragments, and the hull is designed to offer a good measure of protection to the crew in the event of detonating a mine. Access is by doors in the hull sides and rear and roof hatches. Variants other than those discussed below include an ambulance and a repair Ratel. Mortar, anti-tank (missile) and air-defence variants seem likely developments.

Ratel-90

Type: Fire-support vehicle; wheeled, 6×6
Crew: 4+6 infantry; fewer infantry if employed specifically in the fire-support role, when more 90mm ammunition is carried.
Armament: *Main* 1×90mm low-pressure gun in two-man turret
Secondary 1×7.62mm co-axial machine gun; 1×7.62mm anti-aircraft machine gun on turret roof; 1×7.62mm machine gun on ring at rear of vehicle for close-in and anti-aircraft defence; smoke dischargers; firing ports in hull sides
Comments: Derived from the basic Ratel-20 IFV. Employed chiefly as a fire-support vehicle in mechanised infantry battalions; also employed in an anti-tank role in which it has proved itself capable of dealing with T-54/55 series MBTs. The turret is identical to that of the Eland-90. Technical details are similar to those for the Ratel-20.

Ratel-60

Type: IFV; wheeled, 6×6
Crew: 4+7 infantry
Armament: *Main* 1×60mm breech-loading mortar in two-man turret
Secondary 1×7.62mm co-axial machine gun; 1×7.62mm anti-aircraft machine gun on turret roof; 1×7.62mm machine gun on ring at rear of vehicle for close-in and anti-aircraft defence; smoke dischargers; firing ports in hull sides
Comments: Derived from the basic Ratel-20 IFV. The turret is identical to that of the Eland-60. Technical details are similar to those for the Ratel-20.

Ratel-Command

Type: Armoured command vehicle; wheeled, 6×6
Crew: 3+6 command post personnel
Armament: *Main* 1×12.7mm machine gun in two-man turret
Secondary 1×7.62mm anti-aircraft machine gun on turret roof; 1×7.62mm tail/anti-aircraft machine gun; smoke dischargers; firing ports in hull sides
Comments: Derived from the basic Ratel-20 as a command vehicle with greater internal space for communications equipment; artillery command, fire support control and communications centre vehicles are among the sub-variants. Technical details similar to those for the Ratel-20.

Ratel-Logistic (Ratel Log)

Type: 8×8 wheeled, armoured, off-road logistic support vehicle
Crew: 3
Armament: *Main* 1×12.7mm machine gun on a ring mount for both surface and anti-aircraft defence
Comments: Derived from the Ratel 6×6 family as a support vehicle for mechanised formations. The basic logistic variant is designed to carry all the stores needed to keep a mechanised infantry platoon operating for a week under the normal conditions. Its equipment is very comprehensive, to the extent of including a hot shower facility. A recovery variant of the basic vehicle is also being considered. Full technical details are not yet available, as the final production version is still under development.

Above: 8×8 Ratel Log.

Bulldog

Type: Mine-resistant armoured personnel carrier
Crew: Driver + 10 passengers
Armament: Provision for mounting 2 machine guns
Weight: 14 tonnes
Dimensions: Length 5.34m; width 2.3m; height 2.69m; ground clearance 46cm
Engine: 79kW 6-cylinder air-cooled diesel
Comments: Successor to the Buffel; based on the Samil-20 chassis. Armour offers protection against normal small-arms fire and grenade fragments. The Buffel is essentially similar, but is based on the Unimog chassis. Basic technical data for the Bulldog are identical to those for the Samil-20.

G-5

Type: 155mm gun/howitzer
Weight: 13.5 tonnes
Crew: 8
Dimensions: length (towing configuration), barrel turned back, 9.1m; height 2.3m
Mobility: 10t gun tractor, towing speed 90km/h on roads and 50km/h on dirt; self-propelled by 68hp auxiliary diesel engine allowing speeds of 3 to 8km/h
Elevation: +75° to −3°
Traverse: 84° with elevation below 15°; 65° above 15°
Range: 3000m minimum; 30,000 maximum with standard round, 37,500m+ with base bleed
Rate of fire: 3 rounds/minute for 15 minutes, then 2 r/min
Ammunition: High explosive (HE) (45.5kg), HE base bleed (47kg), smoke, illumination, white phosphorous. The HE rounds contain 8.7kg of explosive and their casings release between 3032 and 4756 fragments.

G-6

Type: 155mm self-propelled gun/howitzer
Crew: 5
Weight: 37 tonnes (turret 9 tonnes)
Dimensions: Length 9m; width 3.3m; height 3.25m
Engine: 525hp diesel
Transmission: Automatic or manual (6 F, 1 R) allowing selection of 6×2, 6×4 or 6×6 drive
Performance: Speed 90km/h on roads, 30-40km/h off-road; range 600km on roads; gradient 40%; step 50cm; ford 1m; side slope 30%; ditch 1.5m
Ordnance type: 155mm tube identical to the G-5 but fitted with a fume extractor
Elevation: −5° to +75°
Traverse: 80°
Range: 3000m minimum; 30,000 maximum with standard round; 37,500m+ with base bleed
Rate of fire: 4 rounds/minute; will increase when the intended automatic loading system is fitted
Ammunition: 44 rounds and 50 charges (12 rounds in the vehicle front, 28 in the rear). Same ammunition as the G-5
Comments: 7.62mm or 12.7mm turret-mounted anti-aircraft machine gun; firing ports in turret sides; smoke dischargers.

Valkiri

Type: Self-propelled multiple rocket launcher
Crew: 2 (+2 men in the 5t ammunition vehicle)
Weight: 6.5 tonnes
Dimensions: Length 5.35m; width 2.3m; height 2.7m
Ordnance type: 24-tube 127mm rocket launcher
Range: 7500m minimum (with drag rings); 22,000m maximum

Below: 155mm G-5 gun/howitzer.

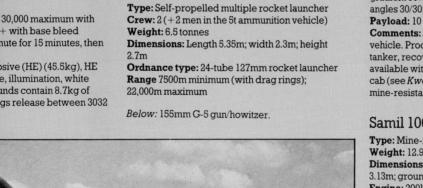

Rate of fire: 1 round per second; individually or in programmed ripples of between 2 and 24
Reload time: Under 10 minutes for full salvo
Ammunition: 60kg fragmentation rocket with 8500 steel balls cast into a cylinder surrounding the explosive charge, effective over 1500 square meters; accuracy is 290m in azimuth and 200m in range at maximum range; 48 rounds are carried in the Samil-50 ammunition truck.
Comments: The basic vehicle is presently the Unimog, but this will soon be replaced by the Samil-20.

Samil 20

Type: 4×4 light general-purpose truck
Weight: 4.58 tonnes
Dimensions: Length 5.34m; width 2.3m; height 2.69m; ground clearance 46cm
Engine: 79kW 6-cylinder air-cooled diesel
Performance: Speed 90km/h; range 800km; gradient 87%; side slope 18°; approach/departure angles 40/40; ford 1.2m
Payload: 2.2 tonnes
Comments: Produced in several variants, including office and workshop bodies and with a mine-resistant cab. Basis of Bulldog APC and Valkiri SPMRL.

Samil 50

Type: 4×4 medium general-purpose truck
Weight: 6.34 tonnes
Dimensions: Length 7.78m; width 2.25m; height 3.1m; ground clearance 35.5cm
Engine: 120kW air-cooled V-6 diesel
Performance: Speed 88km/h; range 1000km; gradient 83%; side slope 18°; approach/departure angles 35/35; ford 1.2m
Payload: 4.8 tonnes
Comments: Standard 5-tonne category logistics vehicle. Available in several variants, including a 6000-litre fuel tanker which has a 400-litre/minute transfer pump. Others include a recovery vehicle, box bodies and dumpers. Several of these are also produced with a mine-resistant cab. There is also a mine-resistant ambulance version.

Samil 100

Type: 6×6 heavy general-purpose truck
Weight: 9.135 tonnes
Dimensions: Length 10.27m; width 2.5m; height 3.35m; ground clearance 35.5cm
Engine: 200kW V-10 air-cooled diesel
Performance: Speed 88km/h; range 800km; gradient 70%; side slope 18°; approach/departure angles 30/30; ford 1.2m
Payload: 10 tonnes
Comments: Standard 10-tonne category logistics vehicle. Produced in several variants, including tanker, recovery and artillery tractor. Several are available with an armoured and mine-resistant cab (see *Kwevoel*, below). An armoured and mine-resistant recovery variant is also in service.

Samil 100 Kwêvoël

Type: Mine-resistant logistics vehicle
Weight: 12.9 tonnes, load 9 tonnes
Dimensions: Length 10.87m; width 2.5m; height 3.13m; ground clearance 35.5cm
Engine: 200kW air-cooled V-10 diesel
Performance: Speed 93km/h; range 700km
Comments: Produced as flatbed, bus, bowser, recovery vehicle and horsebox.

Kriek

Type: Military off-road motorcycle
Weight: 140kg
Ground clearance: 26cm
Engine: 54hp 494cc air-cooled four-stroke
Range: 400km on roads; 250km off-road

ARMY ORGANISATION

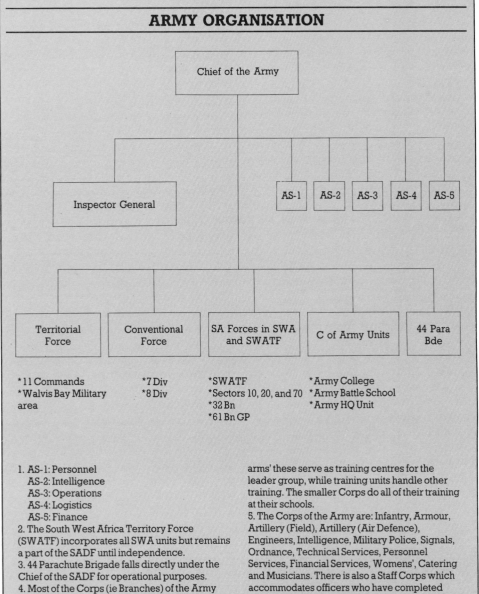

```
                        ┌─────────────────────┐
                        │  Chief of the Army  │
                        └─────────────────────┘
                                   │
          ┌────────────────────────┼──────────────────────────────────┐
          │                        │                                    │
┌──────────────────┐     ┌────┐ ┌────┐ ┌────┐ ┌────┐ ┌────┐
│ Inspector General│     │AS-1│ │AS-2│ │AS-3│ │AS-4│ │AS-5│
└──────────────────┘     └────┘ └────┘ └────┘ └────┘ └────┘
```

Territorial Force	Conventional Force	SA Forces in SWA and SWATF	C of Army Units	44 Para Bde
*11 Commands *Walvis Bay Military area	*7 Div *8 Div	*SWATF *Sectors 10, 20, and 70 *32 Bn *61 Bn GP	*Army College *Army Battle School *Army HQ Unit	

1. AS-1: Personnel
   AS-2: Intelligence
   AS-3: Operations
   AS-4: Logistics
   AS-5: Finance
2. The South West Africa Territory Force (SWATF) incorporates all SWA units but remains a part of the SADF until independence.
3. 44 Parachute Brigade falls directly under the Chief of the SADF for operational purposes.
4. Most of the Corps (ie Branches) of the Army have training schools. In the case of the 'teeth arms' these serve as training centres for the leader group, while training units handle other training. The smaller Corps do all of their training at their schools.
5. The Corps of the Army are: Infantry, Armour, Artillery (Field), Artillery (Air Defence), Engineers, Intelligence, Military Police, Signals, Ordnance, Technical Services, Personnel Services, Financial Services, Womens', Catering and Musicians. There is also a Staff Corps which accommodates officers who have completed their senior staff course.

artillery in this scenario can be readily appreciated. The parachute brigade is not expected to be used en bloc, but this possibility will not be discounted. Its normal role will be that of 'fire brigade' and raiding force, using aircraft and/or helicopters as appropriate.

Not many years ago, a comparison of this doctrine with the available equipment would have produced either amazement or amusement, depending on the circumstances. Today the SA Army is rapidly on its way to becoming one of the best-equipped small armies in the world and is very capable of applying its doctrine of fast-moving, wide-ranging and hard-hitting operations. This has been amply demonstrated by the cross-border operations against insurgent bases in southern Angola. Not least important, the Army has shown its ability to adjust rapidly to changing circumstances: Operation Sceptic, initially planned as a relatively short strike, was later expanded to allow exploitation of intelligence gained in its early phases. This shows that the lessons of

Top, far left: Close-up of a Valkiri rocket launcher showing a missile leaving its launch rack.
Left: Members of a reaction force closing in on 'insurgents' during an exercise in the northern Cape.
Below: World War II-vintage 5.5-inch gun. To compensate for this weapon's lack of range Army training emphasises bringing the guns into action as quickly and as far forward as possible.

Savannah have been well learned and, most importantly, that the logistic system has considerable built-in flexibility.

Some serious gaps, however, do remain in the Army's equipment line-up. Probably the most serious is the continuing lack of self-propelled air-defence equipment. This problem is being addressed, but the Army is not willing to comment beyond stating that the equipment in view will 'not be as complicated as some of those used by the major armies.' The most likely development seems to be an air-defence variant of the Ratel, perhaps on the 8×8 chassis of the Ratel 'Log.' Another possibility would be to use the G-6 chassis, although this is very large. The other major gaps are the lack of a modern MBT – which is only partially addressed by the Olifant programme – the lack of SP artillery until the G-6 can be brought into service and the absence of long-range anti-tank weapons. This is particularly embarrassing in view of the SAAF's lack of any anti-tank helicopters.

Despite these weaknesses, the SA Army is much more capable today than it has ever been and is more than equal to any immediate threat. Given completion of current programmes and closure of the most embarrassing equipment gaps, it should soon be able also to face up to any likely proxy force with well-justified confidence.

THE SOUTH AFRICAN AIR FORCE

The most effective air force in Africa by a wide margin, the South African Air Force (SAAF) has long been reputed to have some of the world's finest military pilots. It is also among the oldest of the independent air forces, having celebrated its 65th birthday on 1 February 1985. The reputation of its pilots actually predates the inception of the SAAF, as their extraordinary prowess had already been demonstrated in the 1914-18 war. Their reputation was further enhanced in the 1939-45 and Korean Wars, and the standard has been maintained ever since through an exceptionally rigorous selection process and training programme.

Military aviation first came to southern Africa in 1885 when British forces employed observation balloons in Bechuanaland. This exercise was repeated during the Boer War and noted with interest by the Boers. The first heavier-than-air machine to fly in southern Africa took off at East London in 1909. Others followed over the next two years, but it was the demonstration flights by the African Aviation Syndicate in 1911 that really aroused interest – not least within the UDF. Thus the Union Defence Act of 1912 made provision for the establishment of an SA Aviation Corps.

Two former Boer generals now gave the major impetus toward the early establishment of South African military aviation. The Commandant General of the UDF, Brigadier Beyers, toured England, France, Germany and Switzerland to observe manoeuvres, with specific instructions from the Prime Minister, General Smuts, to study military aviation in those countries. To this end he visited the new aviation school of the British Army and also became the first SA general to fly when he went aloft in a Rumpler Taube in Germany. He returned to report in part that 'I am firmly convinced that . . . it is impossible for any country to build up a completely successful system of defence without taking due account of this new arm of military science.'

It is hardly surprising that these former Boer generals were so favourably impressed by the military potential of aviation. Mobility, flexibility and wide-ranging reconnaissance had, after all, been the hallmarks of their campaigns – and what could be better suited to that approach to warfare than this new development. The British officers of the UDF had learned many of the same lessons and were thus equally well disposed toward the concept. Thus little time was wasted in acting on Beyers' report once it had been fully studied. The *Government Gazette* of 10 May 1913 carried an advertisement inviting applications for training as 'officer aviators.'

Several hundred applications were received, from which ten were selected as the first group. The actual training programme was let out to the Paterson Aviation Syndicate in Kimberley which had been formed after the failure of the African Aviation Syndicate. Payment would be per student who actually qualified. Instruction was carried out by Paterson and his fellow instructor in a 50bhp biplane which Paterson had de-

Previous page: Mirage F-1CZ of 3 Squadron. Together with the Mirage F-1AZs of 1 Squadron these are the most modern and potent aircraft in the SAAF inventory.

Below, main picture: One of the Imperial Gift DH9 aircraft which gave the SAAF its start.

signed himself. When this crashed early in proceedings, he and the students simply set about building another from the wreckage and some new components. After that too crashed, killing an instructor, a third aircraft was bought with which the course was completed.

Six of the newly-fledged airmen were then selected to attend the Royal Flying Corps' Central Flying School at Upavon for further training. They reported there in April 1914 and made such rapid progress that five had been awarded their RFC wings just before the outbreak of war. By October, with all of 20 flying hours each, they were considered operational and were posted to two of the first four RFC squadrons to go to France. One, Kenneth van der Spuy, soon made his mark, with a Lewis Gun suspended from the wing of his aircraft in place of the usual pistols and shotguns; he was also instrumental in the introduction of aerial photography.

Right: Pierre van Ryneveld and Quintin Brand at the end of their pioneering flight to South Africa.

Above: South African Gladiator biplane fighter at an airstrip in East Africa during the early stages of World War II.

This French interlude was short-lived, however, for early in 1915 they were recalled to form the SA Aviation Corps. This became operational in May 1915 with a number of steel-framed Farman F-27 biplanes and began operations in support of SA forces invading German South-West Africa. Employed mainly in the scouting role, they quickly proved invaluable by enabling General Botha's forces to out-manoeuvre the German Schutztruppe, which surrendered in July of the same year. With this success, the SAAC became dormant and those members volunteering for further duty were formed into 26 (SA) Squadron RFC. After some refresher training, they sailed from England to East Africa on Christmas Day 1915.

Here they enjoyed less success, as the German commander, von Lettow-Vorbeck, proved extremely adept at using the dense bush of the region both to avoid detection and to limit the effects of air attack. The only real success was the spotting of the German warship *Königsberg* in her Rufiji River hiding place by a South African airman – but he was serving with the Royal Naval Air Service. Some-

what disappointed, 26 Squadron left for England in June 1918. By then, almost 3000 South Africans were flying with the RFC or undergoing training. Among those who did particularly well were Captains Beauchamp-Procter – with 54 kills he was the most decorated Empire airman – Kinkead and Venter with 30 and 22 kills respectively and Hugh Saunders, who later became an Air Chief Marshal in the RAF, with 19.

Beauchamp-Procter's aviation career was almost a non-starter after he was told that his height of 5 feet 2 inches precluded him from military service – despite his having served throughout the campaign in SWA as a signaller. In 1917, however, he chanced to meet Major Miller, who recruited most of the South Africans who joined the RFC, and signed on. Trained on an aircraft modified for his size, he went to France with 84 Squadron and claimed his first kill on 3 February 1918. Fifty-three more would follow before a wound on 8 October put him into hospital for the rest of the war. Soon after the war he was arrested when two constables could not believe that one so young could have earned such decorations. He died in 1921, practising for the first Hendon Air Show, when the cushions he needed to reach the controls fell out during a loop.

One of the original five who had gone to France with the RFC and then to SWA, van der Spuy, began 1918 commanding an RFC training wing and was earmarked to command a group. Instead, he was invited to command the RFC element going to Archangel to support the Allied forces fighting with the White Russians against the Bolsheviks. On arrival, he found himself also in charge of the Anglo-Slavic Aviation Corps of former Russian Army pilots – not a few of whom had their 'secretaries' with them in the base. This interesting period came to an unhappy end in April 1919, when van der Spuy suffered engine failure after leading an abortive attack on the Red headquarters of the Vaga Front. Captured after a day and a night of evasion, he was imprisoned under miserable conditions for months before being repatriated.

The first commander of the future SAAF, 'Pierre' van Ryneveld, joined the RFC under his own steam in July 1915 after first being commissioned into the infantry. His early operations were against marauding Zeppelins over England. He then flew at Gallipoli, against the Senussis in the Western Desert, against the Turks in Egypt and Palestine and against the Bulgarians over Salonika. In 1916 he was recalled to England to command 78 (Home Defence) Squadron, one of the first night-fighter units. He ended the war commanding the 11th Army Wing. While not high on the list of scorers, van Ryneveld had attracted attention as a leader and was selected to form the new SAAF. Before undertaking this task however, he and Major Quintin Brand pioneered the air route from England to South Africa, and were knighted for their endeavours.

The new air arm got off to a real 'flying start' courtesy of the British Government, which offered 100 surplus aircraft together with the necessary spares and equipment – the latter including hangars and even vehicles. Van Ryneveld and his new second-in-command, van der Spuy, set at once to defining what aircraft types would be best for inclusion in this 'Imperial Gift.' They finally decided on 48 de Havilland DH9s, 30 Avro 504Ks and 22 SE5a Scouts. The entire gift had arrived by

1921, together with an additional 10 DH4s and one DH9 donated by the Overseas Club of London and the City of Birmingham.

Also in 1921, the first SAAF airbase was established at Zwartkop, near Pretoria. Recruiting proved again to be no problem at all, with a veritable flood of applications received. This allowed for extremely high standards, a practice still adhered to by the SAAF. The new service saw its first action in 1922 under unhappy circumstances, when it was called out to help put down the miners' rebellion on the Witwatersrand. Shortly afterward, aircraft played the major role in putting an early end to the Bondelswarts uprising. Similar operations followed in 1925 and 1932. The employment of aircraft drew criticism in each case, but there can be no doubt that it served to reduce bitterness and loss of life by bringing the situation under control quickly.

Meanwhile, van Ryneveld had succeeded in securing autonomy for the new service – but only after threatening resignation. Interestingly, it was General Smuts who was instrumental in establishing the RAF as an independent service; he was among the first to recognise air power's potential. The SAAF was less successful in its fight against the everzealous Treasury: like the other services, it found its budgets pruned drastically. Thus the single squadron that had been formed soon had to be reduced by a third,

and vital supporting elements were reduced to nuclei.

Despite these difficulties, the foundation for a larger force was laid. A key element in this achievement was the organisation of the only squadron into specialised flights – bombing, close support, reconnaissance – which could readily be expanded into squadrons. At the same time, provision was made from the outset for a reserve of part-time pilots. The full-time pilots kept up their proficiency by assisting the civil authorities in survey work, dusting plantations, spraying locust swarms, flying diamonds from the state diggings and undertaking various mercy and relief operations. The standard of training was brought to a pitch of excellence with establishment of the Central Flying School at Zwartkop in 1932, starting what has become a tradition.

The basic approach adopted by van Ryneveld, that of creating a core organisation which could be expanded as required, was recognised in 1934 when Parliament approved a major five-year SAAF expansion programme – assuming correctly that it could be absorbed by a

force that had long been starved of funds. This was followed by the Air Force Development Programme of 1936 which included a provision for building up a reserve of 1000 pilots and 1700 artisans for the SAAF over six years. In addition, twelve new squadrons with some 1000 pilots, 600 observers and 3000 mechanics were to be formed by 1942. Finally, van Ryneveld himself proposed in 1939 that the SAAF be expanded to 720 aircraft, including 336 fighters.

These goals naturally necessitated major expansion of training activities. The Central Flying School was no longer sufficient; others were established at Bloemfontein, Cape Town and Durban. Some training was also conducted for the SAAF by civilian flying clubs, concentrating mainly on the reserve element. The resultant shortage of training aircraft was met by purchasing from Britain at nominal price a truly motley collection of aircraft, which included Hawker Harts, Hartebeeste and Hinds, Avro Tutors and Westland Wapitis. These were soon followed into service by ex-RAF Audaxes and additional Hinds.

Right: General Sir Pierre van Ryneveld, in many respects the father of the South African Air Force.
Below: South African Boston medium bomber of the Desert Air Force returns to base after a sortie. After the North African campaign the Desert Air Force squadrons saw further hard service in Italy.
Bottom: Junkers Ju 86 aircraft of 12 Squadron after a raid on Italian positions in East Africa.

54

Above: SAAF B-24 Liberator in flight over the Alps. Two SAAF squadrons, 31 and 32, flew this type of heavy bomber. After the war they ferried many South African servicemen home from Europe.

Nevertheless, these good intentions and almost frantic efforts could not undo the damage of years of financial neglect. The SAAF, like the other services, went to war in 1939 woefully ill-equipped and under-manned, boasting all of 104 largely obsolete aircraft and a strength of some 1500. It had only eight combat aircraft – six

Below: Rockets from a SAAF Beaufighter fighter-bomber strike home on the Italian liner *Julio Cesare.*

Hurricane MkIs, one Battle and one Blenheim – none of them the epitome of modern aviation technology. Initial steps to correct the problem included the militarisation of South African Airways and the enlistment of all and any light aircraft that the SAAF could lay its hands on. The latter were passed to training units, while the 11 SAA Ju-52s and 18 Ju-86s were pressed into service as transports and maritime patrol aircraft, respectively.

Thanks to some far-sighted planning in its formative years, the SAAF was soon able to overcome this rather shaky start. First priority went to training, and a Training Command and further flying

schools were established. Then August 1940 saw the Joint Air Training Scheme initiated, whereby aircrew of the SAAF, RAF and other Allied air forces were trained at some 38 flying schools and two operational training units in South Africa – well away from poor weather and potential enemy interference. These measures soon had their effect on the SAAF; by late 1940 it had grown to some 1700 aircraft and more than 31,000 personnel, including 956 pilots and 715 observers. Also, most older aircraft had been phased out.

In the meantime, the ex-SAA aircraft had drawn first blood in December 1939 when the German blockade runner *Watussi* was intercepted by a Ju-86 and scuttled herself. Coastal patrols to cover the vital Cape Sea Route continued to enjoy high priority throughout the war: more than 15,000 such sorties were flown before its end. SAAF maritime patrol aircraft had attacked 26 submarines and been involved in the interception of 17 blockade runners. Their major value, however, lay in their very presence over these sea routes, which severely limited the options for the opposing submarines. The Junkers were replaced by Ansons and some Marylands during 1940. Beauforts followed in 1941 and, finally, Venturas.

With the Japanese entry into the war came fears of a possible thrust toward the Cape. One measure taken with this danger in mind was reinforcement of the coastal patrol force by two fighter squadrons flying Mohawks. The Allies then decided to seize Madagascar from the Vichy French to pre-empt any such Japanese attempt. The first step of this opera-

Above: SAAF Avro Anson on coastal patrol early in World War II. The Ansons were brought into service in 1940 replacing the Ju 86s acquired from SA Airways.

tion was the occupation of Diego Suarez in May 1942. A Beaufort squadron of the SAAF was then based there for much of the campaign. It concentrated on maritime operations, but also destroyed a number of French aircraft in raids on airfields before it moved on to East Africa in November 1942.

The SAAF opened operations on the African continent in May 1940, deploying one fighter squadron (Hurricanes and Furies) and two bomber squadrons (Hartebeeste and Ju-86s) to Kenya. A single flight of Gladiators was detached to the Sudan. Italy entered the war on 10 June, and the SAAF launched its first strike against Italian forces in Abyssinia on the morning of the 11th. With only forty aircraft to set against more than 380, the SAAF was badly outnumbered throughout this campaign. Even the arrival of an additional Hurricane squadron and another of Marylands shortly after hostilities began did little to change this.

Nevertheless, the SAAF succeeded in imposing its will on the enemy, flying 6517 sorties and downing 71 aircraft for the loss of 79 aircrew killed and five missing. These missions were flown from forward bases under extreme conditions that went beyond discomfort and made maintenance a nightmare. To give but one example, the dust on some of the airfields was so bad that wooden propellors were reduced to a life of only twelve take-offs. By contrast, some of the missions were anything but orthodox. One need only think of the Valentia that bombed an Italian fort with a homemade device built into a 44-gallon drum – which displayed an alarming reluctance to go out of the door once the fuse was lit! Then, too, we have the naked Gladiator pilot . . .

The first SAAF elements were trans-ferred northward to the Western Desert theatre even before the campaign in Italian East Africa was over. No 1 Squadron took over the defence of Alexandria from April 1941, while No 24's Marylands joined RAF light bombers in harassing Axis forces. These two squadrons were soon joined by squadrons No 12 and 24 (bomber), 2 and 4 (fighter), 40 (tactical reconnaissance) and 60 (photo reconnaissance). Together, they formed a major and highly active part of the Desert Air Force and were repeatedly singled out for high praise by Allied commanders. Quite apart from the capabilities of the aircrew, the performance of armourers and maintenance crews also drew universal admiration.

Squadrons No 12 and 24 were held in particularly high regard, both for the effectiveness of their operations and for their well-nigh incredible sortie rate. On 4 July 1941, for instance, they flew no fewer than 100 sorties with their increasingly tired aircraft: peacetime theory had held that the possible peak was around 20 a day for four days. The 100-sortie day came after several weeks of more than 20 a day. A major contribution was also made by the Bisleys of 15 Squadron, which did much to interdict Rommel's shipping and thereby contributed greatly to his eventual defeat. The true importance of the SAAF element can be gleaned from sortie figures: on D+1 of the Alamein attack, 3 Wing of the SAAF flew 133 of the 174 light-bomber sorties flown. On the 26th they flew 90 of 122.

Below: Sabre fighters of 2 Squadron preparing to set out on a mission in Korea.

Before the Allies could consider crossing the Mediterranean, much preparatory reconnaissance work had to be done, largely by 60 Squadron of the SAAF. Apart from sorties over Sicily and southern Italy, 60 Squadron also brought the first photos of the oil installations at Ploesti – for which Lieutenant 'Shorty' Miller received the American DFC – and of the Munich-Augsburg area of southern Germany. Squadron No 40, in turn, flew the lion's share of spotting and tactical reconnaissance missions during the invasion of Sicily, while the other SAAF squadrons were kept busy hounding the German forces.

The Dodecanese adventure, when the Allies landed on Cos and Leros, proved

Below: 2 Squadron Sabre being armed for a ground attack mission in Korea. The Squadron's "Flying Cheetah" crest can be seen on the side of the aircraft.

less happy for the SAAF. A detachment of 7 Squadron with Spitfire MkVs joined one from 74 Squadron RAF to provide local air cover and finally had to withdraw over the beach when the Germans retook the islands. Not, however, before it had added to its tally of 'kills.' On the same day that 7 Squadron landed on Cos, 40 Squadron was spotting for the 16-inch guns of HMS *Nelson* and *Rodney* in support of the landings on the Italian mainland. Soon the squadrons of the old DAF were heavily engaged in this campaign. With Britain beginning to prepare for the invasion of France, the SAAF was assigned an increasing proportion of this commitment in Italy to free RAF elements for their new task.

This increased load demanded greater SAAF strength in Italy. To this end, a new heavy bomber wing was formed (31 and 32 Squadrons), plus a light bomber squad-

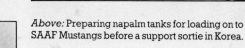

Above: Preparing napalm tanks for loading on to SAAF Mustangs before a support sortie in Korea.

ron (30, with Marauders), three fighter squadrons and an additional transport squadron. These were joined by three coastal squadrons transferred from South Africa, where the SAAF took over 262 Squadron RAF's Catalinas from Durban. Three of these squadrons – 16 and 19 with Beaufighters and 25 with Marauders – were attached to the Balkan Air Force and operated over the Adriatic and Yugoslavia. The others found themselves involved in some of the hardest fighting of the war, with the Marauder squadrons, in particular, having a hard time of it in the face of tenacious and well-organised air defence forces.

During August and September 1944 the two Liberator squadrons flew their hardest and most heroic missions – dropping supplies to the Polish Home Army in Warsaw. Flying 1700 miles through

several night-fighter areas and braving heavy anti-aircraft fire at altitudes of 200 feet above the city, they gave their best to no avail: the Red Army stood on the other side of the river and, many allege, waited for the Germans to crush the Polish uprising before they resumed their advance. The post-war period saw a similar but more successful mission when 20 SAAF crews flew RAF Dakotas in the Berlin Airlift to keep that city alive in the face of Soviet blackmail.

The SAAF ended World War II with some 35 operational squadrons, of which 29 were stationed in the Northern Hemisphere (27 in Italy, 22 Squadron at Gibraltar and 26 Squadron in West Africa). Personnel strength stood at 45,000, to which should be added the numerous South Africans serving with the RAF. The Joint Air Training Scheme had produced 33,347 pilots, including 12,221 for the SAAF. The contrast with the 1939 situation is almost so great as to be unbelievable.

Above: Super Frelon transport helicopter.
Right: The present Chief of the SAAF, Lieutenant General Earp, served as a pilot in Korea and was one of those unfortunate enough to be shot down and taken prisoner.

Unfortunately, the Treasury mentality had not died in SA: little time was lost in cutting the SAAF down to a reasonable peacetime size – and then beyond.

The peacetime SAAF was finally reduced to four full-time squadrons – 1 and 2 flying Spitfires out of Waterkloof near Pretoria, 28 flying Dakotas out of Swartkop (Zwartkop) and 35 (ex-262 Squadron RAF) with its Sunderlands at Durban. With its active strength cut so grossly, the SAAF reverted to pre-war doctrine and became again an expandable core. As a result, a number of CF squadrons were formed into a reserve, manned chiefly by war

Below: Harvards of 7 Squadron shortly after World War II. These aircraft were the only equipment of many squadrons in the years immediately after the war.

58

service personnel who had returned to their civilian occupations but still hankered after flying. Despite the availability of this large pool of aircrew, the SAAF had its eyes firmly on the future and also instituted a pupil pilot scheme to feed these squadrons. Much of the initial training was again carried out by civilian flying clubs.

Action came again for the SAAF with the outbreak of open war in Korea. The SA Government made No 2 Squadron available for service with the UN forces and the 'Flying Cheetahs' sailed for Yokohama late in September 1950. On arrival in Japan

they converted to the F-51D Mustang at Johnson AFB before deploying to Korea. Here they were attached to the USAF's 18th Fighter Bomber Wing operating out of K-9 and K-24 airfields near the town of Pyongyang. When UN forces had to withdraw in the face of Chinese pressure, 2 Squadron relocated to K-10 and K-13 near Chinhae. From here they flew many arduous and dangerous close-support and armed-reconnaissance missions over the next two years. In all, they flew 10,373 sorties, losing 74 of their 95 aircraft, with 12 pilots killed and 30 missing.

Early in 1953 2 Squadron traded in their outmoded F-51s, converting to F-86F Sabres. They began operations out of K-55, first carrying out fighter sweeps along

the Chang-Chung and Yalu Rivers, then reverting to the highly dangerous close-support missions. Before the war ended, the Cheetahs had flown more than 2000 sorties with their Sabres, building up their already formidable reputation as pilots who got the job done no matter how difficult. To quote one US officer who got to know them: 'We always gave them the dirty or tricky jobs that no one else wanted because we knew that they would handle them.' The Cheetahs were so highly regarded that the 18th FBW had standing orders to play the opening bars of the SA National Anthem before their own.

The SAAF passed the remainder of the 1950s uneventfully, concentrating on building up a solid core of both flying and

Below: Harvards have been in service with the SAAF since 1942 and are still used for *ab initio* flying training at the Central Flying School, Dunottar.

ground personnel. There was, however, considerable expansion of the CF element: nine squadrons were re-formed in this guise, chiefly on Harvards, although two operated Dakotas in transport and maritime roles respectively. Several were then disbanded again in 1958/9 as an economy measure; 17 Squadron was re-formed in 1957 with three S-55s and one S-51, the first pure helicopter unit. Acquisitions included Vampire FB Mk52s for 1 and 2 Squadrons in 1950 and 1953 and Canadair Sabre 6s in 1956 to replace them. Shackletons replaced the Sunderland flying boats of 35 Squadron in 1957.

The arrival of the first Alouette IIs in 1961 ushered in a period of almost uninterrupted expansion lasting well into the mid-1970s. During that 16-year period, the SAAF took into service no fewer than 26 different aircraft types and sub-types and re-formed 16 squadrons to operate them. That it was possible to do this without major problems is eloquent testimony to the excellence and wisdom of the previous training effort. That it should have been necessary is equally eloquent testimony to the neglect the SAAF had suffered at the hands of government until then.

Aircraft taken into service during the 1960s included four members of the Mirage III family (CZ, EZ, RZ and BZ), Canberra B(I)12s and T-4s, Buccaneer S-50s, Albatross maritime patrol aircraft,

Alouette III, Wasp and Super Frelon helicopters, Cessna 185 spotters, C-130 Hercules and C-160 Transalls, the locally built Impala Mk I and some old Skymasters. The Super Frelon was at that time the biggest helicopter in the world. In the first half of the 1970s the SAAF acquired additional Mirage IIIs (R2Z, DZ and D2Z), Mirage F-1AZs and F-1CZs, the new Puma helicopter, additional Alouette IIIs, Mercurius and Merlin VIP aircraft, Bosbok

spotters and the related Kudu light transport. Impala production also continued, with the Mk II light attack aircraft following the earlier trainer on the assembly line.

The SAAF is presently organised into two regional commands, four functional commands and a central headquarters in Pretoria. Most squadrons and some of the supporting units fall directly under the central HQ, which also controls those airbases not under one of the regional

Above: Mirage IIICZ of 2 Squadron at Hoedspruit in the Eastern Transvaal. The Mirage III has been in SAAF service since 1963.
Below: A Cactus anti-aircraft missile being fired during trials of the system.

commands. The HQ itself has the usual staff departments handling operations, intelligence, logistics, personnel and finance. An Inspector General – who reports directly to the Chief of the SAAF – is responsible for ensuring operational efficiency. To this end he devises and controls inspections and also plans exercises in conjunction with the staff departments.

Western Air Command handles all operations in support of the counterinsurgency campaign in northern SWA and controls the airbases in that region. Aircraft and personnel are assigned to it as required, generally on a rotation basis,

drawing on all squadrons and other elements of the SAAF. Squadrons will usually send personnel only to man aircraft which are based in the Operational Area. The main aircraft types operated in the area are Impala Mk IIs, Pumas, Alouette IIIs, Bosbok and Kudu. Dakotas, C-160s and C-130s fly 'scheduled' transport missions into and within the Operational Area. Other aircraft types such as Mirages, Buccaneers and Canberras are assigned when needed, usually in support of crossborder operations.

Southern Air Command is responsible for maritime operations and has its HQ at Cape Town, co-located with that of the

SAN Commander Naval Operations in the Silvermine complex. It has the additional responsibility for air-sea rescue operations and also for relief and rescue operations in the vicinity of the coast. Similar operations in the interior of the country are handled by SAAF HQ. Southern Air Command controls most of the coastal airbases, and maritime squadrons (22 – Wasps and Alouette IIIs, 27 – Albatross, 35 – Shackleton, all at Cape Town), two Impala squadrons (6 at Port Elizabeth, 7 at Cape Town) two helicopter squadrons (16 – Alouette IIIs at Port Elizabeth, 30 – Pumas and Frelons at Cape Town) and 25 Squadron at Cape Town with Dakotas, as well as 88 Maritime Operational Training School at Cape Town.

Tactical Support Command has the mission of establishing and operating temporary airstrips, whether newly prepared field strips or on existing civilian facilities. Its main elements are the CF Tactical Airfield Units, which are located around the country and can be speedily mobilised. These units have all the necessary vehicles and equipment – much of it containerised – and can have an airstrip ready for use by most SAAF aircraft types within 48 hours of arriving on site. They

Left: One of 44 Squadron's DC-4s ferrying a press party into the Operational Area.
Below: Mirage IIICZ of 2 Squadron, the 'Flying Cheetahs'. The Mirage has a maximum speed of more than Mach 2 at altitude.

Above: 35 Squadron Shackleton.
Right: A Cactus surface-to-air missile launch vehicle. The Cactus was one of the first effective low-level SAMs.

are even faster when setting up on an existing airfield or a stretch of widened and strengthened road. Squadrons bring their own specialised, aircraft-specific support equipment. The SAAF also assists in constructing civil airfields in strategic areas, simultaneously ensuring their suitability to wartime SAAF operations.

The primary task of the SAAF is to gain and keep air superiority from the outset of any conflict. Most air forces have the same primary task, but geographic factors in southern Africa require greater-than-usual emphasis on it. Key among these are

Above: Shackleton of 35 Squadron during a typical mission. Retiring at the end of 1984, these aircraft performed a vital role in South Africa's defence for some 27 years.

the excellent flying weather that prevails for most of the year, the generally open terrain and the vast distances linked by a sparse road net, all of which render ground forces inordinately vulnerable to air attack. Additionally, the poor force: space ratio that will inevitably pertain will make ground-based air-defence extremely difficult to implement effectively.

Air-defence as such is organised as an integrated system and falls directly under SAAF HQ, although the actual deployment of assets is the responsibility of the regional commanders. Army air-defence units 'plug in' to the local SAAF sector to ensure proper control and co-ordination. The main air-defence HQ at Devon in the Transvaal controls Northern Air-Defence Sector and is linked to permanent satellite radar stations at Ellisras, Mafeking and

Mariepskop. Mobile radar units provide additional coverage as required. Targets above 3000 meters are the automatic responsibility of SAAF interceptors. Targets at lower altitudes are normally allocated to ground-based systems where these are deployed.

Pride of place in the air-defence system goes to the Mirages of 2 and 3 Squadrons. The latter is equipped with F-1CZs and is stationed at Waterkloof outside Pretoria; 2 Squadron has the older IIICZs and is presently stationed at Hoedspruit in the eastern Transvaal. It shares this very modern base with the F-1AZs of 1 Squadron, which also have considerable air-to-air capability. The Mirage IIIEZs, formerly operated by 3 Squadron, are now flown by 85 Advanced Flying School at Pietersburg in the northern Transvaal. Surface-to-air weapons include the Cactus low-level SAM and, according to *The Military Balance*, some Tigercat SAMs. Gun systems in use are the 40mm L70 Bofors

and the Army's twin 35mm K-63 Oerlikons and single 20mm cannon.

The same factors that render SA ground forces peculiarly vulnerable to air attack apply equally in reverse. Despite this, deep interdiction does not enjoy high priority in the SAAF – the available Buccaneers and Canberras are too few to mount a really effective deep interdiction offensive. Particularly important or lucrative targets would, however, certainly be attacked. Battlefield interdiction and close air support, on the other hand, enjoy a priority only little lower than that accorded air-defence. This is partly a recognition of their potential under local conditions, but also reflects the difficulties the Army will face providing effective

SAAF FLYING TRAINING

1. Three months' basic training (SAAF Gymnasium).
2. Eleven weeks' officer training (SAAF College).
3. Nine weeks' aircrew orientation – introduction to aeronautics; survival; parachute orientation; etc.
4. Twenty-six weeks at the central Flying School – ground training and some 130 hours on Harvards; selection for Phase Two.
5. Pupils choose one of three categories: Fighters, strike aircraft and transports; helicopters; light aircraft.

6. Six weeks ground training at the appropriate Advanced Flying School, followed by some 120 hours on Impala I, Alouette III or Kudu respectively.
7. Those who qualify are now awarded their wings.
8. Operational training with a squadron.
9. Prospective Mirage, Buccaneer or Canberra pilots must first complete a tour on Impala IIs. Such a tour will normally include operational flying in northern SWA.

artillery support to its widely dispersed forces.

The basic air support system is essentially similar to those employed elsewhere. Overall priorities are determined at the Joint Forces level; actual control lies with the SAAF Air Support Operations Centre (ASOC), which reconciles these with the requests for air support in its tasking of the available assets. A Forward ASOC may be established in support of an independent force or when operations are to be conducted far from existing airbases. Brigade Air Offices control all air support operations in their areas, Forward Air Controllers ensure that close air support meshes with the requirements of the ground forces and does not go awry. When aircraft are detached to support a particular Army element, a Mobile Air Operations Team controls them.

Above: Impala II light strike aircraft, the type which has borne the brunt of the SAAF's recent close support missions and has performed very capably.
Left: The Cessna 185 is used by the SAAF to train future Bosbok and Kudu pilots.

The Mirage F-1AZs and IIIEZs are the backbone of SAAF strike capability and important in the close air support role. They can be supplemented with F-1CZs and IIICZs when there is no major air threat. The Impala Mk IIs are the primary close air support aircraft and have secondary light strike capability. The Buccaneers and Canberras have primary interdiction and strike roles, although the former also fly close air support and maritime strike missions. Helicopters provide close air support in counterinsurgency operations. Reconnaissance missions are flown by Impala Mk IIs mounting camera pods, the Mirage IIIRZs and R2Zs and

Below: Canberra bomber and reconnaissance aircraft of 12 Squadron

Canberras. The Bosbok specialises in artillery spotting, FAC work and visual reconnaissance.

The former emphasis in SAAF maritime operations on anti-submarine warfare (ASW) in conjunction with the SAN has changed with the Navy's diminishing ASW capability and the phasing out of the Shackletons which, in any event, are no longer adequate against modern submarines. The pending retirement of the SAS *President Pretorius* might also mean the end for the Wasps if no other suitable vessels are obtained. Today the emphasis

lies on coastal reconnaissance, with the protection of the sea routes round the Cape as a secondary task. Air-sea rescue operations are the other major concern of Southern Air Command.

Within the framework of the new priorities, the Shackletons fly the longer patrols, conduct specific reconnaissance and also shadow passing foreign naval units. The Albatross fly daily patrols of the shipping routes within 75nm of the coast and also carry out meteorological flights. Fishing vessels are checked on as a matter of course during all flights, but

specific fisheries-patrol flights are undertaken only on request. One typical Shackleton mission is the radar and visual reconnaissance from Cape Town to the Cunene mouth. It covers the area within 40nm of the coast and all shipping within 15nm is reported to Silvermine. East coast patrols are conducted from Cape Town to Kosi Bay. Some Shackleton missions may last as long as 12 to 13 hours.

One unusual rescue mission involved collecting an injured seaman from the Sedco 702 off the Cunene River mouth in June 1982. A Frelon flew to the rig from Cape Town via Alexander Bay, Walvis Bay and Terrace Bay – where trucks had been sent with fuel – accompanied by an Albatross to watch over it and assist with navigation. The seaman was given initial treatment and flown to Walvis Bay, whence the Albatross took him to Cape Town. Another operation involved flying two Pumas to Europa Island via Maputo in C-160s, assembling them and lifting the crew off the Danish *Pep Ice* aground on Bassa da India. Less fortunate was the crew of the Norwegian *Berga Vanga*, which sank in 1979 outside the effective range of the Shackletons. Norwegian and US Orions arrived too late.

Transport operations are another major facet of SAAF activity. The small force of

Left: Fire control vehicle for the Cactus missile system. One fire control vehicle will usually direct two or three launch vehicles.

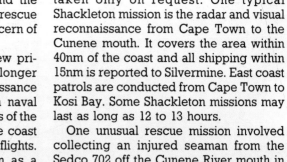

C-130 Hercules and C-160 Transalls shuttles regularly between the major airbases and into the Operational Area. They are complemented by Dakotas flying into smaller bases and Skymasters in the shuttle role. All but the Skymaster also have a paratrooping role. Kudus fly personnel and supplies into the smallest bases and also fly casevac. Frelons and Pumas do the vertical lift work and operate in the tactical trooping role, the latter flying assault and casevac missions. The ambulance role falls to a Merlin and one Dakota.

Present operational priorities are the day-to-day running of the air-defence system, tactical and logistic support for the security forces in northern SWA and coastal patrolling. Pumas play the major

Above: An air-portable photographic laboratory unit designed to allow rapid, high-quality processing of reconnaissance films to be carried out in forward areas.
Main picture: Buccaneer maritime strike aircraft of 24 Squadron.

414

SAAF FLYING SCHOOLS

1. Central Flying School, Dunottar
2. Jet Flying School, Langebaanweg
3. Light Aircraft Flying School, Potchefstroom
4. Combat Flying School, Pietersburg
5. Multi-Engine Flying School, Bloemfontein
6. Helicopter Flying School, Bloemspruit
7. Maritime Operational Training School, Ysterplaat
8. Air Navigation School, Langebaanweg

Above: The veteran Dakota transport serves in a variety of missions particularly supplying some of the smaller bases in the Operational Area.

part in SAAF operations in northern SWA, granting the security forces the mobility they need to react to and counter acts of terrorism by the insurgents. The fact that a Puma is always on standby for casevac is also a great boost to morale. Close air support is provided by a number of helicopters and Impala Mk IIs, while Bosboks fly various missions such as spotting, surveillance, communications relay, road patrol and route reconnaissance. The various transport types provide logistic support to and within the Operational Area.

While it is not as dependent on the CF as is the Army, the SAAF does have a large CF element. This consists, in the main, of personnel in various supporting roles, including ground crew, base defence, operations and technical staff. There is also, however, a growing body of CF aircrew which, while small in overall numbers, is very important. At present no fewer than 10 of the SAAF's 27 squadrons have a large proportion of CF pilots.

These are the six Impala squadrons (4, 5, 6, 7, 8 and 40) and Squadrons 27 (Albatross), 41 (Kudu), 11 (Cessna 185) and 44 (Dakota and Skymaster). There are also 12 Air Commando squadrons, which consist of CF personnel flying and maintaining their own light aircraft. They are employed chiefly for liaison, casevac and mercy missions.

The SAAF's greatest problem is that the fighter force faces block obsolescence over the medium term. The Mirage F-1s all date from the mid-1970s, the Mirage IIIs nearly all from the early to mid-1960s. More immediate problems lie in the lack of any serious deep interdiction capability, long-range maritime patrol aircraft and anti-armour-capable helicopters. Finally, both the helicopter and fixed-wing transport fleets need expanding and modernising. Another area of difficulty is that of personnel retention, as the skills the SAAF needs in its men are also in high demand outside. This is partly alleviated by the fact that the SAAF can retain in the CF many of those who leave the Permanent Force.

The obsolescence problem of the fighter force is arguably the most difficult and the most pressing. The SAAF can live without deep interdiction and maritime patrol as long as it has a good air-defence and strike capability. The difficulty arises from the generation change that is taking place today in fighter technology. Certainly Armscor could 'Chinese copy' Mirages if it really put its mind to it, but this is not the problem. The problem lies in the need for a 'new technology' fighter to replace the Mirages when they finally do become obsolete – and that is going to take ingenuity, money and time. On the other hand, the SAAF has had this problem before and did overcome it, albeit by purchase rather than manufacture.

Purchase will, in fact, almost certainly be the only way the SAAF can address most of its other equipment problems. Heavy transports and long-range maritime patrol aircraft could not reasonably be produced locally. The helicopter situation is less problematic, as they need not

Right: C-160 Transall seen during a delivery to a base in the Operational Area. This C-160 operates from Grootfontein.
Below: C-130 Hercules transport undergoing maintenance at Waterkloof. The Hercules and the Transall fly generally similar missions.

SOUTH AFRICAN AIR FORCE ORGANISATION

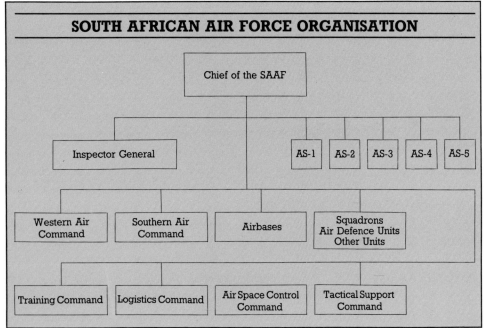

Chief of the SAAF

Inspector General

AS-1 | AS-2 | AS-3 | AS-4 | AS-5

Western Air Command | Southern Air Command | Airbases | Squadrons Air Defence Units Other Units

Training Command | Logistics Command | Air Space Control Command | Tactical Support Command

SAAF SQUADRONS AND AIRCRAFT

1 Squadron	Hoedspruit	Mirage F1AZ	Ground Attack/Day Fighter
2 Squadron	Hoedspruit	Mirage IIICZ	Day Fighter/Ground Attack
3 Squadron	Waterkloof	Mirage F1CZ	All-Weather Fighter/Ground Attack
4 Squadron	Lanseria	Impala II	Ground Attack
5 Squadron			Inactive, to be reformed at a later date with Mirages
7 Squadron	Langebaanweg	Impala II	Ground Attack
8 Squadron	Bloemspruit	Impala II	Ground Attack
11 Squadron	Potchefstroom	Cessna 185	Liaison/Battlefield Recce/Utility
12 Squadron	Waterkloof	Canberra	Photo Recce/Medium and High Level Bombing
15 Squadron	Swartkop	Super Frelon	Troop and Equipment Transport/Naval Support/Search and Rescue Support
16 Squadron	Port Elizabeth	Alouette III	Battlefield Support/Counterinsurgency/Search and Rescue
17 Squadron	Bloemfontein	Alouette III	Battlefield Support/Counterinsurgency/Search and Rescue
19 Squadron	Swartkop	Puma	Troop Transport/Casevac/Search and Rescue
21 Squadron	Waterkloof	HS125 Mercurius/Swearingen Merlin Viscount	VIP Transport
22 Squadron	Ysterplaat	Alouette III/Wasp	Anti-Submarine Warfare/Search and Rescue
24 Squadron	Waterkloof	Buccaneer	Naval Strike/Interdiction
25 Squadron	Ysterplaat	Dakota	Short-Range Tactical Battlefield Support/Air Support
27 Squadron	Ysterplaat	Piaggio 166S Albatross	Inshore Maritime Patrol/Air-Sea Rescue
28 Squadron	Waterkloof	C-130 Hercules/C-160 Transall	Medium- and Short-Range Tactical Air Support/Search and Rescue
30 Squadron	Ysterplaat	Puma/Super Frelon	Transport/Search and Rescue/Casevac
31 Squadron	Hoedspruit	Alouette III/Puma	Battlefield Support/Counterinsurgency/Troop Transport/Casevac/Search and Rescue
35 Squadron	Cape Town	Shackleton	Long-Range Maritime Patrol/Air-Sea Rescue
41 Squadron	Lanseria	Kudu	Light Battlefield Support
42 Squadron	Potchefstroom	Bosbok	Battlefield Recce
44 Squadron	Swartkop	Dakota/DC-4	Passenger Transport

Above: An Albatross of 27 Squadron on a coastal patrol. As well as patrol duties the Albatross has also proved useful in the search and rescue role.
Below: Impala II strike aircraft. The Impala carries two 30mm cannon and up to 1814kg of other stores.

be on the frontiers of technology to be effective. In fact, Armscor have announced their intention to begin producing an initial helicopter type for the SAAF, although they have not revealed type or timescale. Lighter transports and an Impala successor are also well within local capability and will almost certainly be tackled if there is no relaxation of the arms embargo.

Given these problems, the SAAF does not face a future quite as bright as its immediate past, for much of which it was the only SADF element with a credible conventional warfare capability. Nevertheless, it is still a very potent force indeed, and its fleet of some 75 assorted Mirage fighters and 75 Impala Mk II close support aircraft will remain useful for many years yet. The approaching obsolescence of the Mirages is to be countered by modernisation and by the provision of new weapons systems. One early example is the Kukri AAM with its helmet-linked fire control system, which gives a Mirage pilot a considerable edge over his opponents. With other systems in the pipeline, there is no reason to suppose that the SAAF will not be able to cope with anything less than intervention by a major power.

SAAF AIRCRAFT

Mirage F1AZ and CZ

Type: Fighter, fighter-bomber
Country of origin: France
First flight: Prototype 1966; production 1973
Delivered to SAAF: From 1975
Dimensions: Length 15m; span 8.4m; height 4.5m
Weight: 14.9 tonnes
Power plant: 5035kg static thrust turbojet; 7166kg with afterburner
Maximum speed: Mach 2.2 (2335km/h) at 12,000m; Mach 1.2 (1472km/h) at sea level
Service ceiling: 18,500m
Radius of action: Between 700 and 900km; 3 hours and 45 minutes endurance
Armament: 2×30mm cannon
Air to air 2 Kukri, Matra R-550 or Sidewinder; F-1C also 1 or 2 Matra R-530
Air to surface various bombs, rocket pods, AS-30 ASM up to 3650kg

Mirage IIICZ, EZ, RZ, R2Z, BZ, DZ and D2Z

Type: Fighter, fighter-bomber
Country of origin: France
First flights: Prototype 1956; production IIIC 1960
Delivered to SAAF: From 1963
Dimensions: Length 13.85m; span 8.22m; height 4.2m (IIICZ – others differ slightly)
Weight: 11.8 tonnes (CZ); 13.5 tonnes (EZ, RZ)
Power plant: 4025kg static thrust turbojet; 6000kg with afterburner (CZ, BZ); 4280kg and 6200kg (EZ, DZ and RZ); 5035kg and 7166kg (R2Z and D2Z)
Maximum speed IIIC Mach 2.1 (2230km/h) at 11,000m, Mach 1.22 (1490km/h) at sea level; IIIE Mach 2.2 (2336km/h) at 12,000m, Mach 1.1 (1390km/h) at sea level
Service ceiling: IIIC 16,500m; IIIE 17,000m
Radius of action: IIIC between 290 and 700km; IIIE between 290 and 600km; up to 1200km with external fuel;
Armament: 2×30mm cannon
Air to air 2 Sidewinder, R-550 or Kukri and 1 R-530
Air to surface Various bombs and rocket pods up to 1800kg; also AS-30

Buccaneer S Mk 50

Type: Maritime strike, strike aircraft
Country of origin: UK
First flights: Prototype 1958; production 1962; production S Mk 50 1963
Delivered to SAAF: 1965
Dimensions: Length 19.33m; span 13.41m; height 4.95m
Weight: 28,123 tonnes
Power plant: Two 5035kg static thrust turbojets and one 3630kg thrust rocket motor for additional take-off power under 'hot and high' conditions
Maximum speed: Mach 0.85 (1038km/h) at 60m
Service ceiling: 15,200m
Radius of action: Between 805 and 965km; up to 3700km with additional fuel
Armament: 4 bombs of up to 450kg each in bomb bay plus bombs, rocket pods or AS-30 ASMs on four underwing pylons up to a maximum of 7257kg

Canberra B(1)12

Type: Bomber, reconnaissance aircraft
Country of origin: UK
First flights: Prototype 1949; production 1954
Delivered to SAAF: 1963
Dimensions: Length 19.96m; span 19.51m; height 4.74m
Weight: 24,950 tonnes
Power plant: Two 3357kg static thrust turbojets
Maximum speed Mach 0.83 (901km/h) at 12,200m, Mach 0.68 (821km/h) at sea level
Service ceiling: 14,630m
Radius of action: 1300km; range of 6100km
Armament: 2720kg of bombs internally and up to 454kg on a hardpoint under each wing

Impala Mk II

Type: Light strike
Country of origin: Italy; built under licence in South Africa
First flight: Prototype 1957; MB.326K on which the Mk II is based 1970
Delivered to SAAF: From 1974; Impala I trainers from 1966
Dimensions: Length 10.65m; span 10.15m; height 3.72m
Weight: 5216 tonnes
Power plant: One 1547kg static thrust turbojet
Maximum speed Mach 0.82 (843km/h) at 6100m
Service ceiling: 11,900m
Radius of action: Between 130 and 600km
Armament: 2×30mm cannon; up to 1814kg of bombs or rocket pods on six underwing hardpoints

Shackleton MR3

Type: Long-range maritime patrol, anti-submarine
Country of origin: UK
First flights: Prototype 1949, MR3 1955
Delivered to SAAF: 1957
Dimensions: Length 26.59m; span 36.58m; height 5.11m
Weight: 44.45 tonnes
Power plant: Four 2455hp piston engines driving contra-rotating propellors
Maximum speed: 439km/h at 3650m
Service ceiling: 5852m; typical operating altitude 460m
Range: 6782km
Armament: 2×removable 20mm cannon in nose turret; various bombs, depthcharges, homing torpedoes and sonobouys in the bomb bay

Above right: The Canberras of 12 Squadron are employed chiefly for photo-reconnaissance work but still retain a useful bombing capability.
Below: 3 Squadron Mirage F-1CZs on final approach to land.

Albatross P-166S

Type: Inshore patrol
Country of origin: Italy
First flights: Prototype 1957; production P166S 1968
Delivered to SAAF: 1969
Dimensions: Length 11.6m; span 14.25m; height 5m
Weight: 3.68 tonnes
Power plant: Two 340bhp piston engines
Maximum speed: 357km/h at 2900m
Service ceiling: 7780m
Range: 1290km
Armament: None

Super Frelon

Type: Medium transport helicopter
Country of origin: France
First flights: Prototype 1962; production 1965
Delivered to SAAF: 1967
Dimensions: Length of fuselage 19.4m; rotor diameter 18.9m; height 6.7m
Weight: 12.5 tonnes
Power plant: Three 1550hp turboshafts
Maximum speed: 275km/h at sea level
Service ceiling: 3500m
Hovering ceiling: 2250m in ground effect; 550m out of ground effect
Range: 650km with 2500kg payload; endurance 4 hours
Payload: 4.5 tonnes freight; 27-30 troops

Puma

Type: Medium transport helicopter
Country of origin: France
First flights: Prototype 1965
Delivered to SAAF: 1969
Dimensions: Length of fuselage 14.06m; rotor diameter 15m; height 4.18m
Weight: 7.4 tonnes
Power plant: Two 1575hp turboshafts
Maximum speed: 294km/h at sea level
Service ceiling: 4800m
Hovering ceiling: 4400m in ground effect; 4250 out of ground effect
Range: 570km
Payload: 2.5 tonnes freight or 16-20 troops

Alouette III

Type: Light helicopter
Country of origin: France
First flights: Prototype 1959
Delivered to SAAF: 1962
Dimensions: Length of fuselage 10.03m; rotor diameter 11m; height 3.09m
Weight: 2.1 tonnes
Power plant: One 550hp turboshaft
Maximum speed: 210km/h at sea level
Service ceiling: 3250m
Hovering ceiling: 1700m in ground effect; 550m out of ground effect
Range: Between 100 and 500km
Payload: 820kg freight or 6 troops

Wasp

Type: Light ASW helicopter
Country of origin: UK
First flights: Prototype 1959; production 1962
Delivered to SAAF: From 1963
Dimensions: Length of fuselage 9.25m; rotor diameter 9.83m; height 2.64m
Weight: 2.495 tonnes
Power plant: One 710hp turboshaft
Maximum speed: 193km/h at sea level
Service ceiling: 3720m
Hovering ceiling: 3720m in ground effect; 2680 out of ground effect
Range: 435km
Armament: Two homing torpedoes or two depth charges

C-130B Hercules

Type: Medium transport
Country of origin: USA
First flights: Prototype 1954; production 1958
Delivered to SAAF: 1963
Dimensions: Length 29.78m; span 40.25m; height 11.66m
Weight: 33 tonnes
Power plant: Four 4050hp turboprops
Maximum speed: 618km/h
Service ceiling: 9150m
Range: 3942km with maximum payload; 7676km maximum
Payload: 46.30 tonnes freight or 92 troops or 64 paratroops

C-160 Transall

Type: Medium transport
Country of origin: France – joint ventures with other European companies
First flights: Prototype 1963; production 1965
Delivered to SAAF: 1969
Dimensions: Length 32.4m; span 40m; height 11.65m
Weight: 51 tonnes
Power plant: Two 6100hp turboprops
Maximum speed: 513km/h at 5000m
Service ceiling: 8500m
Range: 1850km with maximum payload; 4400km with 8 tonne payload
Payload: 16 tonnes of freight or 93 troops or 81 paratroops

Dakota

Type: Transport
Country of origin: USA
First flights: Prototype 1935
Delivered to SAAF: From 1943
Dimensions: Length 19.65m; span 28.96m; height 5.18m
Weight: 13.15 tonnes
Power plant: Two 1200hp piston engines
Maximum speed: 368km/h at 2590m
Service ceiling: 7300m
Range: 2170km
Payload: 3.4 tonnes of freight or 28 troops

DC-4

Type: Transport
Country of origin: USA
First flights: Prototype 1942
Delivered to SAAF: 1966
Dimensions: Length 28.63m; span 35.81m; height 8.39m
Weight: 33.113 tonnes
Power plant: Four 1350hp piston engines
Maximum speed: 441km/h at 4300m
Service ceiling: 5791m
Range: 2414km
Payload: 14.515 tonnes or 50 troops

Kudu

Type: Light transport, liaison aircraft
Country of origin: Italy, built in South Africa under licence
First flights: Prototype 1961; C4M Kudu 1974
Delivered to SAAF: 1974
Dimensions: Length 9.04m; span 13m; height 3.66m
Weight: 2.041 tonnes
Power plant: One 340hp piston engine
Maximum speed: 260km/h at 2440m
Service ceiling: 4150m
Range: 1297km
Landing run: 260m
Take-off run: 215m
Payload: 650kg freight or 7 passengers

Bosbok

Type: AOP and liaison aircraft
Country of origin: Italy, built in South Africa under licence
First flights: Prototype 1967
Delivered to SAAF: 1973
Dimensions: Length 9.09m; span 12.64m; height 2.72m
Weight: 1.75 tonnes
Power plant: One 340hp piston engine
Maximum speed: 278km/h at 2440m; 260km/h at sea level
Service ceiling: 8400m
Range: 1037km
Landing run: 66m
Take-off run: 85m

THE SOUTH AFRICAN NAVY

Once the vigilant 'Guardian of the Cape Sea Route,' the South African Navy (SAN) of today is essentially a coastal force. Starved of major vessels and maritime air support, it lacks the 'blue water' capability to oversee this vital trade artery effectively. SA's changed defence priorities, and the prohibitive cost of developing major vessels locally, seem likely to ensure that this unhappy situation will prevail indefinitely. It is debatable whether relaxation of the arms embargo or even defence aid could change it within a useful time-frame. Once run down, such capability is not readily or speedily restored. However, this is not the first time the SAN has been in straitened circumstances. The outbreak of World War II found it with a Permanent Force of five and a few hundred reservists. By 1945 this had grown to more than 10,000 manning some 89 assorted vessels.

The history of the SAN can be traced back to 1885, when the first successful naval volunteer unit was formed in Durban for port defence. The Natal Naval Volunteers were mobilised for shore service in the Boer War and the 1906 Zulu rebellion. A second naval volunteer unit was formed in Cape Town in 1905 as the Cape Colonial Division of the Royal Naval Volunteer Reserve (RNVR). The SA Defence Act of 1912 established a South African Division of the RNVR into which both units were absorbed. Twelve officers and 267 men of this Division served with the Royal Navy in all theatres during World War I.

Meanwhile, the SA Government had decided that the Union should form its own naval service rather than continue its annual payment of £85,000 toward the RN. At the 1921 Imperial Conference, it was agreed that South Africa would establish a seagoing PF element, expand the SA Division of the RNVR to provide personnel for local defence flotillas and similar services, bear a portion of the cost of developing the Simonstown dockyard and assume responsibility for hydrographic survey of its waters.

The first three ships of the new service, lent by the RN, arrived off Simonstown late on 11 January 1922. Personnel were recruited via the SA Division of the RNVR and appointed effective 1 April 1922; on this date the ships were recommissioned and the South African Naval Services (SANS) began. While this is accepted as the Navy's birthday, it was not officially established until 1 February 1923.

Whether being 'born' on All Fools Day has had an effect is open to discussion, but the SAN has certainly faced more than its share of difficulties from the outset. In its earliest days the Secretary for Finance approved the expenditure of £50 to repaint the names on its first three ships – but disallowed the £100 requested for the recommissioning ceremony!

The most trying time for the new service came with the Depression that began in

Previous page: Three strike craft at speed. They each carry two 76mm OTO-Melara guns.
Left: HMSAS *Protea* during the successful hunt for the Italian submarine *Ondina* on 11 July 1942.
Below left: Natal Naval Volunteers in 1902.
Below: The training ship *General Botha*.

1929/30. With government funds increasingly scarce, the SANS could not escape cuts in spending. Continuous training of CF units, including the SA Division of the RNVR, was stopped in 1932. The largest of the SANS ships, the 800-ton HMSAS *Protea* which had done sterling survey work, was paid off and handed back to the RN in April 1933, followed by her two consorts in 1934. Even when the financial situation began to improve, the SANS as such did not benefit, although the SA Division of the RNVR did receive funds for bases in the four major ports.

Thus the SANS had virtually ceased to exist by the outbreak of war in 1939. The SA Division of the RNVR, however, was in better health and could also call on its War Reserve. Like the other services, it was not mobilised, but permission was granted for volunteers to serve with the RN locally and, in limited numbers, overseas. The response was good enough to allow for the protection of SA ports and for the partial manning of four armed merchant cruisers which were to be fitted out in SA ports.

The SA Government now decided to re-establish its own naval force. Comprising both PF and CF elements, it was called the SA Seaward Defence Force (SDF). Unlike the SANS, which came under the RN, this new force was under

direct control of the SA Department of Defence in Pretoria. The Admiralty was asked to release members of the SA Division of the RNVR for service with the new force – which request was approved – and the five remaining members of the SANS were automatically transferred.

The new SDF was formally constituted on 15 January 1940 with 15 ships and several shore bases in commission. This

Above: The sea fisheries research vessel *Africana* performed valuable survey work after the demise of the SANS.

new force, too, would have a difficult start. In addition to the usual problems of establishing a new organisation, there were those resulting from the lack of naval expertise at Department of Defence Headquarters. Thus a requisition for bosuns' chairs drew the reply that as no

Above: Taking depth soundings with the lead in the
traditional manner aboard HMSAS *Protea* c. 1923.
Below: HMSAS *Gamtoos*, the salvage vessel
responsible for much of the important harbour-
clearing work in the Mediterranean during World
War II.

provision was made in the Army for special sergeants' chairs, it would be impossible to provide special seating for the SDF's bosuns!

More seriously, much work remained to be done on the 29 ships authorised; many of the minesweepers (M/S) were still unarmed. The first two anti-submarine (A/S) vessels became available only in April. But the paper expansion of the SDF went on apace, with the establishment increased to 12 A/S and 28 M/S vessels in October 1940. The authorised personnel establishment was doubled to 183 officers and 1049 ratings.

Concentrated at Simonstown, the SDF had only small initial detachments at Port Elizabeth, East London and Durban. Each of these consisted of a signal station, an examination service and a few minesweepers. This picture changed with Italy's entry into the war, as she had eight submarines stationed in Red Sea ports. Two A/S vessels were then assigned to Durban. January 1941 saw a detachment at Walvis Bay with two A/S vessels, and expansion continued when Japan entered the war.

The Admiralty, meanwhile, had approached the SA Government for A/S vessels to reinforce the RN in the Mediterranean. Despite the shortage of such vessels, four were made available. Formed into the 22nd A/S Group under Lt Cdr A F Trew – later a well-known novelist – HMSAS *Southern Seas, Southern Isles, Southern Floe* and *Southern Maid* reached Alexandria on 11 January 1940. Originally seconded until May 1941, their duty in that theatre was repeatedly extended. The last to return, *Southern Maid*, reached SA on 12 December 1945, almost five years after her departure.

These little converted whalers saw hard service on escort and other duties, which included towing barges into Tobruk. HMSAS *Southern Floe* was lost to a mine in February – HMSAS *Protea* later replaced her – and all suffered frequent attacks by Italian and German aircraft. HMSAS *Southern Maid* and *Protea* evened the score by sinking the Italian submarine *Ondina* on 11 July 1942.

Six months after their arrival the 22nd A/S Group was joined by four of the eight SA minesweepers requested by the Admiralty in May 1941. These also saw hard service in opening the ports of Mersa Matruh, Bardia and Tobruk for Allied use. One of them, HMSAS *Parktown*, would have the distinction of being the last Allied ship to leave Tobruk, towing a disabled tug full of escaping troops. Unfortunately, she fell foul of a group of E-boats and was lost. HMSAS *Bever* and *Treern* were lost to mines in Greek waters.

Above: The first contingent of the SA Division of the RNVR ready for overseas service parading outside their Cape Town headquarters on 9 October 1915.

Above: Men from HMSAS *Transvaal* arrive on Marion Island in 1947. The island is now the site of one of the most important weather stations in the southern oceans.

Another SA vessel in the Mediterranean was the salvage ship HMSAS *Gamtoos*, commanded for much of her service by Hugo Biermann, who was to rise to Chief of the Navy and then Chief of the SADF. Commencing operations on 20 December 1942, she quickly made a name for herself. *Gamtoos* was the first Allied vessel of any size to enter Tripoli, Tobruk, Marseilles and La Ciotat, ports she was largely responsible for opening. Her service also

Below: HMSAS *Blaauwberg*, one of the converted whalers that served in the anti-submarine role during World War II.

included the salvaging of an Italian circling torpedo for study, patching the battleship *Italia* after she fell into Allied hands and raising HMS *Maori* from the bottom of Malta's Grand Harbour.

Operations in home waters, while less dramatic, were important in view of the volume of shipping on the Cape route. Mines were an early problem, with the first field laid on the Agulhas Bank in May 1940 by the famous commerce raider *Atlantis*. A mine-clearing flotilla was formed to deal with this and subsequent fields laid by German ships. The cleared channels around the ports were kept open by local minesweepers. The degaussing ranges at Cape Town and Durban handled almost 20 vessels a month between them

at their peak, but by August 1944 mines had ceased to be a serious problem.

A totally different type of operation was the interception of Vichy French shipping. This served to stop contraband from reaching Europe and also gained ships for the Allied cause. The first to be requisitioned was the *Sontay* out of Saigon for Marseilles. Others followed, until the French instituted a convoy system. One of their convoys was intercepted by SA A/S vessels and RN cruisers in November 1941, yielding five ships – the most successful mission of this type.

The submarine threat in SA waters did not become serious until October 1942, when the Germans opened with a spate of sinkings. The shortage of A/S vessels placed emphasis on protecting the Cape Town and Durban anchorages: by late 1942 they averaged some 80 to 90 ships between them on any given day. Escort could be provided only for ships of exceptional importance, such as troop transports. Several RN destroyers and corvettes were later provided for escort work around the Cape.

By September 1943 the threat was believed – prematurely – to be over. Independent sailings were resumed until April 1944, when renewed attacks resulted in the resumption of 'group sailings.' All sailings north from Durban remained on that basis throughout, the escorts being provided by the 3rd and 4th Escort Groups, seconded to the RN for this purpose. In all, 132 ships were sunk within 1600km of the SA coast, totalling 743,544 tons. Only three submarines could be sunk in return, although many were destroyed en route to or from the Cape.

Meanwhile, the SA Government had decided to maintain a navy after the war and had renamed the SDF the SA Naval Forces (SANF). The SANF's first major warships were acquired in 1944, when Britain presented three Loch-class frigates for operations in SA waters. In return, SA agreed to provide 3600 recruits for RN service over the next twelve months. Renamed HMSAS *Good Hope, Natal* and *Transvaal*, the three frigates were commissioned in 1944/45. The SANF also manned two RN frigates, HMS *Teviot* and *Swale*, which were already in SA waters.

HMSAS *Natal* distinguished herself by a feat unique in the annals of naval warfare when she sank a U-boat within hours of leaving port for her trials. On 14 March 1945, while going to the assistance of a torpedoed ship, she received asdic confirmation of a submarine contact. The first attack brought up oil, as did the second, after which contact was lost. Examination of the debris confirmed the destruction of a U-boat later identified as *U-714*. *Natal* was also the only SA frigate to cross the Indian Ocean; she performed convoy duty in the Far East theatre until her return in November 1945.

Right: HMSAS *Protea* (foreground) and HMSAS *Southern Maid* in the harbour at Alexandria immediately before their return to South Africa at the end of the war.

With the war over, the SANF returned the ships borrowed from the RN or requisitioned. Others were sold off or broken up. Only 17 remained in service – the three frigates, the minelayer *Spindrift*, the boom defence vessels *Barbrake* and *Barcross* and 11 harbour defence motor launches. The port bases were closed down and reverted to a CF training role, with the exception of the Saldanha Bay base which was retained as the Navy's main training establishment.

Thus trimmed, the SANF was re-established as a part of the PF on 1 May 1946. Many chose to stay on and join the PF after their war service expired; others were directly recruited. The fleet was expanded in 1947 by the purchase of two ocean minesweepers, renamed HMSAS *Bloemfontein* and *Pietermaritzburg*, and a Flower-class corvette from the RN. The latter, renamed *Protea*, was converted into a hydrographic survey vessel. That same year the SANF carried out the occupation of Marion Island.

The SANF moved from Simonstown to Salisbury Island at Durban in early 1948. This extensive base, begun for the RN after the fall of Singapore, was completed after the war. An addition to the fleet came

Below: SAS *Transvaal* during a visit to Sydney, Australia, in 1950.

with the 1949 purchase of the W-class destroyer *Wessex* from the RN. Renamed HMSAS *Jan van Riebeeck*, she was recommissioned in 1950. Her sister ship, *Whelp*, followed in 1953 as SAS *Simon van der Stel*. Meanwhile, the SANF had become the SAN (1 January 1951); the prefix changed from HMSAS to SAS in June 1952. In July of the same year, a South

African Corps of Marines was formed, but this was disbanded in 1955.

With an independent SAN firmly established, the situation of Simonstown as an RN base had become anomalous. This was a topic of discussions which culminated in June 1955 in a series of letters generally referred to as 'The Simonstown Agreement.' In essence, these dealt with

Above: HMSAS *Natal* photographed during her trials at Newcastle (UK) in 1945. *Natal* was the only SA frigate to serve on escort duties in the Pacific.

the defence of the shipping routes round southern Africa and the transfer of the Simonstown base to the SAN. This latter aspect provided for the purchase of the base for £750,000 on the understanding that the SAN would be considerably expanded and that the RN would retain the use of the base. The formal handover of the base followed on 31 March 1957.

The other major aspect concerned measures governing future RN/SAN relations and details of the SAN expansion. There would be a strategic zone approximating to the RN South Atlantic Station and including the Mozambique Channel. Both the RN and the SAN would earmark forces for operations in this zone under the operational authority of the RN's Commander in Chief (CinC) South Atlantic. Within this zone lay a 'South African Area' which remained the direct responsibility of the SAN. A Joint Maritime War Planning Committee would work under CinC guidance in consultation with the SAN. The CinC's peacetime responsibilities would include planning and conduct of combined exercises and supervision of the readiness of selected forces.

The agreed expansion of the SAN comprised six anti-submarine frigates, ten coastal minesweepers and four seaward defence boats (SDB) to be purchased from British yards by 1963. The first of these, the SDB *Gelderland*, had already been commissioned in 1954. The others followed in groups: two minesweepers and an SDB in 1955, the frigate *Vrystaat* in 1957, four minesweepers and an SDB in 1958, four minesweepers and two SDBs in 1959 and the three President-class frigates in 1963/4. Fifth and sixth frigates were not ordered as a result of escalating costs, but the SDB order was increased to five.

The ten years following the Simonstown Agreement were happy ones for the South African Navy. New ships arrived almost continuously and regular exercises were

held with the RN. The SAAF acquired Shackletons in 1957 to replace its elderly Sunderlands and Wasps in 1964 for operations with the two destroyers converted to anti-submarine vessels between 1962/6. Many of the older vessels were also modified – SAS *Good Hope* into a despatch vessel, *Transvaal* for training, and *Natal* and the SDB *Haarlem* for the hydrographic survey role. Finally, the first locally built vessel, the tug *De Noorde*, entered service in 1962 and the new training base, *Simonsberg* at Simonstown, was commissioned in 1963.

In 1965 the closing down of the RN's

South Atlantic Station foreshadowed less happy times to come. Nevertheless, the SAN continued to grow at an only slightly slower rate over the next decade. A Maritime Headquarters was established in 1965 to combine the functions of the SAN Operational Directorate and the SAAF Maritime Group; the Chief of the Navy assumed the additional title of Commander, Maritime Defence. In 1969 the SAN took over the SAAF rescue base at Langebaan, renaming it SAS *Flamingo*. Salisbury Island was reopened in 1972, and major expansion of Simonstown followed from 1974. Finally, a sophisticated maritime headquarters in the hills outside Cape Town was commissioned in 1973. Combined exercises with the RN also continued, a South African officer commanding for the first time in 1971. Training cruises were undertaken to Argentina in 1967 and Australia in 1968.

Acquisitions during this period included the tanker *Amman* in 1965. She was converted into a replenishment ship and entered service in 1967 as SAS *Tafelberg*. Others were the locally built diving tender SAS *Fleur* and the tug *De Neys* in 1969; the Daphné-class submarines SAS *Maria van Riebeeck* (1970), *Emily Hobhouse* (1971) and *Johanna van der Merwe* (1971); the

Right: One of the many harbour defence motor launches used by the SANF during World War II for local defence.

Above: HMSAS *Hektor* was one of the minesweepers used to keep South African harbours open during World War II.

Hecla-class hydrographic survey ship SAS *Protea* in 1972 and two rescue launches in 1973. It was decided to acquire a number of fast coastal craft, and a project study undertook to define the requirement and consider the question of building these vessels locally. The maritime element of the SAAF was greatly strengthened by the purchase of Buccaneer aircraft in 1965 and Albatrosses and additional Wasps in 1969.

The fleet was further strengthened by upgrading several vessels already in service. The three President-class frigates were completely refitted and modernised between 1968 and 1973. This programme included fitting helicopter facilities and a new electronics suite comprising air-search radar, fire-control system and ECM/ESM and communications equipment. All of this work was carried out in the Simonstown Dockyard and remains one of its more remarkable feats. The minesweepers SAS *Kaapstad* and *Pretoria* were also refitted and simultaneously converted to a patrol minesweeper

configuration. In 1973 SAS *Maria van Riebeeck* began her first refit and modernisation programme. The SAAF Shackletons were modernised during 1968/9.

The acquisition of the *Daphné*-class submarines was, however, the most important development of this period. This decision was taken in 1967, after it had become clear that the SAN could not rely on support from any major power. A purely A/S fleet would no longer suffice. Further analysis indicated that a submarine flotilla would be the most effective strike element the SAN could either afford or man. The *Daphnés* were selected as much with an eye to the political situation as for their qualities, but have certainly proved themselves in service, performing well on both exercise and patrol.

The decision to acquire them set in train a major effort. They would be not only the SAN's first submarines, but the first major vessels not acquired from Britain. With a large contingent to stand by them during building, and their crews to be trained in France as well, a language laboratory was one priority item. A later step was to provide a primary school at Toulon. A major construction programme at the Simonstown base provided the necessary

Below: The SAN's last remaining frigate SAS *President Pretorius* refuelling from the replenishment ship *Tafelberg*.

accommodation, office space and workshops. This complex includes what was then the only marine lift in Africa, which lifts the submarines to the level of the overhaul shed into which they are then moved on rails. First named *Drommedaris*, this base was renamed SAS *Hugo Biermann*.

Any doubts the SAN might still have had about the attitude of the British Government were cleared away by late 1975. Britain not only refused to supply further ships and aircraft, she terminated the Simonstown Agreement in July of that year. With the SAN now definitely on its own, fleet expansion had become even more necessary than before if any 'blue water' capability was to be maintained. In the event, it had already been decided to order two *Agosta*-class submarines and two A-69 corvettes from French yards; these orders were placed during 1975. While the *Agostas* would certainly have extended the reach of the SAN, the selection of the A-69s represented a clear shift away from an open ocean role.

Six missile-armed fast attack craft had already been ordered in 1974. Now the SAN expressed its intention to obtain new MCMVs to supplement the existing minesweepers. Two of these had been brought

SAN VESSELS IN SERVICE

1. 10th Frigate Squadron
Home base: Simonstown
F 145 SAS *President Pretorius*
A 293 SAS *Tafelberg*

2. Submarine Flotilla
Home base: SAS *Hugo Biermann*, Simonstown
S 37 SAS *Maria van Riebeeck*
S 38 SAS *Emily Hobhouse*
S 99 SAS *Johanna van der Merwe*

3. Strike Craft Flotilla
Home base: SAS *Scorpion*, Salisbury Island, Durban

out of reserve in 1973 and four more followed by late 1976. In 1975 the Maritime Defence Command was abolished, the respective functions reverting to the Chief of Staff, Naval Operations and SAAF Maritime Command. SAN headquarters itself moved to Pretoria in 1977 to facilitate SADF co-ordination. The drift toward a coastal navy was clearly well under way. This became inevitable when France bowed to UN pressure in 1977 and cancelled the *Agosta* and A-69 contracts.

SA Minister of Defence P W Botha had warned as early as 1972 that the SAN and SAAF could cover only those sea routes that lay close to the South African coast. In 1978 the Chief of the Navy was rather more blunt: he made it clear that the SAN could no longer fulfill its earlier role but would have to concentrate entirely on protection of the SA coast, harbours and fisheries. P W Botha, now Prime Minister, was even more blunt: 'In future the safety of the West's tanker and cargo fleets will be its

own responsibility in the southern Indian and Atlantic Oceans. We have been forced into this situation by the Western arms boycott against us and from now on our attitude can be summed up like this – no arms, no service.'

Thus passed an era, sealing the South African Navy's reversion to a coastal force. The deletion of the old destroyer *Jan van Riebeeck* in 1978 underlined this emphatically – she was the last of the older 'big ships' and there were no replace-

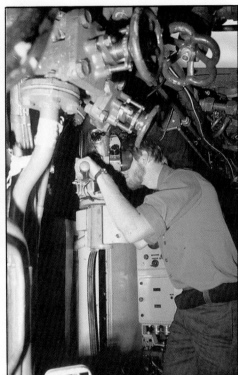

Above: Two *Daphné*-class submarines uncharacteristically operating together on the surface.
Right: The captain of a *Daphné*-class submarine at the periscope.
Main picture: the strike craft SAS *Jim Fouché* passing the former *Jan van Riebeck* after the *Riebeck* had been used as a target in a test of the Skerpion sea-skimming missile.

P 1561 SAS *Jan Smuts*	M 1498 SAS *Windhoek*	d. Three tugs
P 1562 SAS *P W Botha*	M 1499 SAS *Durban*	*De Mist*
P 1563 SAS *Frederick Creswell*	P 1556 SAS *Pretoria*	*De Neys*
P 1564 SAS *Jim Fouché*	P 1557 SAS *Kaapstad*	*De Noorde*
P 1565 SAS *Frans Erasmus*		e. Two hydrographic survey vessels
P 1566 SAS *Oswald Pirow*		A 234 SAS *Protea*
P 1567 SAS *Hendrik Mentz*	**5. Other vessels include:**	SAS *Haarlem*
P 1568 SAS *Kobie Coetzee*	a. Four seaward defence boats	f. Four air/sea rescue launches (home base: SAS
	P 3105 SAS *Gelderland*	*Flamingo*, Langebaanweg)
4. Mine Countermeasures Flotilla	P 3120 SAS *Nautilus*	P 1554
Home base: SAS *Chapman*, Simonstown	P 3125 SAS *Rijger*	P 1555
M 1207 SAS *Johannesburg*	P 3127 SAS *Oosterland*	P 1551
M 1210 SAS *Kimberley*	b. One boom defence vessel	P 1552
M 1212 SAS *Port Elizabeth*	P 185 SAS *Somerset*	g. One diving tender/torpedo-recovery vessel
M 1213 SAS *Mosselbaai*	c. A large number of Namacurra-class harbour	P 3148 SAS *Fleur*
M 1214 SAS *Walvisbaai*	protection launches	h. One experimental patrol vessel
M 1215 SAS *East London*		P 1558

ments. Symbolically, she met her end in 1980 as a target for one of the new strike craft. The remaining 'blue water' capability has since all but disappeared. Of the President-class frigates, only SAS *President Pretorius* is still in service, *Steyn* having been paid off as a source of spares and *Kruger* lost in 1982 after a collision with *Tafelberg* during an exercise. Even the long arm of the SAAF, the Shackleton, has come to the end of the road with no replacement in sight.

This was certainly not a turn of events welcomed by the SAN. SA is after all a maritime country with an enormously long coastline and considerable dependence on seaborne trade. The SAN also has the doubtful pleasure of seeing its predictions on Soviet activities in this area borne out. Nevertheless, the end of a 'blue water' SAN was inevitable under the circumstances. The 'Cape Sea Route' per se has no intrinsic value to SA, as she could never protect, at best, more than a tiny segment of it herself. Then, too, the threat of overland attack, conventional or insurgent, is far more real and immediate than any maritime peril.

In the years since 1978, the SAN has adapted steadily to its new role. The first

Left: Marines training with the 60mm mortar which is one of the weapons which they will use when they take their turn on border duty in northern SWA.
Below: The magnificent but grossly under-used facilities at Simonstown.

SAN BASES AND SCHOOLS

SAN Headquarters:
SAS *Immortelle*, Pretoria

CF Bases:
SAS *Unitie*, Cape Town
SAS *Yselstein*, Simonstown
SAS *Port Rex*, East London
SAS *Donkin*, Port Elizabeth
SAS *Inkonkonsie*, Durban
SAS *Rand*, Johannesburg
SAS *Mogaliesberg*, Pretoria

Naval College:
Gordens Bay, Cape Town – Officer training
Muizenberg, Cape Town – Command and Staff

Training Bases:
SAS *Saldanha* – Basic
SAS *Simonsberg* – Gunnery, Anti-Submarine,
   Communications, Diving, etc.
SAS *Jalsena*, Durban – Indian personnel
   Durban – Radar
SAS *Wingfield*, Cape Town – Technical

of the strike craft was delivered in 1977, and seven more were in service by late 1982. Five were built in the Durban yard of Sandock Austral, and there are hints of at least four more to allow 'operations on both the west and east coasts.' This would also imply the establishment of a satellite base at Simonstown. The main base of the Strike Craft Flotilla on Salisbury Island – SAS *Scorpion* – has been fully operational for some years and, like the submarine base, caters for all the Flotilla's needs. Other developments of this period include the conversion of the minesweepers SAS *Kimberley* and *Port Elizabeth* into mine hunters and the reappearance of the marines.

Established in 1979, the Marine Brigade is an outcome of the growing prevalence of insurgency as a form of warfare. It is intended primarily for harbour and base protection, against both wartime sabotage or raids and peacetime terrorism. To this end the Marines are trained and equipped essentially as light infantry, although they also man a large number of the locally developed twin-hulled Namacurra harbour patrol boats. These are road-transportable for ease of deployment and carry a variable armament of 7.62 and 12.7mm

Below: Firing sequence of the Skerpion missile from the *Jim Fouché* during tests in March 1980. Note the low-level flight path adopted by the missile after the initial stages.

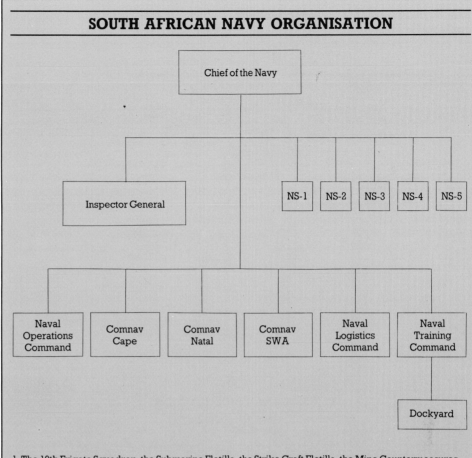

SOUTH AFRICAN NAVY ORGANISATION

Chief of the Navy

Inspector General

NS-1 | NS-2 | NS-3 | NS-4 | NS-5

Naval Operations Command | Comnav Cape | Comnav Natal | Comnav SWA | Naval Logistics Command | Naval Training Command

Dockyard

1. The 10th Frigate Squadron, the Submarine Flotilla, the Strike Craft Flotilla, the Mine Countermeasures Flotilla and individual vessels are assigned as required. Marine Protection Units are stationed in all of the ports while a further element is generally deployed in the Operational Area.

machine guns. The Marines receive their basic training at Saldanha, after which most serve in the Operational Area to gain experience. Thereafter they are posted to various SAN bases for security duties. Most are NSM who continue in this role during their annual periods of duty.

The return of the Marines has brought the NSM and CF element of the SAN back into some prominence, although the sea-going navy remains largely professional. CF personnel do, however, play an important part in various duties, which include partial manning of some mine-sweepers, diving and shore posts. One vessel, the SDB *Gelderland* at SAS *Donkin* in Port Elizabeth, has a Citizen Force captain. The general feeling, nevertheless, is that part-time personnel cannot effectively man modern vessels like the strike craft. But any development toward a

coastal insurgency problem could see a need for numbers of simpler, CF-manned patrol craft.

As the SAN stands today, its chief elements are undoubtedly the Submarine and Strike Craft Flotillas, which bear the brunt of current operations. These concentrate on patrolling SA and SWA waters and their approaches. With a coastline of 1500 nautical miles and 300,000 square nautical miles of economic zone, this is quite a task for a small navy: between 7000 and 8000 ships sail around the Cape annually. While the Suez Canal was closed, this figure reached 25,000. The Mine Countermeasures Flotilla shares the load by handling much of the inshore work. SAAF Albatrosses fly daily intensive shipping patrols off the Cape and also regularly cover other parts of the coast. Shackletons fly long-distance patrols and conduct specific reconnaissance.

On occasion there are forays deeper into the South Atlantic and Indian Oceans. Soviet naval movements in the region are

shadowed routinely. With the 10th Frigate Squadron effectively nullified by the loss of SAS *Kruger*, these tasks now fall mainly to the submarines. Apparently they have grown quite adept at them, not least *vis à vis* other submarines. All elements alternate operations with frequent exercises to ensure that they remain thoroughly practised in their wartime roles. Many of these exercises include the maritime elements of the SAAF.

While a future corvette squadron has often been mentioned: little has been said about the type of vessel in view. They have been variously described as 'small and armed similarly to the strike craft' and as 'similar to the corvettes on order in 1977.' It seems certain that they will have anti-submarine capability, as the SAN has expressed considerable concern at the prospect of its loss if the frigates are not replaced soon. It is possible that two variants may be built, one optimised for coastal A/S work, the other for those surface tasks for which the smaller strike craft lack the endurance or the seakeeping. Whatever their nature, they are likely to follow on to the end of the strike-craft contract at the Sandock Austral yard.

The Submarine Flotilla presents a problem of somewhat greater magnitude in view of the costs and complexities of

Below: Accommodation aboard a *Daphné*-class submarine can be very cramped for the complement of 6 officers and 41 men.

Below: SAS Rijger, one of the seaward defence boats bought under the terms of the Simonstown agreement and still in service with the SAN.

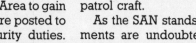

Above: The SAN minesweepers have a reputation for being very 'lively' in even a moderate sea, in part because of their light wooden hulls (designed to give a low magnetic signature).
Right: Fire-fighting and other damage control measures are practiced often and effectively.
Below: Chief of the Navy, Vice-Admiral Putter.

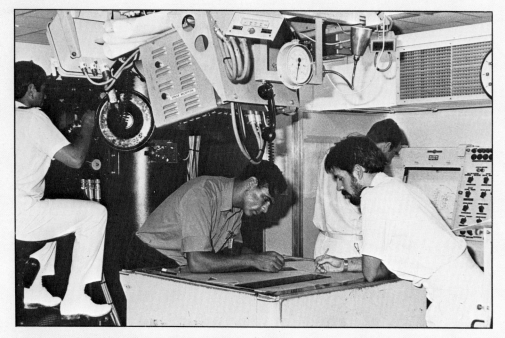

Above; A submarine attack team training in the simulator at the Simonstown base. Simulators provide highly realistic training at very low cost and in complete safety.

developing or even merely building submarines locally. Nevertheless, the SAN is determined not to lose this element of its capability. The present *Daphnés* are felt to have another twelve years of service ahead of them, which does leave some little room for manoeuvre. There is another aspect to this question, however, in the fact that the Flotilla lost its intended expansion and long-range element when the *Agosta* order was cancelled. Even apart from the questions of range and endurance, three boats are not adequate to maintain a useful deployment.

When this aspect is considered, together with the absence of any long-range maritime element once the *Pretorius* and the Shackletons are retired, the situation becomes more urgent. Even a coastal navy does need a stand-off element. Thus the SAN may come to believe that it should look beyond the 'easy way' of, in effect,

NAVY VESSELS

President-Class Frigate

Displacement: 2800 tons full load
Length: 112.8m
Beam: 12.5m
Draft: 5.3m
Speed: 29 knots
Range: 7200km at 12 knots
Propulsion: 2 geared turbines giving 30,000shp
Armament: 1 Wasp helicopter; 2×115mm guns (twin turret); 2×40mm Bofors; 6×Mk32 torpedo tubes (2 triple) for A/S Torpedoes; 1×Limbo 3-barreled A/S mortar
Complement: 13 officers; 190 ratings

Daphné-Class Submarines

Displacement: 869 tons surfaced; 1043 tons dived
Length: 57.8m
Beam: 6.8m
Draft: 4.6m
Speed: 13.5 knots surfaced; 16 dived
Range: 7200km snorting
Propulsion: 2 diesels giving 1224bhp; 2 electric motors giving 2400bhp
Armament: 12×55cm torpedo tubes (8 bow, 4 stern)
Complement: 6 officers; 41 men

Minister-Class Strike Craft

Displacement: 450 tonnes, full load
Length: 62.2m
Beam: 7.8m
Draft: 2.4m
Speed: 30 knots +
Range: 2400km at 30 knots; 5800km at economical speed
Propulsion: Four diesel engines totalling 12,000bhp
Armament: 6 Skerpioen SSMs; 2×76mm dual-purpose guns; 2×20mm cannon; 2×12.7mm twin machine guns
Complement: 7 officers; 40 ratings

Mine Countermeasures Vessels

Displacement: 440 tonnes, full load
Length: 46.6m
Beam: 8.5m
Draft: 2.5m
Speed: 15 knots
Range: 3700km at 13 knots
Propulsion: One diesel of 3000bhp (P1556/7 – 2500bhp)
Armament: 1×40mm Bofors; 2×20mm (one twin, some 1×20mm)
Complement: Varies according to role – sweeper, hunter, patrol

Above: Dramatic view of a strike craft showing the forward 76mm gun and the 20mm cannon on either side of the bridge. A variety of radar and ECM aerials can also be seen.
Below: Early stages of a Skerpion missile's flight.

replicating the *Daphnés* when they are due for replacement. The logical step then would be to use the experience gained in standing by, operating and refitting the *Daphnés*, together with the documentation that was received on the *Agostas*, to develop something more akin to those boats – using the latest technology available to update the basic design. There

have been numerous statements on the subject of building submarines locally, particularly in the last few years. Therefore, it should not come as a surprise if this project is tackled even before the corvette programme is completed.

Other projects likely to materialise over the not-too-distant future could well include the long-intended building of a new

NAVY DIVERS

The divers are to the SAN what the Paras are to the Army. They are also the oldest of the 'elites': the first SAN diving school was founded in Cape Town harbour in 1941, and SAN divers saw distinguished service with the salvage vessel HMSAS *Gamtoos*, which cleared several important Mediterranean harbours during World War II After the war the diving unit was allowed to run down drastically, being reduced to one qualified diver before wiser counsels prevailed in the mid-1950s

Like other elite elements of the SADF, the divers set a very high standard for candidates – many hopefuls get no further than the selection phase. Those who pass the stringent medical and psychological tests must still pass one of the toughest PT tests in the SADF if they are to progress to the swimming tests. These are the final decider and include underwater and long-distance swimming, swimming with a water-filled mask and free diving. Successful candidates enter the three-month basic diving course, which is extremely demanding both mentally and physically.

The course covers diving techniques, basic underwater construction work, demolitions and a good measure of physics. Frequent and hard physical training continues through the course and includes such delights as four-hour swims and combined swimming/running excursions which can include a session on the assault course. Log PT is a regular feature. The final practical examination includes such tasks as cutting a chain underwater wearing a blacked-out mask and using a hammer and chisel, tunnel

Below: Preparing for a training dive. Note the scrambling net, used for physical training, in the background.

Above: As well as their routine use in diving and diving training, the SAN's decompression chambers are also used in the event of civilian emergencies.
Right: Divers during winching exercises with a SAAF Wasp helicopter off Simonstown. Helicopter jumps and recovery are practiced for possible search and rescue tasks among others.

diving in a tunnel too narrow to turn around in, a one-mile swim with snorkel, mask and fins and helicopter jumps.

Successful completion brings Class One Diver rating, qualifying the new member to 30m with compressed air and for basic underwater construction, repair and demolitions work, bottom searches and checking ships for underwater damage or possible charges. National service divers generally stop at this level and spend the remainder of their two-year service and later CF camps on routine diving tasks. Most are posted to the various harbour protection units which are stationed in major ports. Civilians may also apply for this training if they undertake to join a CF unit.

Those wishing to qualify as Class Two Divers must sign on for a minimum of four years in the PF. They will then become eligible to start the Class Two course after completing 100 hours of diving. This qualifies them to 54m with either compressed air or an oxygen/nitrogen mixture and to 10m with pure oxygen. The training covers various advanced techniques and includes an intensive demolitions course that also deals with mine countermeasures and explosive ordnance disposal. Other aspects are compass swimming and 'standard diving' with a helmet and a surface-controlled air supply.

After a minimum of four years' experience, the best divers may apply for Class Three and instructor training. This covers much the same ground as earlier courses but in considerably greater detail. It then progresses to salvage, underwater bomb disposal and charge laying, and a supervisor's course, including recognition and initial treatment of decompression sickness and diving injuries and the use of the decompression chamber. The qualified Class Three Diver can then be posted to command one of the operational diving teams, or as an instructor at the Diving School in Simonstown or the ancillary school at Salisbury Island, Durban.

Above: SAS *Somerset*, an SDB and a minesweeper
out of water for maintenance courtesy of the
Simonstown synchrolift.
Above right: The devastating effects of the Skerpion
hit on the *van Riebeeck*.
Below: The *Jan van Riebeeck* in happier days.
She was decommissioned in 1978 and expended as a
target ship in the Skerpion test shown above right.

generation of MCMVs to supplement and later replace the existing minesweepers and the expansion of the available fleet of coastal patrol craft. This latter category could be on the basis of a smaller, less heavily armed strike craft. The navy is also likely to seek a purpose-built replenishment vessel to replace SAS *Tafelberg*. Another subject close to the SAN's heart is the question of replacing the SAAF Shackletons. Again, even a coastal navy does need a long-range and high-endurance reconnaissance capability if it is to react in time to be effective.

All going well, then, the second half of the eighties should see the SAN enlarge its fleet and enhance its striking power. Despite this, the difficulty of entirely offsetting the effects of the arms embargo will still create some gaps. Ironically, the most dangerous of these will not be within SAN's domain as such, but within that of the SAAF. One other problem that could become serious for the SAN is the continuing shortage of general-duties officers, which bodes ill for any expansion programme. By the mid-nineties, however, the SAN should have recovered from the embargo-induced setbacks to stand as a very potent coastal defence force. However, any question of a return to 'blue water' capability during this century will depend not on the SAN but on the West.

Like any military establishment, the SADF has its elite units which distinguish themselves both in their performance and in their 'rites of passage.' While there is only one true special-forces element – the Reconnaissance Commandos – several other units maintain similar standards in personnel selection and training and in their operational performance. None of them is eager to discuss its doctrines or tactics, but most have released occasional information on selection procedures and training. Both 32 Bn and the elite police counterinsurgency unit, 'Ops K,' have given some insight into their operations. Apart from Ops K, one other non-SADF unit is discussed here: the SWATF's unique SWA Specialist Unit. Finally, it is worth noting that both the South African Police (SAP) and the Transport Services Police maintain highly efficient anti-terrorist units which shun publicity entirely.

1 Reconnaissance Commando – The 'Recces'

With the paratroops moving toward a more conventional airborne-forces role, the SADF felt a distinct need for an SAS or Fernspäher type of unit. This need was met by the establishment of a small specialist unit in Durban (1 October 1972) called 1 Reconnaissance Commando. Since then, a number of additional Recce Commandos have been established, including a CF element and 4 Recce, based at Langebaan in the Cape and trained for amphibious operations. All have amply proved their worth on operations, and the 'Recces' have earned the admiring re-

Previous page: Mounties in the training area of the Equestrian Centre.
Below: Ops K personnel waiting on their Casspir APC in the course of a patrol.

Above: An Ops K patrol takes a break while trackers in the background cast about for fresh traces of insurgents.

spect even of the tough 'parabats' and the bush war experts of 32 Bn.

One of the tasks of the Recce Commandos is that of gathering intelligence on activity in enemy rear areas. The execution of special operations in the enemy rear also falls within their ambit. In general, they could be described as specialists in strategic intelligence, although the war against PLAN insurgents has seen them carry out tactical intelligence-gathering missions. On occasion, they have also been used as an elite combat element, as was the case in operations during 1982 which were aimed at the elimination of two PLAN front headquarters. Normally, however, the superbly trained Recces are too valuable to risk in a combat role despite their undoubted efficiency. As is the case with their equivalents in other countries, they are best employed in a covert observation role.

Little has been released about how the Recces are organised or how they operate. It has been said, however, that their basic element is the five- or six-man team wherein each member is a specialist of some kind. A typical team might include a tracker, a navigator, a medic, an explosives expert and a signaller. On the other hand, there have also been occasional references to reconnaissance teams as small as two men operating well inside Angola, which can safely be taken to refer to the Recces.

Operational and tactical details are nonexistent, which is only natural considering that the Recces must rely always on stealth for the success of their missions and often for their very survival. Broadcasting their methods would be one way of committing suicide. The only information available in this regard is that they are trained in the use of boats, and that they do have some armed and modified vehicles among their equipment. Given the thinly populated nature of much of southern Africa, it does not take too much imagination to see them sometimes operating in a style not dissimilar to that of the British Special Air Service (SAS) of World War II.

Both the selection procedure and the actual training of the Recces are very stiff indeed, putting even the Paras and 32 Battalion in the shade. Above all, every effort is made to avoid roughnecks or 'muscle-bound morons.' While the Recces must be very fit indeed, they also need more than an average intellect to carry out their mission. Strong character and a considerate nature are additional requirements for their role: any weakness of

Right: A rare picture of members of a Reconnaissance Commando on exercise. Both soldiers facing the camera have had their faces blacked-out for security reasons.

character or inability to get along with other team members could all too easily spell the failure of a given operation. The toughness of the selection process is demonstrated by the fact that a typical year may see up to 700 applicants – in themselves a select group – of whom perhaps 45 make the grade. It is also interesting that more than 75 percent of the Recces have their matric, and not a few hold university qualifications in very diverse subjects.

Two selection courses are held each year, prior to which recruiters visit various units to outline the nature and role of the unit and its training programme. They also show films of the process to ensure that there are no false impressions among potential applicants. Potential candidates then undergo thorough medical and psychological examinations and are quizzed about their reasons for wanting to join and what they think they can contribute to the unit. Even prior to this very searching interview, they must pass a PT test which includes:

a) 30 km with normal kit and rifle and a 30-kg sand bag in 6 hours;
b) 8 km in long trousers and boots, with rifle, in 45 minutes;

Left: Like the Recces, 32 Battalion is little photographed. This picture shows a 32 Bn officer, Captain Jan Hougaard on one of the unit's few public displays with a selection of captured weapons.
Below: Mounties of the SWA Specialist Unit in training.

c) 40 push-ups, 8 chin pulls and 68 sit-ups within a specified time;
d) 40 shuttle runs of 7 m each in 90 seconds;
e) Swim 45 m freestyle.

Those who pass this PT test, plus the medical and psychological examinations, and convince the selection board that they have something to offer the unit, can then enter the three-week pre-selection programme course! This kicks off with two weeks of strenuous PT for eight hours a day to prepare aspirants for the rigours of the selection programme proper. Some lectures on relevant subjects are thrown in with the same purpose. Usually some 20 percent of the applicants drop out during this phase – eloquent testimony to its harshness, given the standard of fitness required even for entry.

This is followed by a one-week water orientation programme in Zululand. This tests the candidates' adaptability to water and their adeptness in small boats. Instruction is given in the use of kayaks, two-seater canoes and motor boats. Navigation exercises take candidates many kilometers through swamps, and there is an 8-km race with poles over the dunes – one four-man pole per two men. Candidates are allowed to form up into teams of their choice during this phase and are watched closely for teamwork and leadership; a buddy rating is called for toward the end of the phase. Rations are gradually reduced during the week. Candidates are rated for adaptability, swimming and

Above: Parabats jumping from a Dakota. Despite their age the Dakotas still give good service.

other water skills, ability to work under difficult circumstances and stress, resistance to cold, claustrophobia, co-ordination and fitness. At this point another 20 percent drop out.

The remaining candidates are then flown to the Operational Area for the final phase of the selection programme. The

first week here takes the form of a bush orientation/survival course during which they are taught which plants are edible, which give water, how to get a fire going without matches and how to cope with lion and elephant. The first day of this course sees the candidates stripped and searched for cigarettes, tobacco, sweets and toiletries – only kit and medical items are left to them. They are then given time to build a shelter with their ground sheet – which must be dug in 45 cm – and are marked on its neatness, practicality and originality. Rations are further reduced and water is limited to five litres a day per man.

Apart from the survival training, PT stays with them throughout: a typical day might include an hour of PT before a breakfast consisting largely of water; observation tests wherein candidates are given a fixed route to follow on which they must identify and note down ten different objects; three runs over an assault course – the last with a 35-kg pack, including a mortar-bomb container filled with cement; a five-km run along an *oshana*

Below: Ops K men waiting to take up positions along a road while another group pushes an insurgent patry toward the road where they will be attacked in the open.

(gully) without their kit, followed by loading up again and carrying a tree trunk back to their camp. During this phase the candidates are evaluated for adaptability; water discipline; bush navigation; fear of the dark, animals and heights; ability to do without food; care of weapons and equipment; memory; powers of observation; leadership; and the ease with which they move in bush. Particular emphasis is placed on the ability to get on with others

Above: Dog handler and dog on patrol training at the SADF Dog Centre.

while under stress. A second buddy rating is called for.

This phase ends in a spate of automatic rifle fire that heralds the next stage which is intended to try the candidates psychologically to the uttermost – and succeeds. Then comes the 'crunch' phase. One morning the men are told that 'The course

is 51 degrees magnetic. You walk 38 km and your RV is 1900 hours this evening at a dirt landing strip. If you make it, you may get some food.' Twenty km along they are met by some of the instructors and allowed to fill their water bottles – while the instructors drink and spill ice-cold soft drinks. On arrival at the RV, each man is given eight biscuits – only to discover that they are contaminated with petrol and totally inedible. Meanwhile, the instructors have a happy barbecue picnic which any candidate can join – if he is only willing to drop out.

Finally, the candidates are put into the bush for five days with a tin of condensed milk, half a 24-hour ration pack and twelve biscuits, eight of which are soaked in petrol. Elephant, lion, and bush fires are among the problems of this final stretch. When they finally get to their last rendezvous, the men are given a new bearing and told there are another 30 kilometres to go. Those who go on find the instructors around the next corner. Seventeen percent make it.

Those who survive the selection programme must then complete and pass the parachute course before being accepted into the Recces. The actual Recce training lasts some 42 weeks and includes tracking, survival, weapons handling, explosives, unconventional warfare, unarmed combat, mountaineering, guerrilla tactics, bush- and field craft, map reading, day and night navigation and signalling. Throughout this training they are also taught how to handle enemy equipment in each of the categories. Physical training naturally also stays with them and, in fact, reaches new peaks in what is demanded and achieved. The final test is a night or

Below: Para trainee on the assault course.

two in lion country with rifle, ammunition and a box of matches.

The new Recce is now posted to a team in one of the existing Recce Commandos specialising in whatever he proved best suited to during his training. After serving in such a team for a while, members can choose to specialise further in this direction or in other areas like military free-fall parachuting or sea training. The latter includes combat diving, kayak work, small boat handling, coastal and deep-sea navigation and sailing.

Given the demands of their selection and training, the Recces will always be a very small group of men, a group that others look up to as examples of the ultimate individual soldier. Envy plays no part in this, for their work is easily as demanding and often as unpleasant as their training. Only a special sort of man would seriously want to join, and only those are taken on. This is as it should be, and the Recces will continue to produce fine results out of all proportion to their numbers.

Above: A recruit's impression of life as a trainee with 1 Para (drawn on a hangar wall) showing the standard features of the training programme.

44 Parachute Brigade – The Parabats

Long the elite of the SA Army, the 'Bats' retain their image as one of the toughest and most efficient elements; it is really only the advent of the Reconnaissance Commandos that has removed them from the top-dog position. Their own Pathfinder element, however, runs the Recces a close race for that slot. By any measure, the Bats are a highly effective and respected fighting force that has caused PLAN considerable heartache.

While individual South Africans served in various airborne and commando units during World War II, SA did not have any such elements in its own army until the first parachute battalion was formed on 1 April 1961. Comments on that date, it might be added, are unlikely to endear the maker to any paratroops within earshot.

Formed by the man who would become Chief of the Army – W P Louw – after he and a small contingent had trained with Britain's 'Red Berets,' the new unit was based at Tempe in Bloemfontein. The Parachute Battalion soon established its own extremely high standards of fitness and military skill and became the elite – a unit many might wish to join but which

Below: A mixed party of Koevoet and SWATF personnel resting on a Ratel during operations against insurgents in the Tsumeb area in 1982.

would accept only a few of the best. Soon it acquired a nickname to go with its status, Parachute Battalion being shortened to 'Parabat' or even just 'Bat.'

In 1963 the Battalion was split to create an independent Parachute Training Centre and thereby allow the Battalion as such to become a purely operational unit. By 1967, however, this experiment had been discarded and both training and operational elements were back under one roof with 1 Para. The next development came when the unit's CF element outgrew the

reasonable administrative capacity of the Battalion. One particular problem arose from the fact that its CF members were scattered throughout the country and thus difficult to get together apart from annual camps. Esprit and fresh training in all aspects of their task being vital to the paras, this situation could not continue. Accordingly, a CF Para Bn was formed as 2 Para in July 1971, with an HQ company at Tempe and five rifle companies based in different South African cities.

This battalion received its baptism of fire during Operation Savannah and performed very creditably indeed. With the military situation becoming less favourable, the size of the available airborne force was increased again, and a second CF unit – 3 Para - was therefore formed. Finally, the three battalions were grouped with supporting elements including heavy mortars to form 44 Parachute Brigade, with HQ at Bloemfontein, in 1978. Ironically, this took place at much the same time that the British Army lost its 44 Para Brigade (Volunteers) of the Territorial Army to budget cuts. The new 44 Brigade saw its first action at Cassinga during Operation Reindeer, with elements of all three battalions jumping. Since then the Bats have figured in their primary role in the course of several external operations, including Sceptic, which saw six companies of 1 Para deployed in southern Angola simultaneously, Protea and Daisy.

Elements of all three battalions are also employed on internal operations, usually

some differences: PT twice a day, no walking in camp under any circumstances and a 5-10-km run to end each day. Some 10 to 20 percent drop out during this phase, returning to their original units for the duration of their national service.

This phase is followed by some six weeks of advanced individual training, during which such subjects as driving and maintenance, supporting weapons, signalling and unarmed combat are covered. The level of physical training is now intensified to prepare the candidates for the PT course to follow. During this period they are also formed into companies. The two-week PT course that follows is the final crunch for many of the applicants; few who survive will drop out later. These two weeks see something like seven-and-a-half hours of PT a day, including 16-km runs with tar poles and/or 'dogs' – the latter are motor-car tyres which the trainees drag around with them at the end of a rope. A little later comes 'the marble' – a hessian-covered concrete paving slab which the trainees are required to take everywhere with them. During this phase, trainees work in 'sticks' of 12 to enhance the buildup of *esprit* among the survivors. Reporting sick for any reason results in an immediate RTU (returned to unit). Something like 50 percent of the initial survivors drop out during this phase.

Above: Mounty in dense bush in central Ovambo. This is the type of terrain most suited to mounted operations because the horses can pick their way round obstacles quicker than vehicles can plough through them.

Parachute training proper starts only now with two weeks of hangar training. This commences with instruction on how to land and roll without injury and progresses via harness training; aircraft drills and exit training with mockup aircraft; gantry training for air drills; active landing drills in the hangar to simulate different types of landing; parachute orientation;

Above: SWASpes motorcyclists in training.
Right: A Koevoet fighter group leaving its base to begin a patrol in central Ovambo. The leading Casspir is fitted with a captured 14.5mm machine gun.

providing the airmobile reaction forces in different parts of the Operational Area. In this role, as in much of their external activity, they are generally flown to the scene of a contact or fresh spoor by helicopter. Once there, they relieve the troops in contact, who have often been out for long periods and are no longer fresh. Newly arrived, exceptionally fit and highly trained, with the added advantage of fresh trackers, the reaction force elements leave the insurgents little chance of escape. Another aspect related to their success is the fact that their average age ranges in the mid-twenties, granting an edge in maturity over the very young National-Service troops without sacrificing fitness and expertise.

The selection and training of today's parabats remains exceptionally rigorous to ensure that the standard of combat efficiency is retained at its very high level. Generally, members of 1 Para will visit the various National Service battalions each year early in the training cycle to look for volunteers. These must then pass a PT test at their unit prior to appearing before a selection board, which looks at their character and motivation. Those who are accepted are then transferred to 1 Para, where they first complete the normal three-month basic training course, with

aircraft orientation; and post-jump drills. A recurrent feature of these two weeks is the training tower or Aapkas. This begins with fan jumps, in which the descent is slowed by air resistance on a fan attached to the harness winch, and goes on to full-harness exit training for both port and starboard exits. Finally, exit drills are practised in sticks.

The first real jump comes after about ten days of hangar training and is generally from some 2000 feet, with the trainees jumping in pairs under the watchful eye of the instructors, who also jump. Seven more jumps follow – including two at night and four with equipment – before the prized wings are awarded. On a typical course, fewer than one in three of the

original applicants will have reached this stage. Volunteers among the new para-bats can then go on a six-week Pathfinder course before rejoining their companies for sub-unit training and eventual operational employment.

The pace of training never really slows, however, and pressure is kept on right through the two years of national service and later during CF training. The knowledge that the annual camps will not be any softer is enough to ensure that the men keep themselves fit during their civilian lives. Another important factor is that none would wish to be transferred out of the unit they fought so hard to enter. The *esprit* of the CF units is also outstanding. Far from the usual spate of weak excuses heard by some units when they issue a call-up, the two CF Para Bns often find that more men report than were called up.

Below: 1 Para's training tower – the 'Aapkas' – used to give basic instruction and practice to trainees.

32 Battalion – The New 'Buffalo Soldiers'

First to bear this name were the two regiments of black troops recruited into the US Regular Army after the Civil War to help deal with the Indians. Authorised in 1866, these two regiments saw service throughout the Indian Wars, much of their action on the troublesome Texas frontier and in Arizona. By most accounts they performed with some distinction. Almost 120 years later the same name again refers to a group of black soldiers fighting on a troubled frontier. Wearing a buffalo head badge on their camouflage berets, the soldiers of 32 Battalion have established themselves as probably the finest light infantry in the world today.

Thirty-two Bn was formed as the SA intervention in the Angolan civil war of 1975/6 came to an end. Once SA forces had been withdrawn, the combined FAPLA/Cuban forces advanced quickly southward toward the SWA border, dealing ruthlessly with any remaining opposition. Jonas Savimbi's Unita movement was on its home ground and managed to survive these hard times to become a major force in Angola by the early 1980s. Those FNLA troops and supporters caught in the south of the country were rather less fortunate, lacking Unita's large tribal base in the area. With nowhere to go, many chose exile in SWA rather than face a singularly uncertain future in a Marxist-ruled Angola. Large numbers of them settled in Kavango and Owambo, whence some were moved to the sparsely populated West Caprivi.

Among these refugees were many ex-FNLA soldiers and their families. Not happy to subsist on charity until they could establish themselves economically, not a few of these men offered their services to

the SA forces in the fight against SWAPO, which had sided with the MPLA. Some did so for purely economic reasons, but most also had a strong desire to fight against the system that had cost them their country. A number also had unhappy memories of SWAPO excesses against family and friends. Whatever their individual reasons, many of them were highly experienced bush fighters and almost all had an intimate knowledge of parts of southern Angola which had been their home until so recently.

With Marxist rule in Angola boding ill for the future of peace in Owambo, this was an opportunity the security forces could not pass by. Accordingly, a new battalion was formed at Rundu in Kavango to make the best use of these potentially very valuable volunteers. With most of the recruits having no experience of the SADF's procedures and systems and with only few former leader cadres among them, the new unit was perforce initially staffed almost exclusively with white officers and Non-Commissioned Officers of the SA Army. Since then, an increasing number of the NCO posts has been filled from within the ranks of the battalion; now only officers and senior or specialist NCOs are posted from elsewhere.

These personnel are carefully selected, with emphasis on eliminating the 'cowboys' and 'killer' types who would only be a hindrance at best and a menace at worst. While the senior posts are generally filled by Permanent Force personnel, National

Above right: Pack hounds under training at the SADF Dog Centre.
Right: Ops K trackers running on a very fresh spoor, a photograph taken from one of their supporting vehicles.
Below: Paras making a mass jump. As well as such large-scale operations, training also deals extensively with tactics and techniques for operating in smaller units.

Servicemen fill many of the platoon leader and platoon sergeant slots as well as some of the staff ones. These men are very carefully selected from volunteers from among the infantry school graduates each year and are then required to pass an extremely tough orientation-cum-final-selection phase before being accepted into the unit. This is followed by further advanced counterinsurgency training and orientation to allow the new junior leaders to fit into the battalion. A measure of proficiency in Portuguese is also reached during this period.

The orientation phase lasts roughly one week but varies according to the particular group. It sees the prospective platoon leaders and sergeants divided into syndicates of six and taken to 32's training area near Buffalo, where they are briefed on the requirements of this phase, the danger of wild animals and the procedures to be followed in an emergency. Each group is then issued with a medical satchel and briefed on its use by a medical orderly. Radios and signals instructions issued, questions are called for and answered and then the instructors are let loose on the men.

Each man has his normal kit and

Below: Members of the Para reaction force waiting on the apron at Ondangwa air base in the Operational area. Their normal means of transport here is the helicopter but para jumps are also sometimes used.

equipment and is issued in addition with two mortar rounds and five tins of food that must last him five days. The next few days pass in a blur of marching, physical training, patrolling, river crossing exercises, navigation problems and anything else the instructors can think of. Sleep is frequently interrupted at half-hour intervals for further PT sessions, base defence drills or no reason at all except to try the trainee's patience to the utmost. The daily march is often 23-28 km, sometimes with tar poles in addition to the prescribed

Above: Frans Conradie, one of Ops K's best group commanders, has had his Casspir fitted with an ex-Vampire 20mm cannon 'organised' through friends in the SAAF.

load. At the end of this period the men are loaded into a truck bound for the temporary base where they will undergo further training before being deemed operational with the Battalion. Part way there, they are put back on their feet – with poles – to walk the rest of the way.

The purpose of this procedure is to ensure that only those who can stand up to

Above: A typical paddock at a SWASpes company base in Owambo. Considerable care is obviously taken to tend to the horses' fitness.

the physical and psychological rigours of extended bush operations are accepted into leadership positions. Small groups are out in the bush for five weeks or more at a time locating PLAN's bases and transit camps in southern Angola. While there is always the comforting thought of the SAAF helicopters that will fly in urgently needed supplies, conduct casevac mis-

sions or extract a patrol under almost any circumstances, 32 Bn men can never forget that for most of their time they are well inside hostile territory, far from the support available to other units and almost invariably outnumbered by the enemy.

The proof of the pudding, so goes the saying, is in the eating. On that basis the 'Buffalo Battalion' has amply demonstrated its value. Its almost continuous presence in southern Angola has gone far toward rendering that region inhospitable to PLAN and has also been a key element in

the success of the major operations conducted against the larger PLAN base areas by mechanised forces. In the process, it has also done more than its share of cutting PLAN down to size. By November 1981 the battalion had accounted for more than 1000 insurgents for the loss of 24 of its men and 9 of its officers and NCOs. A 'kill ratio' of more than 30 to one is not easy to match. The disproportion of junior leader casualties to troop casualties also says much for the style and standard of leadership in this unique battalion.

Like all successful military units, 32 Bn has come in for a very thorough campaign of vilification by its opponents and their helpers – both willing and duped. The key element in this campaign has been the claim by a deserter from 32 Bn that it spends much of its time and energy on terrorising the civilian population of southern Angola. This claim says much for the intellectual capacity and military knowledge of those who swallow it. Operating on foot, generally in relatively small groups without heavy weapons, and occasionally well inside southern Angola, 32's soldiers simply cannot afford to antagonise the locals. They rely on them for some of the information that leads them to PLAN, for local terrain knowledge and

Below: One of the more unusual variants of the 10-tonne Kwêvöel truck is this horsebox used to support the Mounties' operations.

for their own security. A hostile civilian could all too easily advise the enemy of their presence, or simply fail to warn them of the presence of a larger enemy force.

Among 32 Bn's operations, only Super (discussed in some detail in another chapter) has received a degree of publicity. Most cross-border operations see reconnaissance patrols looking for signs of PLAN activity that could indicate hostile intentions or lead to a target, and keeping tabs on FAPLA to forestall clashes during later operations. In all of this the troops' knowledge of the area, dialects and customs is invaluable, as is their affinity for people who were once their neighbours and are not infrequently their relatives.

Once a target has been identified, subsequent patrols set about developing the available information. They establish the precise nature, location, size and perimeter of the target, the forces within it and what forces are sufficiently near to interfere with an operation. Terrain reconnaissance of the area and its possible access routes also forms an important part of their task. Finally, these patrols and/or others may also be employed to provide a screen for the actual operation. This will often be conducted by one or even two companies of 32 Bn if the target is sufficiently large to warrant it. Smaller targets will be dealt with by the original patrol, or by a small force flown in to support it. The attacking force will generally either approach the target on foot after being transported to the general area, or heli-assault it. Very large targets are left to the mechanised forces.

Most recently, the new-found accord between Angola and the RSA has seen the creation of a joint military commission to control the withdrawal of SA forces from southern Angola, their replacement by FAPLA and the prevention of PLAN movement through the area. Not surprisingly, the SA element of the commission's military forces has been provided by 32 Bn.

South-West African Specialist Unit

The SWA Specialist Unit – SWASpes from the Afrikaans – is one of the most unusual units of any army. A specialised follow-up unit, it grew out of the peculiar requirements of the protracted counterinsurgency campaign in northern SWA. Its basic concept is to combine and blend the skills of highly trained infantry and expert trackers with the mobility granted by horses and motorcycles and the special abilities of well-trained dogs and their handlers.

As in any counterinsurgency campaign, the major difficulty faced by the security forces is actually coming to grips with the insurgents. Once this has been achieved, dealing with them presents few problems. This difficulty is addressed in part by the policy of striking at the insurgents in their base areas and camps rather than waiting

for them to enter SWA and commit some act of terrorism. Another aspect is the protection of likely targets – in effect making the insurgent come to the security forces instead of having to look for him. Cross-border operations cannot, however, stop all infiltration, nor can every conceivable target be protected. It must also be remembered that most of PLAN's insurgents enter SWA either with a general 'armed propaganda' mission or to lay mines, neither of which occupations lends itself to prediction. They will always enjoy the initiative and can often be dealt with only by pursuit.

This problem is aggravated by the extremely flat nature of much of the Operational Area, which grants exceptional mobility on foot. Naturally, this also applies to pursuing infantry, but they will almost invariably have some measure of time lag to make up. By the same token, it is difficult effectively to 'leapfrog' the pursuit in terrain which has no naturally canalising effect. Finally, the often heavy bush severely restricts visibility, further slowing the pursuit if ambush is to be avoided and account is taken of countertracking on the part of the quarry. With the Angolan border often only some 50 km from the scene of most incidents, speed of pursuit is both essential and difficult to achieve.

Both armoured cars and APCs have enjoyed some measure of success in high-speed follow-up operations, but they do have several disadvantages. One is the self-advertising amount of noise they make, particularly in bad going. While this has not prevented them from achieving some remarkable successes against groups of insurgents who have either not heard them in time or assumed that they had heard civilian vehicles, fleeing insurgents are more alert and less trusting. Then too, vehicles are hampered by thick bush and also allow only a limited degree of tracking on the move. Finally, vehicles have very limited utility in this role in the mountainous parts of the Kaokoland, where PLAN has made some incursions.

Mounted infantry, on the other hand, showed quite early in the campaign that it could offer almost comparable mobility over much of the terrain in the Operational Area – and better in the mountainous areas – without the disadvantages. By mid-1977 the security forces had enough operational experience in its employment to refine the basic concept. Some of the Army's most experienced infantrymen were tasked with this project, and SWASpes was the result.

A composite unit, SWASpes has three main wings – mounted, motorcycle and tracking. Potential members are selected from among infantrymen who have completed their basic and phase-two training with distinction. Selection procedures are thorough and requirements tough – physically, psychologically and mentally.

Above: Para trainees at work on the assault course. The highest standards of physical fitness are maintained throughout the training period.

As one example, the motorcycle wing accepts only some 40 percent of applicants for the training programme and washes out a good proportion of these. Prospective members of the mounted wing and future dog handlers are first sent to the SADF Equestrian Centre and the SADF Dog Centre respectively to learn the rudiments of their new trade.

Once they have mastered the basics of handling their horses and dogs, they move on to the SWASpes base near Otavi. Here they undergo an intensive advanced counterinsurgency course optimised to suit the characteristics of their speciality. The motorcyclists and trackers go straight to SWASpes from their training batttalion, receiving all of their specialised training at Otavi. The standard of training at SWASpes is in line with that of their selection procedures and demands the utmost from the men. Once operational, they are posted to the battalions in the Operational Area, usually by platoons.

The primary advantage the 'mounties' enjoy over their 'foot-mobile' opposition is that of mobility, in terms of both speed and endurance. A horse is obviously much faster than a man – the Arabians and Boerperde most commonly used can cover some 60km a day without difficulty. This mobility edge is exploited to the full by SWASpes, who learn the art of tracking from horseback. The horse's load-carrying ability also allows a mounted patrol to stay out longer between resupplies – thus making it difficult for insurgents to predict its movements. Another advantage accrues from the height of the horse, which grants the rider a greatly increased field of vision in bush, which can often be translated into a very useful advantage in a contact.

The horses' relative silence – they are not shod when used in sandy areas – has resulted in the riding down of several groups of insurgents who heard nothing until the mounties were among them. A final edge results from alert observation of the horse's behaviour – very often a mount will warn of an otherwise unsuspected human presence which could well be an enemy ambush. Not a few soldiers have enjoyed the benefit of this travelling alarm system throughout the history of warfare. One example from the Operational Area saw the horses of a patrol that had camped for the night grow increasingly restive, all of them facing nervously to one side of the temporary camp. When the insurgents launched their attack at first light from that side, they were welcomed by an entirely unsurprised defence.

The motorcyclists enjoy much the same mobility advantages as the mounties, modified by greater potential speed bought at the cost of noise. The latter has, in fact, proved less of a problem than was anticipated. For one thing, the machines are very thoroughly silenced before operational use.Then too, the bush has a muffling and deflecting effect on noise which makes its direction difficult to judge. The motorcyclists' habit of moving widely dispersed at the best speed the terrain will allow helps leave little effec- tive warning time for the insurgents. The confusion factor can be so great that some insurgents have run right into the very pursuers they were trying to flee. Once in among the insurgents, the motorcyclists discard their machines and deal with the opposition by normal infantry tactics adapted to suit the style of their arrival on the scene.

While the selection and training of the mounties and motorcyclists are highly demanding, prospective trackers face a programme designed to daunt or elimi- nate aspirants unequal in calibre to the Recces. Superb physical condition must be accompanied by perseverance, con- trolled aggressiveness, tight self-disci- pline, above-average intelligence and more than a dash of individuality. The hopeful tracker candidate will also need to be intimately familiar with the veld and its inhabitants – and able to live off it for days at a stretch.

The basic tracking course builds on this to provide a knowledge of spoor interpre- tation, enemy countertracking techniques and the local flora and fauna. Emphasis is placed on instilling the concept that track- ing is more than merely following a physi- cal spoor – no matter how difficult that may be. Effective military tracking also requires an above-average tactical sense and alertness to the almost indiscernible changes in wildlife behaviour that can indicate the presence of the enemy, or give an idea of whether he has passed and when.

To pass, the candidate must be able to follow a tricky test spoor for at least one kilometer in a set time. Evaluation is on an individual basis, with instructors rotated daily to eliminate the chance of a biased evaluation – either way. Real tracking competence naturally then comes with increasing experience. An advanced course emphasises the more esoteric tracking and countertracking techniques and survival in different environments. This course usually winds up with a sur- vival test.

What even the most skilled trackers cannot achieve, well-trained and -handled dogs often can, a fact not lost on the security forces. SWASpes uses several breeds of dog in different roles. The Alsatian remains the favourite patrol dog, combining a good nose with discipline, intelligence, controllable aggressiveness and an alert nature. Preference in tracking goes to the Labrador and the Australian Sheepdog, although Alsatians, Blood- hounds and a Doberman/Rottweiler cross are also used with success. Other tasks assigned to these canine counterinsur- gents include mine detection and explo- sives sniffing – the latter during searches and at roadblocks.

Below: Mounties in the training area at the Equestrian Centre.

A relatively recent development is the counterinsurgency application of the Irish Packhound concept, using the dogs to track, run down and corner the quarry for infantry or, more practically, mounties, to deal with. While these dogs are not well disciplined and respond somewhat erratically to commands, they track well and can keep up a speed of 15 km/h for over four hours, peaking at 30 km/h for some 15 minutes. It takes little imagination to realise that the combination of mounties and packhounds is one few insurgents will be able to elude.

It is, in fact, very much this combination of the mobility of the mounties via horse or motorcycle and the skill of the tracker/dog combination that makes SWASpes what it is. To illustrate this by an example: A tracker team on a follow-up picked up a relatively old spoor early one morning. A section of mounties with their own trackers took it over from them and fol-

lowed the spoor through the day. By last light, they had made up so much ground that the spoor was fresh enough for dogs to pick up and follow. A team of handlers and infantry was then brought up by vehicle and followed the spoor through the night. Early the following morning, the insurgents found their entire day ruined by the arrival of troops just as they were about to move on.

Operation K: The Police's Intelligent Crowbar

Any counterinsurgency campaign has one excellent and virtually foolproof measure of a unit's effectiveness: the effort and viciousness with which the insurgents vilify it. Much as the Army's 32 Bn became the target of a campaign accusing it of wholesale rapine and pillage in southern Angola, so the Police's 'Operation K' has been widely accused of totally barbarous behaviour inside Owambo. The fact that

both units practise a style of operation that relies largely on at least the neutrality, if not the friendship, of the local population is quietly ignored. Unfortunately, the ignorance of military matters among many of the vociferous is such that even the honest if misguided ones among those who carry much of the campaign cannot see just how far afield they are. The less honest ones would not worry anyway.

'Operation K' grew out of routine Security Police operations in Owambo; it was founded officially in June 1979 with a strength of 10 security policemen – both black and white – and 64 locally recruited special constables. The fundamental concept was to provide for the fastest possible development and exploitation of information gained through various channels and also a speedy reaction to the identification of spoor in the course of routine operations. Initially the unit concentrated on this intelligence work and on

Above: SWASPES Mounty at speed in training. The combination of the horse's mobility and silent movement has proved particularly valuable in action. *Left:* A mass jump by members of 1 Para.

tracking. Support came from a small fire force provided by a Recce Commando. Even this entailed some delays in following up intelligence and spoor, so by early 1980 Operation K had formed its own small fire force. Operating at first on foot, this element soon acquired a number of Hippo APCs. When stronger support was required, the Para reaction force was called upon.

The new operation brought in 36 contacts in its first 90 days, and success has been the norm ever since. During 1980 it accounted for 511 insurgents killed for the loss of only 12 members of the unit. Toward the middle of that year, the new unit's name 'Koevoet' – Afrikaans for crowbar – had already become well known to the forces on both sides, although their attitudes to it were rather different. By early 1984 the Minister of Police could report to Parliament that Operation K had accounted for 1624 insurgents killed in some 721 contacts since its inception. Police casualties in these contacts have remained low.

Presently there are three units involved in Operation K, one each based in Opuwa, Oshakati and Rundu. Each controls a number of roughly platoon-strength fighting groups plus a small intelligence element which also conducts supporting covert operations. Overall control is exercised from Oshakati by the operation's founder, Brigadier 'Sterk Hans' Dreyer, who has succeeded in building unrivalled *esprit* among his men. This central HQ continuously monitors and evaluates the situation throughout the Operational Area and decides upon the most promising areas of concentration. The groups of all three units are then deployed accordingly, although no area will ever be totally denuded of Koevoet elements. The key here lies in the fact that these groups are not bound to specific areas, even to the area of their unit; they can be and are employed wherever they will be most useful.

The groups themselves generally comprise four Casspir APCs – each carrying a section of ten men – a Blesbok mine-protected supply truck and a Duiker mine-protected fuel bowser. Command of a group falls to an officer or warrant officer, while the sections are commanded by sergeants or, in some cases, constables. The section 2iCs (seconds-in-command) are special sergeants or warrant officers promoted from the ranks on merit. Each section includes a medical orderly. Personal arms were initially a matter of choice, but more recently it was decided to standardise on the R-5 (a short R-4) to simplify ammunition supply. FN LMGs, M79 grenade launchers and some 60mm mortars are carried as supporting weapons. The vehicles themselves are fitted with machine guns, two in each group with a .50-cal or a twin .50-cal/.30-cal mount and two with a single .30 cal.

The integral logistic element allows groups to operate for a week or more, roving over the length and breadth of the Operational Area if need be without worrying about resupply. The bowser is often dropped off at the nearest security forces camp and called out as necessary, but it does accompany the group on forays of more than two days. The groups are sometimes reinforced if this seems necessary, but it is more usual simply to attach another group for the particular operation or contact. In the past, elements of the SWAPOL Task Force were often attached to groups to gain the best possible experience, but this is no longer a regular feature as this force has now built up its own core of highly experienced men.

Generally, the groups alternate a week on operations with a week back in the unit base for rest, repair and maintenance. On operations, the groups will overnight in a police or Army camp if there is one conveniently situated. Operationally, Koevoet relies to a very great extent on information from the local population to set it on the trail of insurgent groups. Not only is this the most efficient way of obtaining accurate up-to-date information, it is also the normal way in which police operate: their approach to counterinsurgency is the eminently logical one that this is essentially police work which happens to involve also a measure of combat, not warfare that relies more than usually on intelligence. The principle of setting a thief to catch a thief is also applied in that most groups include one or two former insurgents. These men are invaluable for their almost automatic insight into the likely movements and reactions of the insurgent groups.

An interesting related aspect is that the insurgents have learned not to wear boots with identifiable treads. Many now wear ordinary tackies or shoes, or commercial boots, some even go barefoot. As a result, it is increasingly rare to find an identifiable enemy spoor by chance. Spoor today is picked out on the basis of intelligence, and only then does tracking come into the picture. The necessary intelligence comes mostly from the local population. An exception to this is naturally when spoor is followed from the scene of a contact or incident, but even then it is often local informants who aid the trackers in ensuring that they are on the correct spoor.

Once a spoor has been picked out of the general mass of tracks littering Owambo, the Koevoet group will follow it to a conclusion at the best possible speed. Unlike most other elements of the security forces, Ops K teams are not restricted by battalion, company or even Sector boundaries. Tactically, the trackers will walk or run on the spoor with the rest of the group following mounted in the Casspirs. If the spoor is lost at any stage, the group will spread out

Above: Koevoet trackers resting during operations along the 'Red Line' that demarcates the southern edge of the Operational Area.

into line abreast and put more people on the ground among the Casspirs until the spoor is regained. A similar procedure is followed when there is any likelihood of the quarry having made a sharp turn off to either side. If the spoor is lost altogether, a widening search is conducted until it is regained, and information is sought from local civilians.

Contacts with single insurgents or very small groups are generally handled by the trackers themselves. If necessary, one or two vehicles will provide support while the rest will either hold back and wait for the matter to be settled, or continue following up the spoor of the rest of the insurgent group, if any. Larger contacts usually take the form of an ambush by an insurgent group that feels powerful enough. Occasionally, this becomes obvious early on from the nature of the spoor. On these occasions the trackers will be pulled back into the vehicles and work from there as far as possible. The actual contact with the ambushing party is then handled as mounted action. Should contact be made before this can be done, the trackers will attempt to remount or will pull out of the contact area, picking off any fleeing insurgents while they wait.

Combat against large groups is carried out mounted if at all possible. The logistic vehicles pull clear of the area and see to their own security, while the Casspirs assault the enemy and then circle through the area of the contact, moving continuously and putting the maximum firepower down on any visible enemy until there is no further resistance. The area immediately surrounding the actual contact is also quartered in search of insurgents who may have split or been split away from their group. Reasons for fighting mounted

include mobility, protection, firepower and clarity. The latter is achieved by keeping all one's troops either mounted or clear of the area, thereby eliminating most of the confusion as to friend and foe that usually accompanies a major contact in flat, heavily bushed terrain.

That these tactics work – totally belying the notion that the insurgent can be fought only on his terms once he is deployed - is clear from the results of Ops K to date. To give but one additional figure: the most experienced fighting group had produced or was involved in some 99 kills by early 1984. The biggest single success to that date had been 34 out of 34. This particular contact arose when a Security Police investigation team from Onessi called for support after its information brought it onto the trail of a large insurgent group. One nearby Koevoet group joined up with them and quickly established that the group numbered 34.

The insurgents were by now aware of the two Security Police Casspirs following them and were very sure of themselves indeed – to the extent of leaving taunting notes rolled around SKS ballistic rounds. Once they reached a likely looking spot, they settled down to lay an ambush. Soon after, they came to the realisation that there were more than two vehicles following them. Suspecting the worst, they decamped and attempted to flee. By now, however, a spotter aircraft was in the air and two Alouettes had also arrived to help spot the enemy and control the contact. One of the helicopters immediately spotted the insurgent group only some 300m ahead of the advancing police. Contact followed almost immediately, with other Ops K groups arriving in time to participate. The action went on for some 40 minutes and extended over a 2km radius. Thirty-four bodies were collected and no spoor could be found leaving the area.

Other contacts have been different but

no less successful. One resulted from the follow-up after a Kaokoland Ops K team had detonated a mine and the recovery vehicle sent to the scene repeated the trick. Groups from Owambo were called in and quickly picked up and followed spoor heading from the scene into the nearby mountains. One vehicle circled far ahead and came up behind the group of insurgents, who were standing behind some bush looking toward the advancing APCs. Sixteen out of 22 were killed in the ensuing contact, one survivor being captured a little later at a waterhole by the bowser crew on their way back to Opuwa after refueling the fighting groups. Bowser crews, in fact, sometimes appear to lead interesting lives – one reportedly entered a fire-fight and killed several insurgents by the simple expedient of chasing them and running them down.

An important and interesting point about Ops K is that most of the men involved do not see themselves as an elite; they tend to disclaim any such notions and insist that they are merely ordinary policemen engaged in what is essentially police work – protecting the law-abiding bulk of the population against the depredations of those who seek to electioneer with guns and mines. Such is the calibre of these men, who have earned the respect of their Army opposite numbers to such an extent that they are even immune to the usual Army versus Police jokes after hours.

Insofar as they can be said to have their 'secret of success,' they feel that it is a combination of several factors. Most important in their view is the fact that all Ops K personnel are volunteers and are in the Operational Area on a permanent basis, not drafted transients who barely get to know the region before their tour is over. Other aspects are their freedom of movement, the higher average age of their personnel and the fact that most of their men are from the region and therefore totally familiar with it.

The white personnel are volunteers, many of them recruited by friends who are in Koevoet. Preference is given to those who already have some years of police experience, but not necessarily in counterinsurgency or COIN. All must first complete the normal SAP COIN training before being trained up more or less 'on the job.' Once with Koevoet, personnel generally stay several years; some now have almost five years with the unit. Transfer out of Koevoet is also up to the individual, who is free to decide when he has had enough. Most of the old hands returned after short spells of normal police duties, but the newer personnel seem more inclined to finish their tour and then settle back into normal routine without problems. It is worth noting that there is nothing to stop a black policeman from volunteering for Ops K. But he would have to be very good indeed to make up for the distrust of a 'foreign' black face in tribal areas.

Black personnel are recruited chiefly from among the special constables serving in various capacities in the Operational Areas - essentially, the best are 'poached' from other elements. Some are taken directly from the training centre if they have really stood out there. Their promotion is purely on merit as demonstrated in the field, there being no formal promotion courses or exams. They can, however, choose to go into normal police work and must then naturally complete the relevant training and pass the exams. Some have done this. In general, Owambo personnel are employed in Owambo and Kavangos in Kavango, but the groups are not made up of personnel from any particular area within these regions. If anything, it is preferred to mix them a little in order to have at least one or two men from each area who will be familiar with it and its people, dialect and customs.

New members of the unit are assigned to one of the groups and receive their 'polish' up to Koevoet standard in the form of 'on the job training.' When a new group is formed, it is around a skeleton of experienced personnel, and some three weeks of intensive group training follow before it will be deployed operationally. Even then, such a new group will not knowingly be deployed in an area where difficult contacts might be expected until it has had a chance to gain experience as a group. Refresher training is fitted into the rest periods to ensure that all groups maintain their edge. Groups are kept

together for as long as possible, their strength maintained with new recruits, rather than being disbanded and replaced by a new group. In this way both unit cohesion and collective experience are kept alive, as is a valuable degree of *esprit*.

Crowbars, it is true, can be and frequently are used to bludgeon victims into submission. In the hands of an expert, however, the crowbar becomes a very flexible tool indeed, capable of extremely delicate application in order to do the necessary with the minimum of collateral disturbance or damage. If there is any-

Above: A Koevoet Casspir fitted with a captured 14.5mm machine gun. The Casspir is heavier than the Army's Buffel and is preferred by the Police for its greater stability.

thing to be read into the code name of this operation, then it should be this – the skilled application of just the amount of force needed to do the job. This interpretation is borne out both by the statistics and by the anguished screams of 'foul!' issuing from the mouths of the insurgents and their supporters.

Below: Ops K trackers following an increasingly faint and doubtful spoor.

RELATED FORCES

As a result of its history of European settlement and African migration, South Africa is host to several population groups of very different backgrounds and traditions. Government policy is to address the resultant potential conflict by separating the major groups sufficiently to enable each to go its own way, aiming toward some form of communal structure in the long run. As far as the various black groups are concerned, this takes the form of national states in the areas which they controlled when first encountered. This is essentially a continuation of the process started by the British when they in effect excised Botswana, Lesotho and Swaziland from what was to become South Africa.

One outcome of this policy has been a requirement to assist in designing and setting up national security systems for the new states. The SADF has approached this task by setting up a regional battalion for each group moving toward independence. This battalion is gradually filled out with trained personnel and finally handed over to the newly independent state. SADF personnel are then seconded to the new force until local officers and NCOs have accumulated the necessary knowledge and experience. Training and organisation are generally on the basis of SA Army practice with allowances made to conform to local conditions, culture and military history.

Initial training for the core of a regional battalion has generally been provided by 21 Battalion at Lenz in the Transvaal. Recruits undergo five months' basic training followed by technical, administrative or instructor courses. Throughout, they are encouraged to further their schooling and time is set aside for this. Potential officers are selected during this phase

Previous page: Soldiers of 1 Transkei Btn. on their first battalion-level manoeuvres in mid 1984.
Below: The Transkei Army's standard 5-tonne troop carrier.

Above: Bophuthatswana Army drill sergeant at work. There is considerable emphasis on discipline and smartness on the parade ground.

and then enter the SA Army officer training programme, usually being commissioned on independence. Once the basic core has been trained, the battalion is formed at a suitable location and begins to train personnel for the future defence force. Recruits who prove suitable during their basic training are sent to 21 Bn on specialist and advanced courses, and further training is provided at training units and schools of the SADF.

Apart from the forces already established, this programme has also resulted in the formation of three other regional battalions: 111 Bn situated at New Amsterdam in the Eastern Transvaal and drawn from among the Swazis; 113 Bn at Impala Base near Phalaborwa (Shangaans) and 121 Bn at Josini near Mtubatuba in northern Natal (Zulus). In addition to military train-

ing, these battalions offer vocational training to give the soldier a career after he leaves the service. The departure of good soldiers is, in fact, not entirely regretted, as they are felt to be a valuable catalyst to the economic growth of their regions. A related aspect is the education of the white officers and NCOs in the language and culture of their troops: 113 Bn, for example, operates a language laboratory run by a Shangaan who taught for 19 years before joining up.

Transkei Defence Force

The TDF was founded in 1975 with the establishment of 1 Transkei Battalion. The first intake underwent basic training at the SACC depot at Eerste Rivier near Cape Town from August before being transferred to 21 Bn where the second intake commenced training. 1 T Bn was built up to a strength of 254, including 71 NCOs and 7 Candidate Officers, the latter being commissioned on Independence Day, 26 October 1976. The battalion had meanwhile been transferred to a new base near the capital of Transkei, Umtata.

Tension between the SA and Transkei Governments led to withdrawal of all seconded SADF personnel by the end of 1977, the last instructors leaving by March 1978. Much to the credit of the first Transkei officers and NCOs – and of their SADF instructors - the TDF did not collapse. On the other hand, it had its work cut out to continue functioning, and further development and growth were out of the question until the available officers and NCOs had passed on their training to expand the cadre to a sustainable level.

Above: Venda troops being put through their paces by a South African instructor during the early stages of their training.

Several officers went to Rhodesia on courses and their exposure to a larger – and combat-experienced – army quickly convinced the TDF of the need for some external expertise.

The outcome was the appointment of the founder of the Selous Scouts, Lt Col Ron Reid-Daly, as GOC. Assuming command in May 1981, he quickly settled down to his task – collecting about him one of the most concentrated bodies of military expertise anywhere as his advisory team: chiefly former members of the SAS, Selous Scouts and RLI. The TDF then

embarked upon a period of consolidation and slow growth into a small but increasingly efficient counterinsurgency force. Today it comprises an infantry battalion optimised for the counterinsurgency role, a Special Forces Regiment with one operational squadron, an Infantry School and basic command and staff elements. The first squadron of a future mounted infantry regiment is to be formed during 1984. This unit will have essentially the same role as 1 Bn, but will be optimised for operations in the mountainous parts of the country. Future planning for the TDF includes a small air wing, and various supporting elements including engineers, signals, military police, a medical corps, a pay corps and a maintenance unit.

Bophuthatswana Defence Force

The decision to form the Bophuthatswana Defence Force was taken in December 1976. The first elements were formed as a unit of North-Western Command at Potchefstroom. Training commenced on 15 February 1977 with some 250 Batswana for a National Guard unit which was formally handed over to the newly independent Bophuthatswana on 6 December 1977. A Bophuthatswana Department of Defence was established in 1979, the National Guard becoming the BDF on 30 November. Supreme command falls to President Mangope. Both the Minister of Defence and the Commander of the BDF are still seconded SADF officers and others hold key staff and instructor posts until local personnel have gained the necessary qualifications and experience.

A Maintenance Unit, 1 Infantry Battalion, and a Military School were established on 1 January 1981. An Air Component followed in March, with an Alouette III as initial equipment and seconded SAAF personnel. This was expanded to an Air Wing in 1982, receiving three Helio Couriers for command and control, reconnaissance, liaison, transport, resupply, casevac and search-and-rescue missions. In 1983 a Technical Services Unit was established to control the Workshop and the Building and Construction Companies, a third rifle company was added to 1 Inf Bn and a Partenavia P-68 was procured for the Air Wing. Military academic training began in January 1984, with a diploma

Below: The Commanding Officer of 1 Transkei Battalion briefing his officers during their exercise Crocodile Tears II in mid 1984.

course offered by the Military School in conjunction with the SADF's Military Academy. Medium-term planning is for a force of two mobile counterinsurgency battalions and the necessary support elements.

Venda Defence Force

Venda chose to raise a combined force rather than separate services. The National Force of Venda was conceived as combining Defence, Police, Traffic Police and Prisons services. Planning was initiated by the Department of Co-operation and Development after discussions with the Venda National Authority. The first interservice discussions began in 1978. As the new force would have primarily a police task, with the defence element seen as more of a police field force than an army unit, the combined project committee was under the chairmanship of the South African Police (SAP).

The National Force was organised with two main wings, a Prisons Service and a Security Service. The latter consisted of the Defence Force, the Police and the Traffic Police. The Defence Force comprised a small Mobile Unit and a Ceremonial Company that also had a protection task. Overall control rested with the President as the political head and was exercised by an appointed commander, with this post initially filled by an SAP officer. No SADF officers were seconded to the VNF in an executive capacity, all being posted as advisors. The VNF came into being formally with independence on 13 September 1979.

Personnel for the VNF were drawn from the SA Army's 112 Battalion, founded at Messina on 1 April 1979 after initial training had commenced on 7 July 1978 at 21 Bn. It moved to Madimbo in December 1979, consisting by now of a small headquarters and one rifle company. The

possibility of joining the VNF was put to members after completion of their training, those who chose to stay in the SADF being retained in the battalion. On 27 September 1981 112 Battalion was transferred to Venda, after the Venda Government had decided to establish a separate defence force after all. It is still officered largely by seconded SA Army personnel, another change from the earlier approach but essential if Venda personnel are not to be promoted too rapidly to gain the requisite knowledge and experience. Most of the instructors and other NCOs are Vendas who have come up through the ranks in the battalion, one having reached the post of company sergeant major by late 1982.

Ciskei Defence Force

The CDF grew out of the South African Army's 141 Battalion. Like Venda, Ciskei opted for a combined security force.

Accordingly, initial planning for the new force involved not only the Department of Co-operation and Development – which chaired the various meetings and committees – and the SADF, but also the SAP and the SA Prisons Service. The resultant Ciskei Department of State Security comprised Police, Prisons Service, the Ciskei Intelligence Service and the Ciskei Security Service. Supreme command falls to the Head of State, at this writing Lennox Sebe, who also holds the portfolio of Minister of State Security.

141 Battalion originally consisted of a small headquarters and a skeleton company. A subsequent support company was developed into a Composite Depot for the new force. By September 1981 the headquarters had become a small Defence Headquarters with its own staff divisions, so that by independence (4 December 1981) the fledgling CSS could function independently of SADF control.

Logistic support and training continued to be provided largely by the SADF. In the course of 1982 the CSS developed into a separate department under a Minister of Defence.

Today the CSS is organised into three major components: the Ciskei Security Force – essentially a small army; *Ikhele we Sizwe* (The Sword of the Nation) – a special-forces element ceated in 1982, with a small parachute-trained force and an air-wing; and a youth movement titled Pillar of the Nation. While nominally under the CSS and dependent upon it for administrative and logistical support, *Ikhele we Sizwe* operational control is directly under the Head of State. The Air Wing operates two Short Skyvans and a Bk 117 helicopter. An interesting aspect of the CDF that emerged during 1984 is the apparent involvement of Israeli 'experts.'

Below: Transkei soldiers in training.

ARMSCOR

Armscor caused something of a stir in late 1982 when it cast aside much of its former protective veil of secrecy to make a surprise appearance at the Athens Defendory Exhibition. This in itself aroused interest, but not so much as the unexpected breadth of Armcor's production palette, the high standard of its armaments and the highly sophisticated products among them.

An outstanding example is the 155mm G-6 self-propelled gun. The second major-calibre *wheeled* equipment of its kind, it totally outclassed existing artillery – bar its own relatives - in range and accuracy. Other equipment drawing favourable comment included the 127mm Valkiri self-propelled multiple rocket launcher, frequency-hopping communications equipment and a fire-control system for fighters that slaves the seeker heads of air-to-air missiles to the movements of the pilot's head.

Armscor owes its existence largely to the UN-inspired South African arms embargo that forced South Africa into producing and developing arms and related equipment. During World War II, South Africa had developed a respectable armaments capability, producing over 5770 armoured cars, some 600 guns and ammunition of all types in enormous quantities. All of this, however, was the result of emergency measures. Once the war was over, South Africa soon fell back into its earlier complacent state.

Nevertheless, an Advisory Committee on Union Defence Equipment Requirements was appointed in 1948 to report on South African industrial potential in this field. It became the Defence Resources Board in 1949 and remained active until replaced in 1966 by the Defence Council. A Defence Production Office was established in 1951 as the main link between the

Above: Samil 50 truck. The Samil 50 is the standard transport vehicle in the 5-tonne category. It is available in numerous variants.
Right: Although the original Centurion design, from which the Olifant is derived, is some 40 years old, the Israelis and others have shown that updated versions are still most effective.

Department of Defence and industry, and as a nucleus from which a larger procurement organisation could be created when needed. It also administered the production and repair of stores and equipment for the UDF by local industry.

The Defence Production Office established a Defence Ordnance Workshop in 1953 to supply some of the UDF munitions requirements and to function as a source of technical knowledge and manufacturing techniques. The next major step came in 1964, when the Defence Production Office was replaced by the Armaments Production Board. This body controlled the manufacture and procurement of all armaments and took over the Defence Ordnance Workshop and the ammunition section of the South African Mint. Defence research and development at this time fell to the National Institute for Defence Research under the Directorate of Projects and Combat Development of the Chief of Defence Staff. The voluntary arms embargo of this period lent a measure of urgency to all developments in this area.

Three other bodies active in this field were replaced by the Defence Council in 1966. These were the Defence Resources Board, the Defence Research Council and the Committee for the Procurement of SADF Requirements. The new body was under the chairmanship of the Minister of Defence and included the Commandant General and the General Manager of the Armaments Production Board among its members. Others were heads of scientific and technical organisations and of some government departments. The chief functions of the Defence Council were to define research and development requirements, finance and control such projects, control stockpiling and consider the desirability of local manufacture on a case-by-case basis.

In 1968 the Armaments Production Board became the Armaments Board, assuming responsibility for acquisition of all equipment and technical stores both from within South Africa and from abroad. It also took over the co-ordination of defence research. The necessary co-ordination was assured by having the Commandant General serve on the Board and its chairman attend meetings of the Supreme Command. The same year also saw foundation of the Armaments Development and Manufacturing Corporation to take over the Board's two existing factories and certain strategic facilities owned by industry.

Armscor, as the new corporation was

Previous page: Ratel 90 (right) and Command Ratel are tested for their gradient climbing performance.
Below: Armscor's A-55 radio was one of the first military radios to have frequency hopping capability.

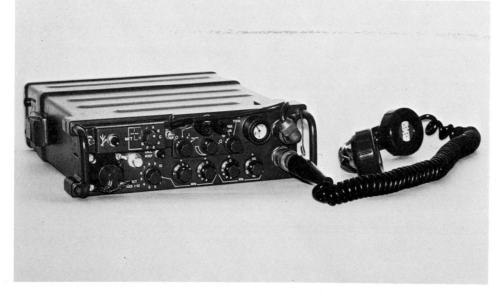

Right: Ratel-20 Infantry Fighting Vehicle. The Ratel-20 has already inspired numerous variants and additional repair, anti-tank missile and air defence versions may be produced.

termed, was an instrument of the Armaments Board. Its role encompassed the manufacture of all arms and equipment too sensitive to entrust to private enterprise or too uneconomical to attract interest from the private sector. The Armaments Board retained direct responsibility for the procurement of all other arms and equipment. The SADF was to establish and programme a definite requirement which was then passed to the Board for execution. The Board first had to establish whether the requirement could not be met by local private industry before turning either to Armscor or to a foreign supplier.

This basic organisation was streamlined in 1975/6. As a first step, a joint committee of SADF and armaments organisation members was formed to co-ordi-

Main picture: Although it dates back to before the First World War, the Vickers machine gun continues to give reliable and effective service to the infantry battalions.

nate purchases. In 1976 the Armaments Board and the Armaments Development and Manufacturing Corporation became the Armaments Corporation of South Africa Ltd. The function of the new body was defined as being 'To meet as effectively and economically as may be feasible the armaments requirements of the Republic, as determined by the Minister, including armaments required for export and firearms, ammunition or pyrotechnical products required for supply to members of the public.'

The original joint committee became the Defence Planning Committee in 1976, with the function of ensuring 'the full participation of all the members of the Defence Family in the planning process.' It consists of the Chief of the SADF as chairman and the Chiefs of the Army, Air

Above: The standard Samil-100 general purpose truck.
Below: G-5 155mm gun firing at maximum elevation. The G-5 is one of the most advanced weapons in its class in service anywhere in the world.

Above: Mine-protected version of the Samil-20 light general purpose truck. Note the sloping sides of the cab to deflect the blast of an explosion.

Right: Ratel-Log support vehicle. As well as carrying enough stores to support a platoon for a week, the Ratel-Log is usually armed with a 12.7mm machine gun for local defence.

Force and Navy, the Chiefs of Staff Operations, Logistics and Finance, the Chairman and the Chief Executive of Armscor and a representative from industry. Its primary function is to ensure that the five-year plan, the current budget and procurement policy are in line with the approved military policy and within the financial limits imposed by the Cabinet.

Organisationally, Armscor comes directly under the Minister of Defence, parallel to the SADF. It is, however, responsible to the Chief of the SADF for armaments procurement, which responsibility he delegates to it. Its direct responsibility to the Minister is for how effectively and economically it performs its task. Management and formulation of

its own policy is in the hands of a board of directors appointed by the State President. The boards of the subsidiary companies are staffed with experienced administrative and professional personnel drawn from the private sector and Armscor's own board and senior management. Armscor's internal organisation is set out in the accompanying diagram.

Current procedure is for a requirement to be formulated by the SADF and approved by the Defence Planning Committee. Thereafter it is passed to Armscor for whatever approach is best suited, employing a matrix organisation of project management which incorporates SADF officers. Armscor continues to contract out to private industry whenever it is feasible to do so, in the case both of acquisition programmes and research and development projects. Only those items that were covered in the original

brief are retained as in-house programmes, to be handled by one of the subsidiaries. Thus even such major projects as the building of the strike craft and Ratel ICV production have been let out. Other examples are to be found in the communications field.

Armscor does continue to acquire know-how from foreign sources, purchase production licences and import certain components. What is obtained, and how, are subjects Armscor prefers not to discuss. What is clear, however, is that this approach to procurement is adopted primarily for economic reasons. It may often be quite feasible to obtain the same result internally, but cheaper, quicker and simpler to obtain it from established specialists in a given field. The first major example of the approach was the Cactus/Crotale low-level SAM system developed by French companies to a South African requirement and specification.

Since its early days, Armscor has grown to become one of the largest industrial groups in South Africa. Today its assets stand at R 1500 million or higher, and it has eight major subsidiaries and some 20,000 employees. Eight hundred major and 300 minor regular sub-contractors have another 60,000 employees among them. Another 1200 firms regularly supply items from their normal production. During the 1982 financial year Armscor undertook production and research and development work to a value of some R 1600 million. Interestingly, its efforts have had a beneficial effect on industry in general. This is a result not only of orders placed with the private sector, but of the fact that it has been necessary to introduce, and in some cases develop, technology which might otherwise not yet have been available in South Africa.

Much of Armscor's growth was too rapid to be absorbed without some major problems, particularly where it involved setting up totally new operations and commissioning new and different plants. Between 1974 and 1981 Armscor's assets grew from R 200 million to R 1200 million and the number of employees from 12,000 to 26,000, while its area of operations became technically ever more complex. Once it became clear that there were major problems unlikely to be solved quickly from within, the Prime Minister approached a top industrial group in South Africa to request the secondment of senior executives. This was readily agreed to, and the influx of fresh minds soon had the desired result.

Right: The Buffel is the standard mine-protected APC of the Army. The example here has the drop sides down showing the harness worn by the troops aboard.

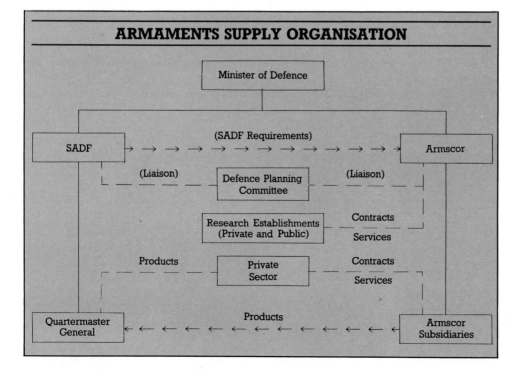

ARMAMENTS SUPPLY ORGANISATION

Minister of Defence

SADF → → → → → → → → → → → → → (SADF Requirements) → Armscor

(Liaison)

Defence Planning Committee

(Liaison)

Research Establishments (Private and Public)

Contracts

Services

Products

Private Sector

Contracts

Services

Quartermaster General ← ← ← ← ← ← ← ← ← ← ← Products ← Armscor Subsidiaries

Above: Olifant main battle tank on the test range. The SA Army intends to keep the Olifant in service until the 1990s.

The first major equipment production project was the licence assembly (and later manufacture) of Panhard AML-60 and AML-90 armoured cars by Sandock-Austral from 1964. Known as Elands, they continue in production in a much modified and improved form. Some 1400 have reportedly been delivered to date, including a number exported to other countries. Modifications have ranged from lengthening the hull nose (to accommodate the fact that South African soldiers have larger feet than their French counterparts), to fitting a local engine and a locally manufactured gun and the production of a derivative mounting the 20mm turret of the Ratel-20.

Also in 1964, South Africa resumed aircraft production, which had ceased after a pre-war start with assembling various trainer aircraft. The new programme too began with a trainer; a licence was acquired to assemble and later to manufacture the Aermacchi MB-326. The Atlas Aircraft Corporation was founded in 1965, and the first aircraft of substantially local manufacture flew within two years of the programme's inception. Named Impala by the SAAF, it remained in production

well into 1982, when the line was closed. Both the two-seat trainer (Impala Mk I) and the single-seat light attack derivative (Mk II) were produced. Total deliveries of the Impala amounted to some 260 aircraft.

Many other programmes were initiated in the mid-1960s, the local production of the FN-FAL rifle having in fact begun in 1961, preceding the establishment of the Armscor structure. The most interesting project of this period was undoubtedly the development of an air-to-air missile, which began in 1966. The first successful interceptions were carried out by 1972, and this project probably formed the basis for what has become the Kukri. The electronics industry took its first steps into the military communications field during this period, producing European equipment under licence. An early success was the B-16 high-frequency manpack radio, which went on to achieve international sales of some 12,000 as the Racal Squadcal. Other programmes were in the fields of infantry weapons, ammunition and spare parts.

With the creation of an industrial and know-how base, several major projects followed in the 1970s. Many were aimed at satisfying the requirements for heavy army equipment. Others included the acquisition of a manufacturing licence for Mirage III and F-1 aircraft and the building

of missile-armed strike craft for the SAN. Events in Angola and Mozambique in 1974/5 underlined the urgency of the situation, and the military lessons of the intervention in Angola showed how far the Army, in particular, had been allowed to fall behind. As a result, several projects were speeded up and new ones initiated.

Even before this, the Army and the Police had requested help in devising means to counter landmines laid by insurgents in the operational area of northern SWA. First, field-expedient and workshop-developed modifications of standard trucks were tested and the most effective standardised. This done, the lessons learned in these tests – and on operations by the SADF in SWA and by the Rhodesians – were applied to the development of mine-resistant and mine-protected APCs and trucks. These tall and rather ungainly looking vehicles have now given some ten years of service, providing near immunity to mines for the security forces and some civilians. The challenge of mine-clearing vehicles has seen several prototypes of varying success and continues to receive attention.

The first major conventional warfare equipment item to enter service was the Ratel-20 ICV. Developed as a wheeled vehicle in deference to the vast area of southern Africa, the Ratel was the first ICV of this type (and the third of any type) to enter service. It was also the first to provide a commander's cupola with a 360° view. It makes much use of standard

commercial components, which has imposed some constraints – notably its height – but has also served to keep the cost remarkably low (around the 250,000-rand level in the late 1970s.) The basic vehicle has been developed into a family which now includes two ICV types, a tank destroyer, a command vehicle, ambulance and recovery variants and an eight-wheeled logistic support vehicle. The Ratel has reportedly also been exported to other countries.

During the Angolan interlude, the Army was indelibly impressed by the superior range of opposing artillery. The performance of the BM-21 MRLs also caused many gunners to reconsider their views in this regard. The results of this sobering experience include the G-5 towed 155mm gun, the G-6 155mm SPG and the Valkiri 127mm SPMRL, with their associated target-acquisition and fire-control systems and ammunition families. Both the G-5 and the Valkiri have been introduced into service, the former replacing the World War II-vintage 25-pounder and 5.5-inch guns. Both have been used in action – apparently to the great satisfaction of both gunners and 'customers.'

The G-5 and G-6 are good examples of how Armscor can blend sophisticated technology from multiple sources to produce a system tailored to suit the SADF. The basic barrel and ammunition of this gun family appear to have been developed by the Space Research Corporation of Quebec. The ammunition was im-

Above: G-6 155mm self-propelled gun at maximum elevation.
Below: G-5 gun being towed by its Samil 100 tractor. The Samil tractor carries the gun crew and their basic equipment as well as a quantity of ready-use ammunition.

Above: Rhino armoured, mine-protected personnel transport/liason vehicle, a Samil-20 variant, undergoes a suspension and mobility test.

proved by incorporating Swedish base-bleed technology; then the unit was mated to towed and SP carriages developed for SA conditions. The Belgian GC-45 and the Austrian GHN-45 are close relatives. Valkiri, too, has an international background – it was developed on the basis of captured Soviet BM-21s.

The first impetus toward development of an indigenous family of soft-skin vehicles came when a 1964 survey revealed

Below: The Bulldog APC is another Samil-20 variant which will gradually replace the Buffel. The side armour folds down to allow rapid debussing if necessary.

more than 200 types in service. Many of these vehicles were wearing out, and with a serious embargo in prospect, new planning was mandatory. As an interim measure, new-vehicle purchases were restricted to a few types and their local components were increased: by 1977 they had reached 66 percent in the Landrover and Bedford – the bulk of purchases. The longer-term aim, however, remained the acquisition of a standardised fleet of vehicles fully equal to South African Army requirements – which were very high in view of the harsh terrain and climate. An analysis of vehicle requirements revealed the need for a family of three basic types: 2-, 5- and 10-tonne.

The first step was to purchase a large number of different, potentially suitable vehicles for testing. One result of early difficulties experienced in obtaining uniform, comparable results was the construction of a special test track at Elands fontein, near Pretoria, which has since grown into a large and comprehensive facility. The tests revealed that no single type fully satisfied the requirements, leading to the decision to develop an indigenous family of trucks for the SADF. The resulting SAMIL (SA MILitary) trucks began to enter service in 1980. To date, more than 12,000 have been delivered in various versions of the SAMIL-20 (2t), SAMIL-50 (5t), SAMIL-100 (10t), the civilian SAMAG and the related road-bound SAKOM (5/10t).

Less visible programmes continued simultaneously, and new ones were initiated. These include the production of light and heavy infantry weapons, various mines and a miscellany of engineering and other equipment and stores. Among the infantry weapons, one of the most recent is the R-4 assault rifle derived from the Israeli Galil. Another project is the Kriek military motorcycle for use as a despatch vehicle and with COIN units. Of the many trailers manufactured for the SADF, two have enjoyed considerable export success – a field kitchen and a glass-fibre water tanker. All types of army ammunition are also produced locally, including a family of long-range ammunition for the 5.5-inch gun.

Another important aspect of Armscor's work is modernising and re-working heavy equipment. The premier example is the Olifant MBT, which has grown out of the Centurion Mk 5s obtained from Britain in 1952 and a number of later models and various hulks reportedly obtained more recently. It has been radically improved by re-working the whole suspension system, fitting a diesel engine and a new transmission and replacing the 20-pounder with a 105mm gun and an up-to-date fire-control system. Another example: the 5.5-inch guns, which have been completely overhauled and re-worked. Of the newer equipment, the Elands, for example, are refitted and updated on a cyclic basis, between batches of new production.

The most visible current project is the G-6 SPG, now being readied for production. Another project that has been acknowledged is an SP air-defence system. This will probably be a Ratel-based gun system, although the G-6 might be considered as the basis despite its size. It has been said that the system 'will not be as complex as [W. Germany's] Gepard.' Armscor has also been candid about the need to develop an Olifant successor. The feeling is that the Olifant will be adequate until the 1990s, when a new MBT will be needed; it is believed that this can be developed locally. Other highly likely near-term projects include a new armoured car and a long-range ATGM, but nothing has been said in this regard.

In the electronics field, SA created a stir when it became known that the SADF was one of the first – if not the first – forces to

Below: Samil-50 mine-protected recovery vehicle which can be used to remove captured vehicles as well as working with SA Army equipment.

Above: Eland-90 armoured car with an Eland-60 in the background. The Eland-90 has proved able to knock out enemy T-54/55 tanks when well handled.

have 'frequency-hopping' communications systems in service. Developed by Grinel, one such system has reportedly been in use since early 1979. Grinel was formed when Racal were taken over by the Grinaker group. Racal had already absorbed SMO, one of the pioneers in SA electronics. Another major supplier of communications systems is Tactel, which has been supplying the SADF since the late 1960s. Tactel, too, have developed several 'frequency-hopping' systems. Other companies are involved in the

supply of antennae and related equipment: antennae built to European specifications do not last in the South African bush.

In addition to radios, full communications systems have been developed, the most recent of which all link up to each other and, indirectly, to a national tropospheric scatter network. Standardised

Above: Eland-90 armoured car. In addition to their main armament 90mm gun and co-axial machine gun, most Eland-90s carry a second machine gun on the turret roof.

communications containers designed to fit the SAMIL trucks are now entering service. All are air-transportable in C-130 and C-160 aircraft and can also be fitted with wheels for towing. Field telephone systems with the necessary mobile exchanges have also been developed.

The bulk of Armscor's work for the SAAF has been carried out by the Atlas Aircraft Corporation. Beginning in the 1960s with the assembly of Impalas, Atlas went on virtually to manufacture these aircraft and, later, to assemble the Mirage F-1AZ. When the Impala production line closed in 1982, the Chairman of Armscor announced that Atlas would soon begin production of an unspecified type of helicopter. Other aircraft projects have been the assembly of the AM-3C Bosbok spotter aircraft and the production of the related Kudu light transport version. Fifteen Bosbok and 25 Kudu were delivered to the SAAF. Other work has concentrated on the production of spares.

Besides aircraft production, Atlas is also responsible for a share of major maintenance, overhaul and repair work. To this end, some Atlas personnel are to be found at squadron level, where they assist SAAF personnel. The larger tasks, however, are generally handled at the factory. One example of this work was the total overhaul, refit and resparring of the Shackletons in the mid-1970s. Another aspect of Atlas's work is research, most of it aimed at improving the effectiveness of available aircraft and lengthening their service lives. In this regard Atlas also assists the SAAF in clearing new aircraft/weapon combinations. It has also done some work in an autogyro project, which may be the basis of the announced intention to produce helicopters.

Another company involved in production for the SAAF is Kentron, whose most visible development has been the Kukri short-range air-to-air missile. Reportedly developed on the basis of the R-550 Magic and incorporating the results of earlier work in this area, it is a fairly standard modern infra-red-homing dog-fight missile with one distinctive edge over competitors. This lies in the target-acquisition system, which slaves the seeker head of the missile to the movements of the pilot's head, thereby allowing the seeker to acquire and lock onto a target well outside the aircraft axis. Once the seeker is locked on, the pilot selects the tracking mode and is then free to divert his attention, firing when ready. Most other SAAF weapons such as bombs, rockets and flares are also produced locally.

The only announced future project for the SAAF is the intended production of helicopters. While nothing has been said as to the type, it seems likely that initial production will be of a medium helicopter to supplement the Pumas. An armed derivative should follow soon after, as the SAAF has no attack helicopters in its inventory, despite the fact that these would be ideally suited to operations in this theatre. The SAAF's other most urgent requirement is for new-technology fighters; efforts toward this end can also be expected in some form. Beyond this, concentration is likely to be on modern weapons systems.

The biggest naval project ever tackled in South Africa is the construction of strike craft by Sandock-Austral in Durban. Derived from an initial Lürssen Werft design via the Israeli Reshef class, these vessels have enhanced the SAN's coastal capabilities and given the local shipbuilding industry experience in building and fitting out naval vessels. This, together with the SAN's own experience of refitting and modernising, and the industry's

experience with commercial vessels of up to 10,000 tons, is the foundation upon which a corvette construction programme may be set up. Submarine building could, perhaps, follow.

Other naval work has included the building of several small tugs and the diving tender *Fleur* for the SAN. More immediate naval projects have included the design and building of a 30m patrol craft and the development of the Namacurra class of harbour patrol boats. These have been designed around an unusual twin hull which grants them very good seakeeping for their size. The same basic hull has also been used for some service boats. Several new 'water tractor' type tugs are also on order for the SAN. As with the other services, most ammunition is produced locally. Torpedoes are one area where this is not the case, the emphasis here being on the replacement of certain components as necessary.

Armscor has also assisted the SAN with the refitting and often very extensive modernisation of its vessels. The biggest of these projects was the modernisation of the President-class frigates. Earlier, the two W-class destroyers had been similarly but less extensively modernised by the SAN. Another major project has been the conversion of several mine-sweepers into mine-hunters, which continues. Refits of the submarines have also been extensive. SA's capability in this field received an accolade when the Iranian Navy had its flagship *Artemiz* refitted in Cape Town in 1973/4.

Future projects are still indefinite, although the SAN has announced its intention to advance the corvette programme to make up for the loss of the *President Kruger* as quickly as possible. There have also been several increasingly more definite statements about building submarines, but this is unlikely to proceed before the corvette programme is at least

well under way. Another programme that has been in the offing for some time is the building of new MCMVs to supplement and later replace the existing vessels. Finally, it appears that the SAN intends to order a new, purpose-built replenishment ship as soon as funds are available.

The breadth of Armscor's output compared to the relatively small size of the SADF reveals what is probably the biggest problem facing South Africa in this field. Any major equipment item is costly both to develop and to manufacture, and much of the latter cost is of a capital nature. Add to this the costs of keeping production lines open after the basic order has been met – which is essential for maintaining the capability to replace wartime losses. Any locally produced major equipment item, then, will be very expensive indeed if all these costs are set off only against the SADF requirement. Thus the decision to enter the export market should not have come as a surprise; it is the only way to address this problem effectively .

Despite the political difficulties attending this approach, Armscor's export organisation will enjoy two major advantages vis à vis the competition. One is obvious: much of the equipment has been developed on the basis of operational experience and has, in fact, been used in action. Arguably more important is the fact that all of it has been developed with the needs, problems and capabilities of a relatively small defence force in mind. Thus it is likely to be far more suited to the needs and resources of a potential buyer than is equipment developed first for the armed forces of a major power.

Another future prospect is that of further co-operation with such other third-level arms producers as Argentina, Brazil,

Below: Command Ratel on the vertical obstacle-climbing section of the test track.

Above: Water tanker on the basic Samil 100 chassis. These vehicles have been extensively employed in recent drought relief operations as well as military tasks.

Chile, Israel, the Republic of China and South Korea. They and some others all face similar problems regarding a secure source of arms and equipment supply and support. No one of them can really afford to develop up-to-date major systems by itself. In most cases some element of necessary technology may also be absent. A grouping of several of these countries, however, would have considerable expertise and potential – no matter how unofficial their understanding might be. While they might not wish to develop identical systems, much of the basic know-how is common within a given field, and this is where such co-operation would pay off handsomely.

Overall, then, it can be said that Armscor faces a busy future. SA defence expenditure still hovers around the 5-per-cent-of-GNP mark despite the growing threat, so it should not be too difficult to persuade the government to increase funds for new equipment. More difficult will be Armscor's task in replacing those items that are not suited to local production at this stage, such as strike aircraft, long-range maritime patrol aircraft and a long-range SAM system. On the other hand, Armscor does have a record of remarkable achievement, having grown from virtually nothing to a major arms producer in a matter of 20 years.

Below: Preparing to fire the new 60mm patrol mortar which is to replace the older bipod-mounted weapon in the company support sections of most units.

INSURGENCY IN SOUTH-WEST AFRICA

The origins of the insurgency now plaguing parts of northern SWA go back to 1957 and to Cape Town – some 2200 kilometres south of the troubled area. That year the Owambo Peoples' Congress was founded in Cape Town by one Herman Toivo ja Toivo, a former railways policeman who had recently been released after serving a prison sentence in connection with his later activities. Several of his advisers and mentors of that period were self-declared members of the South African Communist Party, which may have served to set the scene for current events. The new organisation was renamed Owambo People's Organisation in 1959; in June 1960 it adopted the name South West Africa People's Organisation (SWAPO) in an effort to disguise its tribal character.

While this did succeed in misleading several foreign backers, the name change proved less efficacious within SWA. One

Previous page: Part of the mechanised force preparing for its attack on the 'Vietnam' base near Chetaquera in southern Angola during Operation Reindeer in May 1978, the first major cross-border operation since the 1975 incursion.

reason for this no doubt lies in the continuing mistrust felt by many of the other population groups toward the Owambos – not a little helped along by the attitude of many Owambos toward members of the smaller groups. Thus SWAPO has remained essentially an Owambo organisation, although individuals from other groups have joined over the years and, in some cases, have been placed in senior posts. The probable proportions are reflected in the fact that almost 95% of captured or killed insurgents are Owambos. A young Dama recruit captured during a cross-border operation by security forces told his interviewers that he was happy to be clear of SWAPO because he was 'unhappy with the racism in the training camp,' which is a telling commentary.

One group did commit itself fully to SWAPO: The Caprivi African National Union (CANU), which merged with SWAPO in 1964. Today, many of CANU's leaders find themselves imprisoned in host countries after a purge by the SWAPO leadership. This followed indications – including a letter to the Chief Minister of Caprivi – that CANU intended to break away from SWAPO and re-enter the constitutional process. Other purges have removed most of SWAPO's early and most prominent members, several of whom have returned to SWA in recent years to re-enter legitimate politics.

SWAPO based its platform chiefly on dissatisfaction among the Owambos with both the migrant labour system and the system for electing headmen. On this basis SWAPO campaigned for independence from South Africa – which controls the territory under a League of Nations 'C' Mandate – and for the introduction of a national-level 'one man, one vote' system of government. The fact that the demographic realities of SWA would then inevitably result in Owambo hegemony was – tactfully – not mentioned. Also glossed over to this day is the fact that the 'C' Mandates made no provision for the future independence of the territories concerned because they were considered unlikely ever to be viable as countries.

Despite some political success, several of the new party's leaders left SWA in the early 1960s to prosecute their aims from abroad. Among these was Sam Nujoma, who feared arrest for his involvement in the instigation of a riot at Windhoek. Once established overseas, SWAPO decided on 'armed revolution' as the means towards their end and announced this in 1962, forming a military wing – the People's Liberation Army of Namibia (PLAN) – for this purpose.

Above: Political education plays a major part in the training of FAPLA officers as the posters on the walls of this classroom show.
Below: A mass briefing for troops before the start of an operation in 1980.

Above: A Ratel damaged in a minefield and by FAPLA tank attacks is nonetheless recovered.

Meanwhile terrorism had been initiated by a second group of ten insurgents, who plundered two trading stores near the Angolan/SWA border in February 1966. Their navigational skills had proved somewhat shaky, however, as both shops were on the Angolan side of the border. The two shopkeepers, a Portuguese and an Owambo, were murdered. This group then broke up, but three of the insurgents were apprehended by members of the local population near Rundu in Kavango – east of Owambo – some time later and handed over to the police.

July 1966 saw a third group of ten insurgents enter Owambo to begin operations. Among the incidents that followed were the shooting-up of the border village of Oshikango in September, several attacks on Owambo headmen and an attack on a farm in the Grootfontein district – immediately south of Owambo – in December. That same month the fourth group of eight PLAN insurgents arrived in Owambo. In 1967 there were similar terrorist incidents, as well as armed propaganda activity, more intensive recruiting attempts and the expansion of the insurgency into Caprivi, the eastward-reaching finger of SWA between Botswana and Zambia. This opened in March

Recruiting proved disappointingly slow, and SWAPO soon had to resort to the tried and trusted ploy of offering scholarships tenable in the United States and England in an effort to attract young Owambos. Some 900 recruits were obtained by this method at the time, and it remains in use today. The recruits were flown from Botswana or Zambia to Tanzania, where they were taken to a camp north-west of Dar es Salaam for basic training – the nature of which must have come as a rude shock. Those selected for advanced or specialised training were then sent on to other countries, including Algeria, China. Cuba, Egypt, North Korea and the Soviet Union.

The first six armed insurgents entered Owambo – one of the northern regions of SWA – during September 1965. In subse-

quent months, they moved around the region spreading their message and seeking out likely recruits. Some thirty young Owambos received rudimentary training at several temporary camps during this period, after which most were sent back to their homes to await instructions. Despite the insurgents' best efforts to maintain security, word of their activities reached the police and set in train an intensive intelligence-gathering effort.

Their current camp was finally discovered by a team of police who had spent several weeks moving through the general area disguised as a roadworks party, following up information received from members of the local population. On 26 August 1966, after a period of surveillance, a small heliborne police force raided the camp. Two insurgents were killed and nine captured in the ensuing skirmish. Several others were arrested later after identification by local people.

with the ambush of a police patrol in western Caprivi that resulted in the arrest of almost all of the ambush part.

After this inauspicious start, PLAN suffered a new setback in May when their 'supreme commander,' Tobias Hanyeko, was killed in an exchange of fire on a passenger barge along the Caprivi shore of the Zambezi. Police had boarded the barge for a routine check and recognised him. Two policemen were seriously injured in this incident, of whom one was blinded and the other died two years later of the after-effects. The following ten months brought a series of greater or lesser disasters for the insurgents, 160 having been arrested and two killed in clashes with police counterinsurgency elements by March 1968. That April, in fact, saw the police withdraw their counterinsurgency personnel from Owambo in view of the peaceful conditions then prevailing.

As it turned out, this withdrawal was premature, although Owambo did remain peaceful for some months thereafter. During October, however, two large groups of insurgents entered Owambo and reopened PLAN's campaign, necessitating the renewed deployment of counterinsurgency elements to the

region. While PLAN could claim this as a success of sorts, their change to the employment of large groups was anything but that: no fewer than 56 of the insurgents were arrested within a week of their arrival in the region. As one result, PLAN reverted to its earlier system of operating in small groups. By the turn of the year, however, personnel losses had reached unacceptable levels and, together with the continuing hostility of much of their own tribal base – the Owambos – had forced a virtual halt to the insurgents' operations. This lull lasted throughout 1969 and 1970 with insurgent activity picking up again in 1971, concentrated chiefly on the sporadic laying of mines.

During this period the insurgents also became something of a nuisance in Zambia, indulging in a variety of excesses which finally led the local police to seize their weapons on several occasions. The first of the many mine incidents that northern SWA has suffered came in May 1971, when a police vehicle detonated an anti-vehicle mine near Katima Mulilo in the eastern Caprivi. Further mine incidents – and casualties, both police and civilian – followed sporadically.

By 1973 the insurgents had recovered from their earlier setbacks and renewed

Above: Local leaders often carry arms or employ bodyguards for personal protection.
Below: Collecting weapons and equipment including anti-aircraft machine guns in the Smokeshell base complex.

declared boycott of the 1973 general elections in the region: a poll of only 2.7% was recorded. A similar attempt in 1975 proved less successful, and a 55% poll was recorded. This was quickly countered by SWAPO in the form of stepped-up terrorism, one victim being the Chief Minister of Owambo.

Between the two events had come the beginning of the Portuguese collapse in Angola, resulting in the first large-scale deployment of South African troops in northern SWA. This severely restricted PLAN's freedom of action for a time, although a measure of low-key armed propaganda and 'soft intimidation' could not be prevented. The insurgents' position was weakened further with the beginning of Operation Savannah, the South African intervention in Angola during the latter part of 1975.

During this intervention, substantial elements of PLAN were forced to go 'underground' in those parts of southern Angola which they had just come to regard as safe staging areas for operations against Owambo. Insurgents who

their activities, stepping up pressure on the local population and – particularly in Caprivi – setting the occasional ambush for police patrols. The first intimation of this new vigour came in January of that year, when a police camp was subjected to a brief bombardment from several recoilless rifles before the attackers, having taken some casualties to return fire, withdrew back into Zambia. When the pressure continued to grow, responsibility for the counterinsurgency effort was passed over to the Army, which had the necessary manpower.

The degree to which armed propaganda and intimidation had done their work in Owambo became clear when PLAN succeeded in enforcing a SWAPO-

Above left: Buffels at Xangongo being prepared for the pull-out back to SWA.
Below: Army vehicles in Xangongo, known in former times as Vila Rocadas.

did succeed in entering Owambo during this period concentrated mainly on more or less spectacular activity in an effort to retain media attention. It was hoped that this would both convince foreign backers of the insurgency's vitality and, via the local press and word of mouth, balance out the reduced presence in Owambo. Losses during this period were painful.

Overall, however, developments in Angola have proved highly advantageous for PLAN. Instead of having to infiltrate Owambo by way of Caprivi and the hostile Kavango or, alternatively, having to penetrate a hostile Portuguese-controlled Angola, the insurgents now enjoy direct access to their tribal base. This advantage is even greater than it might appear at first sight in that numerous Owambos live in Southern Angola – separated from their kin only by a line drawn across featureless bush in one of the many unfortunate border decisions of the colonial era. Thus social and minor commercial cross-border traffic is a reality that facilitates infiltrations and hampers the security forces.

Then, too, the open support that SWAPO receives from the MPLA government in Angola goes a long way toward eliminating many of the previous problems. PLAN can now maintain a compre-

hensive network of training camps and forward staging base-areas while sharing parts of FAPLA's logistic system. Access to Soviet and other aid is much easier and movement is simplified by the existence of parallel Soviet – supporting FAPLA and PLAN – and Cuban supply systems. The greater stability in PLAN's training system has also allowed for increasingly effective use of various advisers, instructors and specialists, some of whom may well be shared with FAPLA. Finally, FAPLA appears quite happy to allow at least some of PLAN's bases to 'hug' its own so as to reduce the danger of attack by security forces.

One countervailing result of develop-

ments in Angola, apparently, is that PLAN, euphoric at gaining direct access to Owambo, temporarily neglected its effort in Caprivi. This gave ample opportunity to the security forces and Caprivi authorities, allowing greater emphasis on civic action projects and a speeding-up of civilian development programmes. At the same time, the remaining insurgents were neutralised or driven from the region by vigorous security force action - increasingly aided by the local population as the

Below: A civilian car after a mine explosion. Civilian vehicles suffer far more seriously than those of the army because of the high standards of mine protection that virtually every army vehicle incorporates.

threat of reprisals faded. This same confidence among the local population also hindered renewed attempts at infiltration.

Faced with rapidly declining effectiveness in Caprivi, PLAN apparently decided to stage a major publicity exercise – both to regain a measure of prestige within Caprivi and to bolster its faltering image in the eyes of its foreign backers and its Zambian hosts. This operation finally took the form of several 122mm rockets fired at the base at Katima Mulilo in August 1979. Ten soldiers were killed when the barrack hut in which they were sleeping was hit by the only effective rocket.

The security forces reacted with an

Left: Political posters are routinely found in SWAPO camps whenever they are raided by the security forces.
Below: Buffels in a densely bushed part of northern Owambo. The open top of the Buffel can make life uncomfortable for its passengers in such terrain.

immediate follow-up operation that inflicted some casualties. Shortly thereafter, a major raid was mounted against PLAN bases in south-western Zambia, whence the rocketeers had come. This, PLAN decided not to contest, avoiding contact almost entirely. Nevertheless, they suffered additional damage to their local image – in both Caprivi and Zambia – and to morale. PLAN has made no serious attempt to reopen operations in Caprivi since.

With Caprivi virtually restabilised, only Owambo remains as an active operational area. Kaokoland, in north-west SWA, has experienced incidents of mine-laying and murder as well as some intimidation along the border with Angola. There have also been cases in which insurgent groups used this region as a route to the south and to outflank security forces in Owambo. Overall, however, this area, too, has

remained relatively quiet – perhaps because it is too thinly populated to be of much interest to SWAPO. In any event, the Himba population – essentially Herero – is not generally well disposed toward the Owambos.

Kavango - between Owambo and Caprivi – has long been hostile to the Owambo-dominated SWAPO and its insurgency. Not only does it enjoy considerable development and stability, Kavango also has the contrasting examples of the now-peaceful Caprivi and the terrorism-wracked Owambo on either side. Then too, Kavango is host to a large number of refugees from south-eastern Angola, many of whom have bitter memories of PLAN excesses during operations in support of FAPLA against Unita insurgents. Thus, despite some more or less legal SWAPO activity, occasional subversion of local government officials and increasing expansion of operations from eastern Owambo into western Kavango, most infiltrations have been promptly reported to the security forces for counteraction. However, this has not deterred PLAN from ongoing attempts to 'activate' Kavango.

Elements of the security forces remain stationed in both regions as a precaution. Much of their time is devoted to a variety of civic-action and development programmes, with emphasis on providing the materials and specialised knowledge for a broad spectrum of self-help projects. Naturally, they also spend time patrolling and doing general intelligence/counter-intelligence work. Both Kaokoland and Kavango do remain highly vulnerable to terrorist incursions from Angola, because their populations are largely concentrated very near the rivers that form their

Above: A T-34/85 captured in its hide during Operation Protea.

respective boundaries with Angola. As a result, PLAN's recent operations in these areas should perhaps be seen not as a serious attempt to open new fronts, but as reminders to the local population of their vulnerability.

PLAN's attempts to open operations south of Owambo have been sporadic and not particularly successful. These operations are conducted by PLAN's 'special forces' elements, known by the code names Typhoon and Volcano. The pattern has been for a small group of insurgents to move south through the very sparsely populated eastern Owambo during the rainy season, when surface water is available to them and contributes to the heavier bush that renders tracking and detection more difficult. Once arrived in the farming districts immediately south of Owambo, they have generally concentrated on attacking isolated farms and sabotaging the railway line.

On occasion, these forays have had embarrassing results: in one case a fifteen-year-old schoolgirl drove off an attack after her father had been killed in the opening flurry of fire. She killed one of the insurgents and wounded another, who was later finished off by his compatriots. The most recent of these operations have involved rather larger groups, but have otherwise differed little from their predecessors except in requiring a greater effort on the part of security forces. Exceptions to the norm have been such isolated incidents of urban terrorism as bombs in Windhoek and Swakopmund and the assassination of the widely respected Herero leader Clemens Kapuuo

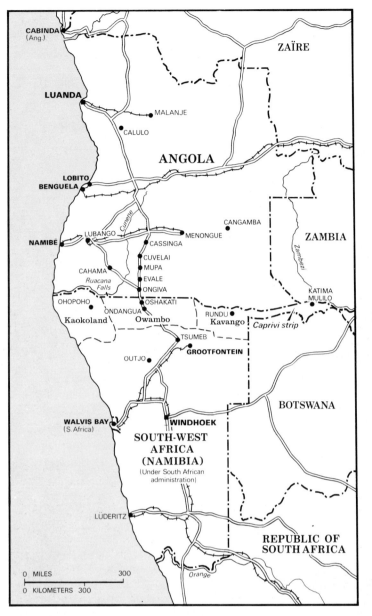

in his shop outside Windhoek. There has also been an attempt to destroy the main road bridge south of Keetmanshoop.

In Owambo itself, terrorism began to escalate seriously not long after SA forces had withdrawn from Angola following Operation Savannah. By 1978 the situation had become so untenable that it was decided to deny the insurgents uncontested sanctuary in southern Angola. On 4 May that year, the security forces launched the first major cross-border operation against PLAN bases to the north of the border – Operation Reindeer. This took the form of two separate but co-ordinated raids. An airborne force, roughly of small battalion size, struck the rear-areas camp code-named 'Moscow' near Cassinga, some 250 km inside Angola, while a mechanised force hit the 'Vietnam' camp complex near Chetequera, 28 km north of the border. Several smaller sweeps were simultaneously conducted closer to the border.

Some 1000 PLAN personnel were killed and 200 captured in this operation, for the loss of six fatalities in the raiding force. Arguably of still greater value was the intelligence gained on PLAN's organisa-

tion, doctrine and aims. Considerable stores of equipment were also destroyed. Despite the great success of the operation, it served as a reminder of the vulnerability of paratroops operating beyond reach of friendly ground forces. Had the opposing armour been handled less ineptly, the operation could well have turned into a costly and embarrassing disaster. As it was, enemy tanks were actually on the landing zone as the last of the force was lifted out by Pumas.

The major effect on PLAN was the massive loss of trained and partially trained personnel, a blow from which it has not yet fully recovered. For a time, this forced PLAN to revert to operating in large groups of semi-trained recruits, stiffened by a few experienced men. While this did allow PLAN to maintain limited operations that conserved surviving trained personnel as instructors, it also brought very heavy losses, as these large groups were relatively easy to detect, fix and destroy. By the end of 1979, losses stood at some 90 a month. Losses have continued to rise since, as a result both of new external operations and more effective internal measures.

Above: A Special Constable of the SWA Police armed with an FN MAG light machine gun.
Above left: General map of Angola and South-West Africa.

The latter part of 1979 saw the second major cross-border operation – Saffron – when elements of the security forces crossed into south-western Zambia in response to the rocketing of Katima Mulilo, discussed above. The third such major operation – Sceptic – followed in June 1980, when a mechanised force struck at a PLAN base area code-named 'Smokeshell' in southern Angola.

Originally intended as a short raid, this operation was extended to last almost three weeks when intelligence indicated the presence of additional base areas and camps nearby. Contacts during the first night had also confirmed the continued presence of insurgents in the area. Overall, some 360 insurgents were confirmed killed and a number of prisoners taken for the loss of 17 members of the security forces killed. Several hundred tonnes of arms, ammunition and equipment were captured and destroyed, while some 150 tonnes – including vehicles – were taken back for evaluation.

While the 'Smokeshell' base area had not been ideally sited tactically – difficult to achieve, in any case, in flat and bushy terrain – it had been thoroughly prepared for defence. Earth and log bunkers, slit trenches and fighting holes were plentiful. The defence itself was apparently quite spirited once the initial surprise had been overcome, with the light anti-aircraft guns – 14.5mm single and 23mm twin – proving especially troublesome in the ground defence role. One ZU-23-2 succeeded in knocking out several Ratels before being silenced.

The attack went in after a brief artillery preparation on identified targets. Three mechanised groups swept through the target area on a roughly east-west axis, thereby largely avoiding the defences, oriented to the south. The sheer size of the base area – some 65 sq kms – dictated that the infantry remain mounted throughout

Right: A destroyed 14.5mm anti-aircraft machine gun in the Smokeshell complex. These weapons also proved troublesome in the ground role.
Below: A dramatic sequence of gun camera photos taken by a SAAF aircraft during the shooting down of a MiG on 5 October 1982.

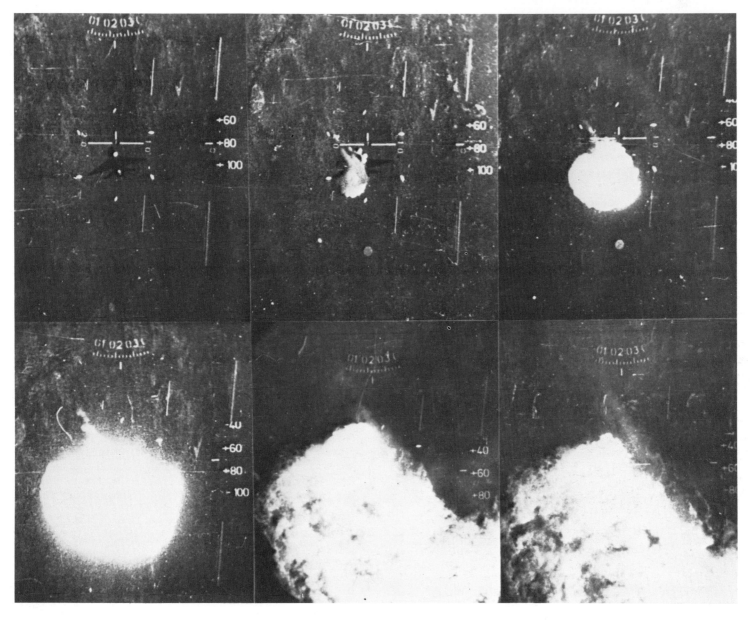

SOUTH-WEST AFRICA TERRITORY FORCE (SWATF)

The SWATF was established on 1 August 1980 as the basis of a future independent South-West African defence force. It remains under SADF operational control for the present; the General Officer Commanding SWATF doubles as SWA Secretary for Defence and OC SWA Command, the latter being an SADF post exercising command over South African forces and the counterinsurgency operations in northern SWA. Budgetary control falls to the SWA authorities, and all administration, national service matters, training and purchasing are SWATF matters. National service for all males has been proclaimed but is only applied selectively, both to avoid potential political problems arising from the insurgency situation and to avoid overloading the limited training facilities. At present, the SWATF provides some 30 percent of the troops in the Operational Area.

The SWATF is structually similar to the SADF in that it is militia-based and has both an area-bound counterinsurgency element (Area Force) and a mobile conventional warfare element (Reaction Force). SWA is also divided into seven Sectors with functions similar to the Commands in South Africa. The three sectors covering the Operational Area (10 – Kaokoland and Owambo; 20 – Kavango Bushmanland and West Caprivi; and 70 – East Caprivi) remain under SADF control for the time being. The remaining four Sectors (30 – HQ at Otjiwarongo; 40 – HQ at Windhoek; 50 – HQ at Gobabis; 60 – HQ at Keetmanshoop) are commanded by SWATF officers.

The Area Force is essentially similar to the SA Commando system. The 26 Area Force Units vary widely in strength and composition, being tailored to suit their particular responsibilities. They fall under the Sector headquarters for command and administrative purposes. The

Above: Like the SADF the SWATF places great stress on fitness with physical training being an important part of the day-to-day routine.

Reaction Force comprises a CF Motorised Brigade – which includes one standing battalion – and six standing regional light infantry battalions manned by volunteers. These are counterinsurgency units whereas the Brigade has a primary conventional role, although its elements also do duty in the Operational Area. Other elements include a specialised follow-up unit and a light aviation squadron. The regional battalions handle their own basic training while other troops are still given their initial training by the SADF at Walvis Bay. A Military School at Okanhandja conducts advanced courses.

Below: 701 Bn troops practicing with light machine guns. 701 is raised locally in East Caprivi and provides security for that area as well as sending elements to the Operational Area.

the assault, debussing from their Buffels and Ratels only to deal with determined dug-in opposition. Particularly stubborn strongpoints were subdued with the aid of both direct (Eland-90, Ratel-20 and Ratel-90) and indirect fire (mortars, 140mm guns). Some close air support was also available, consisting chiefly of Impala Mk IIs firing cannon and rockets.

The operation's extended phase proved both tedious and time-consuming, with objectives widely scattered and well concealed. It was speeded up to some extent by deploying helicopters to move infantry among the various base areas to reduce strongpoints as they were located, leaving the bulk of the mechanised elements free to continue sweeping the area. Other infantry searched the subdued base areas, mopping up and collecting documents and equipment.

This phase also brought two clashes with semi-mechanised PLAN columns which were apparently attempting to conduct a reconnaissance in force. One was detected as it entered the area, the other on attempting to slip away without making contact. Both were fixed by air attacks until ground forces could reach and destroy them. Several BRDM-2 scout cars and BTR-152 APCs were captured or destroyed in these engagements, as were a number of trucks. During the withdrawal phase, a mechanised FAPLA force clashed with one of the raiding elements, engaging it with both direct and indirect fire. This necessitated a brief counter-attack with air support before a clean break could be achieved. The only other FAPLA involvement came when a SAAF helicopter strayed too near one of their camps and was shot down; the pilot made his way back to friendly lines on foot despite a back injury and some hair-raising adventures en route. Contacts with local civilians were few, most apparently having heeded the pamphlets dropped before the operation calling on them to keep clear. Those who were encountered were given food – a valuable commodity in Angola today – and any necessary medical treatment.

The next such operation – Protea, in August 1981 – was rather more complicated in that combined PLAN and FAPLA forces were encountered throughout. Also, FAPLA had assured the local population that there was no danger and had prevented them from leaving the area of the PLAN establishments that were the raid's objectives. By then, too, the new Cuban- and East German-installed air-defence system had become operational and warned PLAN of potentially dangerous air movements.

Operation Protea followed onto a series of foot-mobile search-and-destroy operations against the PLAN infrastructure in southern Angola east of an imaginary line drawn through Ongiva (formerly Perreira de Eca). One of these operations – Carnation – actually continued in tandem with Protea. Although none of these operations had brought any clashes with FAPLA, despite an occasional approach to within a few hundred meters of their positions, the planning for Protea had to accept such contact as a distinct possibility: west of the imaginary line, PLAN and FAPLA facilities and logistics were so closely intertwined as to be virtually inseperable. The situation was complicated by PLAN standing orders that required their personnel to wear FAPLA uniform in or near towns.

Preceded by an air strike on the radar installation at Cahama – some 130 km inside Angola – Protea opened in the early hours of 24 August, when a mechanised force crossed the Cunene River near Ruacana. This force then moved rapidly northward along the western bank of the river to the area of Humbe, where it took up blocking positions to cover the operation against possible interference from the Cahama area and to prevent the escape of any PLAN elements along this route.

A second mechanised force moved from Ondangwa during the night, arriving just south of Xangongo (formerly Vila Rocadas) – 70 km north of the border – around 0900 hours. One element of this force moved farther north to guard against interference by FAPLA elements stationed at Peu Peu, some 20 km to the north-east. Other elements were de-

Below: Captured guns including Soviet-made 76mm field guns and twin 23mm anti-aircraft guns and Yugoslav triple 20mm anti-aircraft machine guns.

tached to deal with PLAN camps south and south-east of Xangongo.

At Xangongo, the site of PLAN's North-Western Front HQ, the main body found a mixed PLAN/FAPLA force dug in on the southern outskirts. This defence was disrupted in a brief but vigorous action, followed by several hours of mopping up remaining defences in and around the town. During this activity, a convoy of more than 60 GAZ-66 trucks was encountered and captured in the town. Most of

Above: A few of the captured trucks parked at Ondangwa prior to disposal.

these trucks were loaded with a variety of supplies, but some had 20mm anti-aircraft cannon mounted on their load beds, a few of which put up a brief fight before being silenced by the Ratels. Two T-34/85s were also encountered during the fighting and were destroyed by Ratel-90s. Meanwhile, the detached element covering against Peu Peu fought off a short attack by

FAPLA armour and infantry trying to break through toward Xangongo.

Once Xangongo had been secured and it was clear that covering forces could handle any interference, the main body of the raiding force took the road toward its next objective, Ongiva, which was the site of PLAN's Northern Front HQ. The detached elements continued their area operations around Xangongo, searching out and destroying PLAN camps and collecting arms, ammunition and equipment for destruction or transport back to SWA. Light relief included a football match against the local Xangongo team, which the raiders won two-nil.

The main body met some resistance near Mongua – 40 kilometers east of Xangongo – on the 25th. Here a mechanised FAPLA force with artillery support attempted to stop the advance toward Ongiva. This resistance was quickly broken down, although one helicopter was lost in the process. Ongiva was reached on the 26th.

Here the raiding force encountered another mixed PLAN/FAPLA force deployed to defend the town. Comprising armour and infantry and enjoying some artillery support, this force appears to have put up a spirited resistance before Ongiva fell during the afternoon of the 28th. Nine tanks were destroyed in the fighting. At one stage a column of some 25 vehicles attempted to depart the area but ran into a blocking group north of the town. Ignoring calls to identify itself, parts of the column then tried to outflank the blocking position. Most of the column – which turned out to be FAPLA – was then destroyed in the air attacks called down upon it. Several Soviet personnel were killed in this incident, and a warrant officer was captured.

With Ongiva taken, the raiding force set about destroying local PLAN facilities and then began withdrawing back to SWA. The covering force and the detached elements around Xangongo followed suit, the last elements of the raiding force having been released by 1 September, marking the end of Operation Protea. The foot-mobile operation to the east was then wound up, and these troops completed their withdrawal by the 8th. It is estimated that Protea inflicted some 1000 fatal casualties on the combined PLAN and FAPLA forces involved. Security-force losses amounted to 10 killed. Among the PLAN casualties were the Deputy Commander in Chief and the Deputy for Political Affairs, both of whom were killed, and the Artillery Commander, who was captured.

Captured materiel amounted to between 3000 and 4000 tonnes, of which some 2000 tonnes was taken back to SWA for study and evaluation. This included eight T-34/85 tanks, three PT-76 reconnaissance tanks, three BRDM-2 scout cars, one BM-21 122mm multiple rocket launcher, twenty-four ZIS-3 76mm field guns, sixteen ZU-23-2 23mm and fourteen Yugoslav M-55 20mm triple-barrel anti-aircraft guns, plus 200 assorted trucks. These included various versions of UAZ-469s, GAZ-66s, URAL-375s, ZIL-131s and

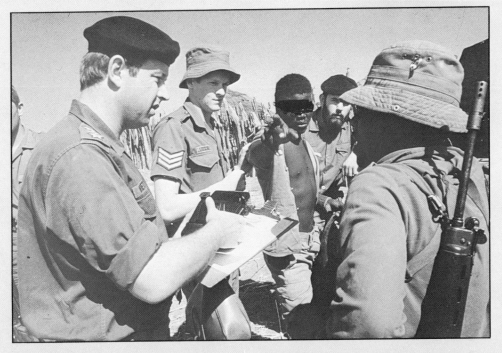

Above: Initial interrogation of a captured insurgent. The prisoner's face is blacked out because he has since been resettled and might be endangered if identified more closly.
Main picture: Railways Police in Buffels escorting a truck convoy to Oshakati.
Bottom: Still more captured equipment, this time D30 122mm howitzers, taken during Operation Askari.

Above: A building in Chitado formerly used by SWAPO is blown up in August 1980.
Right: An Eland-90 armoured car section on patrol in central Owambo.

KrAZ-219s. The materiel destroyed in situ included more than 300 tonnes of various types of ammunition.

The next major external operation, code-named Daisy, followed in November 1981, partly as a result of intelligence gleaned during Protea and from the evaluation of documents seized in that operation. Daisy saw the deepest penetration into Angola since the South African intervention in 1975, Operation Savannah. Daisy's primary objectives were a PLAN HQ at Bambi and a base area in the vicinity of Cheraquera.

Daisy opened on 1 November with a mechanised force crossing the border and moving on Ionde, some 120 km inside Angola. An old Portuguese trading post with an airstrip, Ionde, had been chosen as the site of the tactical HQ which was set up while the main force moved farther north toward Bambi and Cherequera. The latter was attacked on the 4th after an initial air strike by a mixed force of Mirages, Canberras and Buccaneers. Once the objectives had been secured, infantry carried out area operations in their vicinity. The operation wound down, and the raiding force withdrew on the 20th.

While FAPLA did generally stay clear of the forces involved in Daisy, their air force conducted a number of demonstrations toward the general area of the operation. During one of these, a clash with SAAF Mirages resulted in the shooting down of a MiG-21. Coming as it did not long after extensive FAPLA involvement in support of PLAN during Protea, this

incident gave rise to considerable concern for the future. Since then, another MiG-21 has been shot down (October 1982) after four MiGs had engaged two Mirage F-1s escorting a Canberra on a reconnaissance mission.

The sixth large-scale cross-border operation came only in December 1983. Intelligence had begun to indicate that PLAN intended a larger-than-usual rainy season campaign for early 1984, which was confirmed in the course of November. Indicators supporting this intelligence included the withdrawal of insurgents for retraining, stepped up PLAN reconnaissance activity and the pre-positioning of caches on the intended axes. The training of special forces elements intended for operations south of Owambo had also been stepped up. Available intelligence was augmented by reconnaissance flights and also by long-range reconnaissance patrols - some as small as two men – operating quite deeply into Angola.

Several of the reconnaissance flights drew fire from the Angolan air-defences, including the first firings of SA-8s and SA-9s in this theatre. Initial confirmation of the employment of SA-9s came when an Impala Mk II returned from a reconnaissance mission over the Cahama area with an SA-9 warhead stuck in its tail. A complete SA-9 system was later captured near Cuvelai. S-60 57mm guns were also encountered for the first time in any numbers. Several air-defence suppression missions were then flown in areas where an active air-defence could have prejudiced the success of the overall operation. Interestingly, artillery was also used against some of the air-defence sites. One such case saw an artillery element with a covering force approach to within range of the air-defences around Cahama and engage them.

Operation Askari itself got under way around the 6th of December, when additional reconnaissance parties and patrols were despatched to develop hard information on which the security forces could act in order to pre-empt the intended PLAN offensive. Combat elements were sent in as the situation developed, including four mechanised combat groups of around 500 men each and some smaller infantry forces which chiefly operated closer to the border. While the mechanised elements were intended to hit specific hard targets, the infantry conducted routine search-and-destroy area operations.

Initially, there had been some thought of hitting one of the large PLAN training camps deep inside Angola, where many of the insurgents earmarked for the forthcoming incursion were under training. This concept was shelved when, toward the end of December, intelligence was received that seven companies of insurgents (between 800 and 1000 men) had been offloaded from heavy military

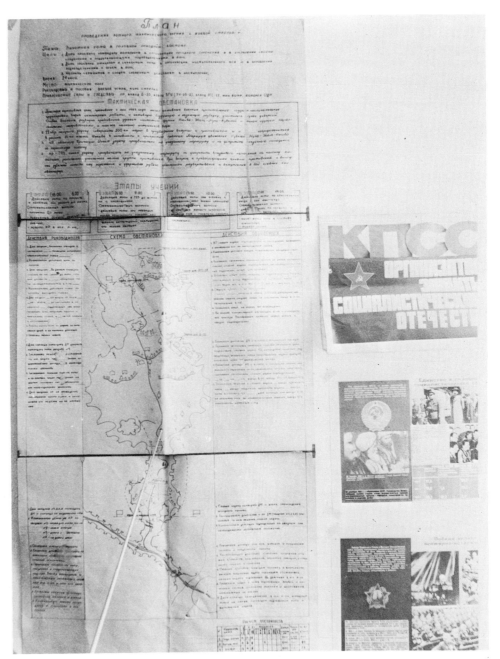

trucks near Jamba and had indicated to fellow PLAN personnel there that they would be moving south. This was obviously the beginning of the expected offensive and operations were adjusted accordingly, emphasis being placed on the area south and east of Jamba.

The major aspect of Operation Askari was the disruption of the PLAN logistic infrastructure and command and control system by air and ground attacks on various bases and headquarters. The HQ near Lubango was also attacked by four aircraft as a reminder of its vulnerability and to create doubt as to whether it might not also become a target for ground forces. Another major part of the operation was wide and deep reconnaissance to locate PLAN elements which could then be engaged and destroyed. High priority was also accorded the location of pre-positioned supply caches and their destruction or removal. Finally, strenuous efforts were made throughout to isolate any PLAN elements from nearby FAPLA or Cuban forces.

Above: Documents captured during Operation Askari – an operational plan for the defence of Cuvelai written in Russian and then translated into Portuguese.

Despite this, there were several clashes with FAPLA elements during the operation. The first came in the vicinity of the small town of Caiundo, when a reconnaissance element was ambushed by FAPLA forces. Another small clash came when FAPLA forces stationed at Mulonde came to the support of PLAN elements in Quiteve when these were attacked. The FAPLA garrison of Cahama also sortied out to cover the withdrawal into that town of some 200 insurgents when their nearby camp came under attack. Most of the PLAN elements that were encountered during Askari attempted to seek shelter with FAPLA and most were, in fact, accorded protection.

The most serious incident occurred on 3 January when FAPLA's 11th Brigade was reinforced with two Cuban battalions and engaged one of the mechanised combat groups near Cuvelai. This had been deal-

ing with a PLAN tactical HQ and base area some five kilometres to the north-east of that town. A heated action followed, during which the Cuban/FAPLA force suffered some 324 fatal casualties and lost 11 T-54 tanks. Most of the 21 fatal casualties suffered by the security forces during Askari were incurred in this clash. The biggest single loss occurred when a Ratel-

Below: Chief of the SADF, General Viljoen, gives a press briefing on the course of Operation Askari. The map shows SWAPO infilatration routes.

20 became enmeshed in a minefield and was knocked out by a T-54, five of the crew being killed.

Askari was wound up around 13 January. The actual withdrawal of forces involved was complicated by heavy rains, which had turned many of the roads and tracks into mud trails and flooded the many streams that had to be crossed. The last combat group out had to build an improvised log bridge over a tributary of the Cuvelai River – not an easy task when some of the vehicles weighed over 20

Above: The last unit to withdraw during Operation Askari was briefly trapped by floods but built an improvised bridge rather than wait for engineering support.

tonnes. Another hazard was that of landmines on the tracks and roads, which often slowed the withdrawal to the walking pace of the sweep teams.

While Askari did not succeed in inflicting as many casualties on PLAN as some previous operations, it did cause severe disruption of the insurgents' logistic backup and thereby was judged successful. Then too, Askari served to demonstrate to FAPLA that intervention, even with superior forces and armour, could be an expensive and unproductive exercise. Askari also produced some interesting information on just how dependent FAPLA is on Soviet assistance. Among the many documents taken at Cuvelai was an operations order for the battle prepared for the Angolan commander by a Soviet adviser – written in Russian and translated into Portuguese.

Apart from these – by local standards – large-scale external operations, the security forces have also conducted numerous smaller-scale ones. The commonest and most typical of these have resulted from the 'hot pursuit' of an insurgent group after a contact, or from follow-up on a contact, reported incident or spoor or acting on information received. Long range reconnaissance patrols and reconnaissance patrols and sweeps nearer the border, have also been conducted regularly in an effort to keep an eye on PLAN activities and intentions. On occasion, minor sweeps and raids have moved out to exploit intelligence while it is still fresh. Hot pursuit and follow-up operations have naturally been carried out most often by troops involved in the initial contact or by the nearest reaction force.

Many of the less immediate external operations have fallen to 32 Battalion. This unusual unit was formed in 1976 and includes many former Angolans who chose exile rather than a life under the Marxist MPLA regime. Most of these are also former members of the FNLA, one of the other two insurgent movements that had fought the Portuguese and then lost out to the MPLA after the Portuguese collapse. Among those who know the business, 32 Bn is widely regarded as the premier light infantry unit in the world today. It is also employed in more routine operations, but 32 has specialised in searching out and destroying PLAN's forward camps and base areas.

Typically, such an operation would follow on location of a PLAN camp by a reconnaissance patrol acting on the report of an earlier team or intelligence gained from prisoners, evaluation of captured documents and the local population. Later patrols then develop this information to establish all possible details on the proposed target and the surrounding area. Finally, they may also act as security and stopper groups during the actual attack on the camp. This will usually be conducted by elements of 32 Bn in strength that varies with the size of the target. An objective too large for an infantry assault would be handed off to a mechanised force, with 32 providing the intelligence and guidance.

While insertion and extraction of 32 Bn elements is usually by helicopter, most of their operations are conducted on foot.

Right: Pastor Cornelius Ndjoba, former Chief Minister of Owambo, was killed in 1983 when the pick up in which he was driving hit a landmine. *Below:* A Ratel 60 crew cleaning up after an action during Operation Askari.

Above: A casualty from a mine incident being rushed to treatment by a medical team.

They are largely occupied with extensive foot-mobile patrols and sweeps, on which the troops involved spend days at a time in the bush with only occasional resupply by helicopter. It is this unremitting reconnaissance effort that has gained 32 the information and local expertise for its highly successful operations. With many relatively small groups on the ground in southern Angola, often for lengthy periods, 32 is also rather dependent on the goodwill of the local civilian population for its security as well as for much of its information.

Another style of minor 'external' is well illustrated by Operation Klipkop. This raid followed various incidents of mine-laying and other terrorism in the Kaokoland, and the rocketing of Ruacana in late July 1980. Intelligence had earlier identified the nearby small Angolan village of Chitado as a PLAN transit point with a small tactical HQ and supply depot. Insurgents were generally brought as far as Chitado in light trucks and received final instructions from the local HQ, as well as drawing the bulk of their heavier stores – such as landmines – from the depot. Some groups would also return to Chitado for resupply and a brief break in the course of their activities.

A considerable degree of correlation had, in fact, been established between PLAN activity in Chitado and the recent events in the Kaokoland. Accordingly, it was decided to destroy the PLAN facility in Chitado. The assault was carried out by a two-platoon force of infantry, which was heli-landed just outside the village on 2 August. A brisk thirty-minute sweep through the village dealt with the opposition, whereafter the intelligence and demolition teams went to work. The infantry, meanwhile, cleared the nearby airfield and also swept an arena within a three-kilometer radius of Chitado. The buildings used by PLAN were then destroyed and the force extracted.

Operation Super (March 1982) was similar in concept. In this case 45 men of 32 Bn were dropped by helicopter some two km from a PLAN camp near Cambeno in south-western Angola at around 0800 hours on the 13th, sweeping through the camp and surrounding area in an eight-hour action. Fire support was provided by a mortar group dropped on a nearby hill by other helicopters. Stopper groups were inserted on likely escape routes and dealt with any insurgents who attempted to decamp. Control proved difficult as a result of the hilly terrain and often heavy bush and was handled for much of the operation by the senior helicopter pilot; others spotted for the mortars and also kept him informed of any ground movements out of his immediate vision. Over 200 insurgents were killed for the loss of three members of the raiding party, and large quantities of stores were captured, putting back a planned offensive in the Kaokoland by many months.

A rather more ambitious operation followed in July and August of 1982 with the aim of destroying PLAN's Central and Eastern Front headquarters. Operation Mebos turned into a frustrating game of hide-and-seek, with PLAN HQs moving every time they had been located by

large quantity of stores. This included some 1000 landmines which would otherwise have wreaked havoc among the unprotected civilian motorists of Owambo. In all, about 345 insurgents were killed and some captured for the loss of 29 members of the security forces. This rather high total resulted from the largest single loss of any operation when a Puma was downed on 12 August, killing all three crew and twelve troops aboard.

The attack at Mupa was, arguably, the most valuable part of the operation, as the secretary to the Eastern Front commander had left his departure a little late. He was killed as he attempted to get into his vehicle and escape, many revealing

Left: The then Chief of the Army, General Viljoen, with members of Combat Group 61 during the Operations against the Smokeshell complex.

special forces patrols: thus each attack resulted in the infliction of few casualties. Finally, the Eastern Front HQ was located in the Mupa area and hit quickly by one of the Reconnaissance Commandos before it could be moved again. Even so, the attack came only just in time, as most of the senior personnel had already decamped. Further attacks on its new locations followed until the operation was terminated, having thoroughly disrupted the PLAN command and control system for some time to come.

Apart from its disruptive effects, Mebos also produced much valuable intelligence and allowed seizure and destruction of a

Right: Paras clearing houses in Cassinga after taking the town during the fighting in 1978.
Below: The Cassinga area photographed from one of the last Pumas to leave the area. The pilot, Major Church, was decorated for his last flight over the by then enemy-occupied town to check no one was left behind.

Above: Pumas lifting the Paras out of Cassinga at the conclusion of the raid. The first enemy armour reached the landing zone as the last helicopter left.

documents being found in his briefcase and in his office. Among these were the minutes of a meeting held at the PLAN HQ near Lubango on 15 June, at which instructions had been issued that all of the 'puppets' in SWA should be 'eliminated' before any cease-fire could come into effect. This document caused something of a stir when it was released, SWAPO naturally claiming that it was a forgery. In view of the earlier murders of such legitimate politicians as Elifas, Kapuuo and Shiyayaga, however, there can be little doubt that it was, indeed, genuine.

The primary purpose of all these 'external' operations has been to pre-empt and disrupt PLAN's incursion efforts before they can lead to increased terrorism inside SWA. In this they have been successful, as illustrated by the steady decline in landmine incidents as PLAN has been forced to move its forward transit camps farther and farther back into Angola. As a result, the insurgents can no longer merely stroll across the border, do their deed and depart; now they face a walk of 100 to 200 kilometers in some cases. This has disrupted PLAN's mine-laying campaign, as a landmine is a heavy and difficult item to carry so far. The attempt to overcome this problem by establishing caches close to the border has been largely countered by thorough reconnaissance and intelligence activity by the security forces. Similarly, most of the recent attempts at major rainy-season offensives have been largely disrupted.

The other major effect of the raids has been to allow the security forces to engage insurgents en bloc. This, in turn has facilitated the use of semi-conventional methods at which the security forces enjoy a substantial advantage. The result has been heavy casualties among the insurgents, who have seen their overall strength decline from around 12,000 to perhaps 7,000 since the late 1970s despite strenuous recruiting efforts. Finally, specific strikes on command and other headquarters have robbed PLAN of many top-line leaders and staff officers, while the attacks on training camps have removed many trained personnel and instructors from the field.

Despite the undoubted benefit of these operations, there are serious problems involved, which result in reluctance to authorise them. Arguably, the most serious of these lies in the potential for a major clash with FAPLA and Cuban forces, which could escalate the conflict to an entirely new and dangerous level. Another problem is that of minimising civilian casualties. Thus far, this has been addressed by means of pamphlet drops and broadcasts prior to any major raid. With FAPLA tending to take a more active part in support of PLAN, and with PLAN itself fielding more heavy weapons, however, this is not a policy that can be continued indefinitely. In any event, it has the undesirable side-effect of allowing PLAN to decide when and where to accept combat and when to withdraw, losing only easily replaced equipment.

Despite these problems and the inevitable international condemnation, there can be no question of the security forces giving up this option – their most effective and efficient means of combatting the insurgents. Were they to wait for commission of an atrocity before acting, the lives of many civilians would be offered up on the altar of political expediency.

Before discussing operations within northern South-West Africa itself, it is desirable to review the peculiarities of Owambo, which is the region most affected by the insurgency. Owambo is one of SWA's four northernmost regions, stretching along some 450 km of the Angolan border and about 120 km in depth. Generally sandy and with some areas of very heavy bush, it is astonishingly flat, with virtually no natural feature higher than an average African anthill. Altitude varies from 1090m to 1150m, and the only real gradient is a very gentle 1 in 2500 levelling to 1 in 5000 from north to south.

As one result, what little rain there is – approximately 500mm in a good year – fills up the innumerable long, narrow and shallow depressions-cum-watercourses called *oshanas* or *omurambas*, putting much of the region under water during the rainy season. In central Owambo there is also a large, generally dry delta, which in some years carries water from Angola south towards the Etosha Pan. The flow within the delta or, indeed, in some of the oshanas, is naturally very slow. Daytime temperatures are in the low 30s (Celsius) in summer, dropping to the upper 20s in the winter months, when the nights can see temperatures in the low single figures.

Owambo is the home of SWA's largest single population group – 454,000 Owambos out of a total of some 973,000 – of whom some 300,000 live permanently in the area. A similar number of Owambos live in southern Angola, with only a neglected border fence to separate the two groups. Although there are some small towns and villages, most of the Owambos live in small family kraals scattered throughout the region. The economy is based on stock farming and some cropping, with smaller industries and organised handicrafts beginning to take hold. The past few years, in particular, have seen a remarkable degree of business development despite the continuing conflict. Then too, there are several thousand small traders running their 'Cuca shops' – some no more than a pile of goods under a convenient Makalani palm, others with modern buildings and a 7-series BMW or S-class Mercedes parked outside.

There are just over 1000 km of roads in Owambo, of which the 207-km main north-south route is tarred, most of the others being surfaced gravel roads. There is also a confusing network of innumerable local vehicle tracks – some no more than a recent set of tire tracks – made by the locals taking advantage of the flat terrain to cut down on travelling time. Sometimes they overestimate the capabilities of their vehicles, and embarrassed visits to army bases requesting a Buffel to tow someone out of the sand are far from rare.

The remaining infrastructure – still rather limited in view of Owambo's early stage of economic development and the difficulties imposed by terrorism - centres on irrigation and electricity supply. The former comprises a system of waterpoints, boreholes, dams, canals and pumping stations which is slowly being expanded. At times it has been a prime target of insurgent activity. The major source of both electricity and water was to have been the giant Ruacana hydro-electric scheme, which was financed by South Africa and Portugal to stimulate development in northern SWA and southern Angola. Unfortunately, this straddles the border and has neither been completed nor taken even partially into service. Ironically, it is SWA that does enjoy some limited benefit from the scheme ever since a civilian helicopter pilot and some friends crossed the border and closed the sluices of one of the minor dams, then threw away the worm gears, thereby preventing them being opened again. Every rainy season now sees some water flow to the turbines.

The Kaokoland, west of Owambo, is a generally dry and harsh region with much rough, hilly country. The small population is concentrated in a few areas, chiefly on or near the Cunene River, and there has been very little economic development thus far. Kavango, east of Owambo, is very similar to Owambo except that it is rather more lush and fertile in the vicinity of the river. Much the same applies to western Caprivi. Eastern Caprivi is also very flat and sandy, but its position in central southern Africa and on the river bank makes it very fertile. It has a healthy agricultural economy, although it does suffer to some degree from isolation from the rest of the territory.

In mid 1984 PLAN fielded some 7000

Below: An Eland 60 struggles through dense bush in the Owambo district. The thorns and branches can make such trips very unpleasant.

Above: South Africa troops in Chitado after clearing the town of opposition during Operation Klipklop in August 1980.

trained and semi-trained insurgents, of whom an average of 300 would normally be found inside Owambo at any given time. Shortly after the agreement between Angola and South Africa to limit PLAN activity from the former country, as many as 800 additional insurgents were infiltrated into Owambo with instructions that they were to go underground until further notice. Those already in the territory were apparently given similar instructions, as the number of incidents dropped to a new low while PLAN waited to see how it would be affected. One possible indication of how PLAN hopes to overcome this problem surfaced in March 1984, when a group of insurgents entered SWA from Botswana; they had been flown via Lusaka to Francistown and then been driven to the border.

Prior to this new development, the insurgents had habitually moved up to the border in groups of up to 60 and then split into section-sized groups of 5 to 15 on entering Owambo. With increasing security-force activity in cross-border operations since the late 1970s, insurgents have been forced to adopt a semi-covert posture even inside southern Angola, moving in smaller groups and often without the benefit of transit camps near the border. Most recently they have been forced to walk from as far north as Jamba – 300 km inside Angola – and in some areas had to break up into small groups well inside Angola, whereas previously they had been able to motor as far south as Ongiva.

Most of the insurgents have entered Owambo directly since access became available through Angola, but some have sought to outflank the security forces by entering through the Kaokoland. Others have entered the Kaokoland specifically to operate there, and some have attempted to use it as a route to the south.

Attempts to infiltrate Kavango continue but have not been particularly successful except in the western part, where there has been some overlap of operations from Owambo and support is available from insurgents and sympathizers in eastern Owambo.

Within Owambo, the insurgents go about their business as unobtrusively as possible, generally seeking to avoid contact with the security forces. Occasionally, however, a group will bring in mortars, recoilless rifles or even, on very rare occasions, single-tube 122mm rocket launchers, and fire a few rounds at a base, town or protected kraal. Less often, larger groups may form up within Owambo specifically to lay an ambush for a patrol. The only deliberate attacks on any element of the security forces have been those on the protected kraals of some of the headmen, and these have almost invariably been beaten off by the special constables of the guard detail – sometimes with heavy losses to the attacking group.

PLAN's major activity within Owambo is aimed directly at the civilian population, with emphasis on conversion at gunpoint and general intimidation of those not well disposed toward SWAPO – armed propaganda, in the jargon of the professional revolutionary. Many of the groups also rely heavily on what food they can obtain or extort from the kraals in their area. The murder of headmen, shopkeepers, businessmen, officials, politicians and often their families, figures prominently in their activities, as does the occasional random killing designed to keep the populace suitably respectful. Owambos deemed 'puppets' of the '*Boere*' are often des-

Above: A member of the SWA Territory Force during refresher training.

patched in particularly gruesome ways, preferably before their families and neighbours. Thus, despite its claims to the contrary, PLAN is still very firmly stuck in the terrorism stage of insurgency and has made no real effort to move beyond it into systematic guerrilla warfare.

Another aspect of PLAN activity is the operation of several very lucrative protection rackets – possibly for the private gain of the groups involved. Finally, recruiting also plays an important part, although this is becoming more difficult as PLAN's military fortunes wane. Where straight recruiting and even the inducement of scholarships fail, abduction is resorted to – sometimes all the children of a given school are marched across the border at gunpoint. Examples of this approach include groups of 119, 200 and 60 abducted in 1978, 1979 and 1980 respectively. Another occasion saw a bus and its passengers highjacked across the border. This kind of activity has decreased in recent years as a result of the cross-border operations and security-force surveillance, which make it difficult to move large groups of unwilling recruits even inside southern Angola.

SWAPO spokesmen, especially the leader Sam Nujoma, naturally deny that their military wing is practising terrorism. Their claim is that they are engaged in guerrilla warfare against the SA forces and that they scrupulously avoid causing civilian casualties. Quite apart from the visible results of the activities outlined above, it is PLAN's love affair with the landmine that ultimately gives the lie to these protestations of innocence.

These sinister surprise packages have become, since 1978, an all-too-familiar feature of road travel in Owambo. Only the

logistic difficulties imposed on PLAN by the cross-border raids have brought some reduction in this particularly brutal application of random terror. One of the worst years was 1980, which saw no fewer than 220 Owambos killed and some 258 injured in mine blasts. The security forces, by contrast, suffer few mine casualties as a result of their liberal equipment with effective mine-resistant vehicles which generally protect their crews from injury and themselves suffer only relatively minor damage. The effect of an anti-tank mine on the average saloon car or light truck is very different and hardly bears description. Even less does the nature of the injuries suffered by their passengers, who are often unidentifiable. It is sometimes difficult to establish how many people were in a vehicle simply because there are not enough identifiable parts left among the debris.

PLAN's affair with the landmine should not come as a surprise to anyone even peripherally familiar with the theory of insurgency. Despite its voluble protestations to the contrary, PLAN does not seem to feel that it has sufficient popular support even in Owambo to move out of the terrorism stage. The landmine fits into this admirably; it is the ideal weapon of random terror. Rendering the normal use of Owambo's dirt roads an extremely hazardous undertaking, the landmine serves both to spread fear and uncertainty among the population and to undermine confidence in the authorities' ability to offer meaningful protection. Additionally, it hinders economic development that might have gone some way toward negating SWAPO propaganda.

Another advantage of the landmine from PLAN's viewpoint is that it achieves all this without the necessity of any contact with the security forces. For this and other reasons, it has also proven a popular assassination tool – a landmine laid in the driveway or under the wheel of a parked car leaves very little room for doubt or counteraction. At least one member of the Owambo Government – Thomas Shikongo – was killed in this way, together with his daughter and some friends. A similar attempt on the life of another Owambo minister – Tara Imbili – was frustrated when the laying team blew themselves up upon being startled by an accidental discharge caused by one of the minister's guards loading his pistol while on his way to commune with nature.

While most of the mines are laid on the many gravel roads – and on their verges, to catch those who think they are clever – there have been many attempts to lay under the tar of the main north-south road. Expedients have included tunnelling under the road from the verge and also heating a 200-litre drum and using it to lift out a section of the surface. None, however, has proved immune to detection by the motorcycle sweep teams which go

over the road every morning. Anti-personnel mines are sometimes laid with anti-vehicle mines in an effort to hamper clearing work. They are also similarly employed in conjuction with sabotage efforts and have been laid in the path of pursuing security forces elements to delay them.

The insurgents' equipment comprises the usual mix of Eastern Bloc small arms, with the AK-47 family and the RPG-7 both particularly well represented. The average group carries an RPG-7 with several reloads, a light machine gun and AK-47 rifles. The SKS carbine has also been used, primarily for its ability to fire rifle grenades. Some Western and older weapons are also encountered from time to time. Both 60- and 82mm mortars have been used, as have some light recoilless rifles and single-tube 122mm rocket launchers. Most recently, some insurgent groups have also taken to carrying SA-7 anti-aircraft missiles. Another recent development is the appearance of Dragunov sniping rifles in some groups.

Webbing and other equipment is kept to a minimum, both to keep down weight and because many groups carry civilian clothes and often wear them for concealment, some routinely changing into civilian clothes on or just prior to crossing the border. Some of the insurgents go so far as to wear several layers of clothing to ensure a quick change capability. Radio equipment is available but not often carried by the smaller groups. Rations are generally in tinned form and are often largely drawn from relief supplies shipped to so-called 'Namibian refugees' in Angola. Most medical stores are from similar sources. Most insurgents also carry money to enable them to supplement their rations with purchases from local shops rather than seizures. Even so, extortion of food and other items is rife, as is looting.

Over most of Owambo the terrain tends to favour the insurgents, the flatness granting them almost unbelievable mobility on foot. This is enhanced by the poor visibility caused by the combination of flat ground and often heavy bush. Finally, in the rainy season, the profuse surface water and frequent rainfall renders tracking extremely difficult. Insurgents have occasionally used bicycles and light trucks 'borrowed' from the local population or provided by supporters. Much of the heavy equipment and most of the mines are moved to preselected caches by porter groups so as to free highly trained specialists for their real tasks and reduce their exposure to the security forces.

When contact with security forces results despite the insurgents' best efforts at concealment and anti-tracking, they generally choose to 'bombshell' - breaking contact and scattering to rendezvous later at a pre-arranged location. Always

Above: Sweep team preparing their equipment prior to work on the Oshivelo-Oshakati road.

very careful about leaving any trail, they become even more so when pursued, employing all of the anti-tracking measures and even changing clothes and shoes more or less on the run. Abrupt changes of direction also feature in their repertoire as, occasionally, does circling back on their own spoor in an effort to ambush their pursuers. A large group may feel sufficiently confident to take on its pursuers in an ambush, usually selecting the L-ambush pattern for this purpose. Here, too, the norm is to decamp if the first burst of fire does not weaken or demoralise pursuers. Overall, the insurgents are simply not well enough trained to take on the security forces in combat, even on relatively favourable terms.

Security-force missions are aligned with modern counterinsurgency doctrine, diverging only insofar as demanded by situational peculiarities. Thus Owambo's flatness, for example, renders many such 'standard' measures as random and mechanised ambushes, observation posts and listening posts of very limited value. The large amount of surface water complicates matters during the rainy season by making the insurgents independent of normal water sources and frustrating tracking efforts. The heavy bush cover, in turn, further restricts the utility of ambushes and also ensures that many contacts are at very close range.

The 'protected village' or 'strategic hamlet' approach is impossible to apply among Owambo's population, scattered as it is through agricultural necessity. The sheer logistic difficulties of seeking to

apply such a system can be appreciated only when the situation has been seen on the ground. The alienation that would result can be readily imagined – as it is, the security forces do not seriously attempt to interdict the routine cross-border visiting that goes on, let alone restrict movement within Owambo. The insurgents' access to most of Owambo's population thus remains to a considerable degree unhindered.

The security-force organisational base is the 'skeleton battalion', of which four are deployed in Sector 10, which has responsibility for Owambo and the adjacent Kaokoland. The 'skeleton' of headquarters and administrative staff is made up of PF personnel on tours of two to three years and some NSM posted to the operational area for the bulk of their national service. Combat elements of the battalions vary in strength and composition according to the situation, with the rainy season, for instance, bringing considerable reinforcement. The battalion areas are broken up into company areas covered by operations from permanent company bases. On occasion, companies will not move into a permanent base, but will remain mobile throughout their tour.

The necessary infantry companies, armoured car squadrons, engineers and other elements are drawn from the training units in SA and from the CF and Commandos. The NSM from the training units usually serve several four-month tours during their national service. CF and Commando personnel can be called up for three-month tours every second year. They usually undergo refresher training in southern Owambo before assignment to a

Below: Special Constables receive initial small arms training. They are mostly employed protecting government installations or people believed to be under threat.

Above: Among the posters in this SWAPO lecture room are portraits of Fidel Castro and of former Soviet leader Leonid Brezhnev.

battalion. Companies are also drawn from the standing battalions and the CF units of the SWATF; these make up an increasing proportion of the total force. Individual officers and NCOs from the CF and Commandos are also called up to fill staff and specialist posts from time to time.

The police, who initially bore the brunt of the insurgency, are still active in the counterinsurgency role, along with normal police tasks in the operational area. They have three different elements involved in the fighting: the normal police COIN units, a guard force and the special unit known as Ops K or Koevoet. COIN units operate much like army rifle companies and platoons, with responsibility

for a specific sector, and are made up of both SWA and SA police – regulars and reservists – serving short tours of duty in the operational area.

A fourth element is involved in counterinsurgency operations against any insurgents who succeed in penetrating through the Operational Area. This is the SWA Police Task Force, headquartered in Windhoek, which has several groups deployed to different parts of northern SWA below the Red Line. It is also responsible for meeting any insurgents who might come through Botswana and for reacting to incidents of urban terrorism. Its groups operate according to much the same tactical principles as those of Ops K. Like the Ops K groups, they are comprised of a mix of regular police and special constable volunteers.

Guard-force personnel are recruited

locally – also in the Kaokoland, Kavango and Caprivi – and employed specifically for VIP and key-point protection. All volunteers, the special constables receive a basic eight weeks' training at the school near Ondangwa before being posted out to guard detachments. Training opens with parade ground work to build coordination and *esprit* and moves on via basic weapons instruction to rural counterinsurgency operations with emphasis on security tasks. Promotion within the force is purely on demonstrated merit: there are no promotion courses as such. Members wishing to join the police force proper can do so, but must first complete the normal police college training.

The guard detachments vary in size from a few men to a reinforced platoon, depending on the level of the perceived threat and the nature of the target. Similarly, the precautions taken at the various protected kraals and installations will vary from a simple fence to an earth wall with proper bunkers and emplaced machine guns. Equipment consists essentially of light infantry weapons up to the light machine gun and the 60mm mortar. Some mine-resistant vehicles are also issued as needed. Despite their relatively short training, the special constables have generally acquitted themselves well in action, and no detachment has ever been overrun or forced to vacate its position.

Ops K is a mobile counterinsurgency unit made up of locally recruited special constables and NCOs and led by regular police officers and NCOs of the SAP or SWAPOL. It originated in the need to provide a speedy reaction to intelligence gained by the security branch. Controlled from Oshakati, it has elements stationed in the Kaokoland and Kavango under local HQs but is, in fact, entirely mobile in its

operations, going where intelligence leads it. The local knowledge of the special constables is backed up by the presence of several former PLAN members serving with the unit. Operations are conducted almost exclusively on the basis of incoming intelligence, and combat is carried out when possible mounted in Casspir APCs. This combination has proved resoundingly successful, and Koevoet is without doubt the premier unit available to the security forces for their internal operations.

The security forces' actual operations, highly interactive by nature, can still be broken down into categories for the purpose of discussion. A broad outline of the typical operations follows.

Border Control: While border closure is impracticable, as discussed above, the border is regularly patrolled, both on foot and by vehicle. The intensity of this patrol activity varies from section to section, depending upon the terrain, the local population density, the proximity of likely targets and the degree of PLAN activity in the area. Popular crossing areas are additionally covered by ambushes and observation posts. The actual border is marked by a rather dilapidated fence and a 'cut line' bulldozed out of the bush. A one-kilometer-deep strip immediately south of the border has been evacuated and is officially a 'no go' zone, although this is not taken too seriously by either the local population or the security forces. Any

tracks found in the cut line are followed up immediately and cutting-off or ambush measures are initiated. Several comparable cut lines have been established inside Owambo and are similarly handled.

Patrolling: As is the case in most counterinsurgency campaigns, patrols of all kinds form the backbone of security-force operations. Apart from those with specific tasks – such as border and road patrols – intensive random patrols are also conducted. These serve both to keep the security forces visible and to heighten the

unease of any insurgents in the area, who cannot effectively predict when or where they might encounter a patrol. Patrols are carried out on foot, on horseback or by vehicle as dictated by the mission and the terrain. Most are carried out in platoon or half-platoon strength, the armoured cars almost invariably operating only by troops.

Search and Destroy: Cordon-and-search, sweep, and search-and-destroy missions are generally carried out in response to intelligence, but may also be

Above right: Casualties from a mining incident lie beside their wrecked vehicle.
Below: Army patrol passing a kraal abandoned because of drought. The kraal has already been partially stripped for firewood by neighbours who have entirely removed the surrounding fence.

Above: A Special Constable guards Herero leader Kauima Riruako at the 1980 Herero Day festivities at Okahandja in 1980.

conducted on suspicion or at random in an effort to stir any insurgents who may be present into movement which will reveal them to the security forces. One variation on this theme are the 'Hawk Ops', which are essentially high-speed cordon-and-search operations with helicopters used to insert the troops and support provided by spotter aircraft or light helicopters.

Ambushes, Observation and Listening Posts: Limited in their effectiveness by the flat and bushy terrain which does almost nothing to channel the insurgents' movements, these are generally employed only in response to specific information or intelligence, although some are placed more or less at random.

Roadblocks: These, again, are employed both at random and in response to information and intelligence; they are also used as a means of gathering information and to restrict PLAN's use of vehicles.

Protection Operations: Largely within the ambit of the police guard unit, these encompass the protection of key installations and individuals: those who have been threatened, whose names have been found on captured 'hit lists', or who seem likely targets for abduction or assassination. Various members of the Owambo Government and many of the headmen fall into these categories. Some installations are protected by Army elements.

Operations in Aid of the Civil Power: Designed to keep the government functioning in the face of sabotage and terrorism, these, too, are chiefly protective operations. Typical examples would include the protection of roadworks teams, cattle innoculation parties and school inspectors. A similar operation is that of

the pension convoys that do the rounds of pensioners under army escort to pay out pensions and allowances. Railways' police with Buffels seconded from the Army provide an escort to the more important groups of railways and private trucks moving goods up to Owambo from the Tsumeb railhead. Another aspect, which falls entirely to the army, lies in the sweeping of roads for mines. The main tarred road is swept every morning by engineers on motorcycles, backed up by a lifting party and an escort in a Buffel. The more important gravel roads are also swept on a daily basis, although this is a rather lengthier process, as a visual check does not suffice. Smaller roads are swept less frequently, some only when major movement is intended or when information is received indicating that mines may have been laid. Unfortunate though this is for the civilian motorist, there are simply too many roads and tracks for all to be cleared constantly.

Civic Action: Less visible in Owambo, where emphasis necessarily remains on directly military tasks, civic-action programmes form an important part of security-forces activity in the operational area. While there are some major projects, the preference is toward providing the necessary specialist expertise, heavy equipment and some of the materials to enable self-help projects to get off the ground. Schoolteachers, agricultural advisors and medical personnel are also provided where necessary. Civilian specialists such as opthalmologists are brought to the area by the SADF at intervals to provide treatment not otherwise available locally. Other activities include youth camps and an ecology awareness programme, which it is hoped was begun early enough to save the region some of

Above: The sickbay at the main 203 Bn base at Tsumkwe. 203 Bn is mostly engaged in civic action work but also provides local security in the area.

the damage that has occurred elsewhere in the name of progress.

One surprising aspect of counterinsurgency operations in Owambo has been the success enjoyed by armour and the other mobile elements of the security forces in what is generally regarded as an infantryman's type of war. This may be due in large part to Owambo's flatness and generally fair going, which grant military

Below: A Convoy of Railways Road Transport Service tankers being escorted by Buffels on the main Oshivelo-Ondangwo road.

vehicles remarkable area-covering ability. This has allowed much of the coverage to be allocated to armoured car squadrons, thereby making it possible to concentrate the infantry effort more effectively. Where such normal vehicles as armoured cars and APCs are not suitable, motorcycles and horse-mounted infantry have proven quite successful.

Perhaps the most astonishing aspect is that parties of insurgents have not infrequently been surprised by armoured cars or APCs in the bush. In one case, a patrol of Elands and Buffels – admittedly coming from downwind – got to within 100 meters of a group of 22 insurgents before being noticed. Once in contact, the armoured vehicles naturally enjoy the advantages of

massive firepower, protection and mobility by comparison with their opponents. Keeping on the move throughout a contact, they are also very difficult targets in the bush for the RPG-7 gunners who may be among the insurgents.

Apart from area patrols, armoured cars are also employed on sweeps, as convoy escorts and in support of cordon-and-search operations. The three main types of mine-resistant APC – Buffel, Hippo and Casspir – are similarly employed in addition to their transport role. A number of Ratel ICVs have also been employed in Owambo and in operations against insurgents who had penetrated into the Tsumeb area. While they proved popular for their weight and power, which allowed them to

plow through bush with little difficulty, their fully enclosed troop compartment has not been well received.

Other mobile forces include motorcycle elements and mounted infantry. The former are chiefly employed on road sweeps and as a reaction force and enjoy considerable mobility in bush that would seriously hamper other vehicles. Interestingly, they have also found that the sound of their motorcycles is not a major problem, as it is apparently muffled and distorted by the bush. The mounted infantry are more often employed on long patrols, or patrols far from the nearest base in areas where vehicle or helicopter insertion is felt to be too noisy. Also, they are even more mobile in dense bush than the motorcycles.

The various mine-resistant vehicles themselves are an interesting outcome of operations in northern SWA. The chief ones presently in use are the Buffel, Casspir and Hippo APCs and the 10-tonne Kwêvöel truck. All have proved themselves thoroughly. Properly strapped into one of these vehicles, the chances of surviving even a multiple mine detonation without serious injury are more than excellent. There is also a profusion of other, lighter vehicles and a number of more or less 'one-off' types. Among these are the logistic variants of the Buffel and Hippo (Zebra), post office trucks with mine-resistant cabs, mine-resistant buses and road graders and others. Many of these vehicles are also used by various government departments and by major contractors working in the operational area. Some of the lighter ones, such as the Ribbok, Rheebok and Rooikat, are also available to individuals.

The SAAF operates in support of both internal and external operations, as well as in the logistics role. Arguably, the most important aircraft are the helicopters, which are very much maids of all work. Pumas are the chief trooping and casevac aircraft and are also used for resupply missions to patrols. The lighter Alouette IIIs are used chiefly for the spotting, command-and-control and liaison functions. Proper gunships are not available, a lack that hampers operations to some degree, as does the small number of all helicopter types. While small arms and light anti-aircraft guns do present a threat, the biggest problem for the helicopters is that of the ever-present dust, which has always presented a major maintenance headache.

Light strike missions and much of the close air support work during external operations are generally flown by the Impala Mk IIs stationed at the main airbases in the operational area. Their pilots are also justly proud of their performance in the night strike and CAS roles, both of which demand extraordinary skill in an aircraft as basic and devoid of modern electronics as the Impala. Many of the

reconnaissance flights used to keep tabs on PLAN activity in southern Angola have also been flown by the Impalas. Even more so than the helicopters, the Impalas have to operate in the face of intense air-defence activity that has included weapons as sophisticated as the SA-9 and SA-8. They are especially wary of the same light anti-aircraft guns – chiefly the 23mm ZU-23-2 – that have also caused problems in the ground role.

Major external operations enjoy additional support in the form of Mirages, Buccaneers and Canberras. The Mirages and, to a lesser extent, the Buccaneers, fly in both the CAS and strike roles while the Canberras operate as medium-level bombers. Weapons used include anti-personel and 450kg high-explosive bombs and rockets. One Buccaneer was instrumental in holding up advancing enemy armour during the extraction phase of the raid on the 'Moscow' camp in 1978, when it flew a series of dummy runs after having expended first its anti-tank and then its anti-personnel rockets in various attacks. Some Mirages have also been stationed periodically at Ondangwa in the air-defence role, when there has been reason to expect possible FAPLA air activity. The Canberras are also flown on long-range reconnaissance missions, usually with an escort of Mirages.

The Bosbok is often employed on a variety of missions including normal army co-operation, road and power-line patrol, scout and spotter. It operates routinely along cut lines, in conjunction with patrols, cordon-and-search, and sweep operations; and in reaction to incidents; also as artillery spotter and forward air control, the latter two roles chiefly during major external operations. Other Bosbok mis-sions include night spotting: watching for possible mining activity or vehicle movement on the main road; and in night airfield security using flares and Telstar or communications relay. The latter operations are flown both for the SAAF during strike missions and the Army. They are the least popular missions, as they can last up to six to seven hours with little to keep the pilot's interest. Another type of mission resulting from the flat terrain is that of controlling the movement of ground forces in contact and providing navigation assistance during the longer moves.

The external operations have provided their fair share of excitement for the Bosbok crews, chiefly in the form of intense anti-aircraft fire from various guns and with SA-7s. Generally, however, the Bosbok's agility has kept it out of harm's way despite its intensive employment. The Kudu is used chiefly in light-transport and liaison roles, but also sees occasional action in some of the Bosbok roles. Just how intensive this can be was demonstrated during Operation Protea, when up to five Bosbok were in the air simultaneously from first to last light. None was hit by the air defences. One neutralised a 23mm gun that had been holding up the ground forces by placing its smoke-marker rockets in the gun pit while marking the target for strike aircraft.

The Kudu is heavily used for a wide variety of light transport, liaison and casevac/medevac roles within the operational area. On occasion, Kudu are also used in some of the Bosbok roles if they are the most readily available aircraft. Pamphlet drops also figure in their repertoire, as do 'skyshout' missions flown with powerful public address systems. The latter have been brought to a fine art in co-operation with Intelligence: it is not uncommon for a group of insurgents to find some members being addressed by name in the course of a skyshout mission.

C-130s and C-160s operate regular transport flights from the Republic to the major transit base at Grootfontein and to such major operational-area bases as Ondangwa, Ruacana, Rundu and Mpacha. C-160s and Dakotas are also used on regular transport services within the operational area and between it and Grootfontein. The DC-4s are generally seen only with visiting VIPs or visitor groups. Apart from logistic support missions, the C-130s are also used to move most of the troops to and from the operational area or Grootfontein in the course of their rotation.

Late 1983 saw a significant development in the then 17-year-old war when South Africa offered to suspend operations into southern Angola if the Angolan Government would undertake to prevent further infiltration from there. This offer met with considerable suspicion, and its credibility was not enhanced by a major raid – Operation Askari – that followed soon after. But it finally bore fruit on 16 February 1984 in Lusaka, when South Africa and Angola reached an agreement based on the original offer. In terms of this agreement, those elements of the security forces then dominating much of southern Angola would be withdrawn as FAPLA forces re-established their control over the region. PLAN elements would be required to withdraw northward and cease operations from southern Angola into SWA. FAPLA would prevent their return to the border region or passage of forces through it en route to SWA.

Control over this disengagement pro-

cess was delegated to a Joint Monitoring Commission that included both SADF and FAPLA officers with several companies of troops – the SADF drawing its contingent from 32 Bn. Its first headquarters was established at Cuvelai – some 250km north of the Angola/SWA border – and the JMC began clearing PLAN elements from the northernmost section of the region after the first official meeting (March 1984). As these operations progressed, the JMC HQ was moved southward, first to Mupa in late March, then to Evale in mid-April and to Ongiva in the first week of May. The final phase will see JMC headquarters at the border post at Oshikango while the remaining strip along the border is secured. Throughout the operation PLAN made attempts to evade JMC patrols and retain some presence in the area and movement through it into SWA. Several of these incidents led to exchanges of fire between the PLAN elements and the joint FAPLA/ 32 Bn JMC patrols.

While it has started off well and weathered several delays and differences of opinion, the success of this diplomatic venture will depend in the long run entirely on whether FAPLA can keep PLAN elements out of the border regions. Should it fail, and infiltration on any scale recur, the security forces will inevitably resume their patrolling of and raids into the area. Success would mean that Angola could begin to restore the economy of one of its richest regions, which has been shattered by the almost continuous operations against PLAN elements since 1978. For SWA, it would bring the prospect of truly 'free and fair' elections that much closer, as SWAPO would be largely robbed of the advantages its terrorism has brought it. The mere fact of Angola having – despite

the Soviet influence – demonstrably turned its back on SWAPO's campaign of terrorism will also hearten peaceful politicians and gravely damage SWAPO's standing in the eyes of its supporters.

It is clear that SWAPO has recognised this danger: early in the proceedings it began a major effort to infiltrate some 800 insurgents into Owambo with orders to 'go underground' until activated. Underlying this operation is the concept that these personnel can be reactivated gradually over a long period of time, thereby maintaining a PLAN presence while SWAPO leaders seek a way around the Angola problem. In an early attempt to deal with it, a small group of insurgents entered SWA through Botswana. However, they were promptly repulsed and the Botswana authorities have shown themselves anything but keen to have such an effort repeated.

With no major infiltration route readily available, PLAN will face severe difficulties in maintaining even its recent level of operations. Its remaining hope will then lie in either Zambia or Zimbabwe allowing

operations from their territory into the eastern Caprivi – full circle to the early and ineffectual days prior to the Portuguese collapse. Neither of those countries, however, is likely to welcome this prospect. PLAN may thus find itself restricted to limited internal operations supported as best possible by evading the security forces of various neighbouring countries.

Under these circumstances, SWAPO's best option would be to enter the election process as quickly as possible to capitalise on the lingering effects of its terrorism. Once the present atmosphere of fear has left the northern regions of SWA – and particularly Owambo – and normal government services have again become practical, its influence can only begin to wane. By the same token it will be very much in the interests of the peaceful political parties to seek to delay elections for at least 12 to 18 months, while these developments take effect. An election held after such a cooling-off period would allow the parties to contest purely on the basis of their political platforms.

Above: Intelligence personnel searching the bodies of insurgents killed in a contact with an armoured car patrol.
Below: The patrol waiting for the arrival of the intelligence group.

INTERVENTION IN ANGOLA

168

The 25th of April 1974 brought an event in Lisbon which was to have far-reaching consequences in Africa – a *coup d'état* that toppled the Portuguese Government and heralded the end of some 400 years of Portuguese presence in Africa. August 1974 brought formal announcement of the decolonisation of the Portuguese African provinces of Angola, Mozambique and Portuguese Guinea, as well as Portuguese territories elsewhere. The richest and largest of these was Angola, which the Portuguese had reached in 1482 and begun to settle from 1575.

Impending independence found Angola in a rather confused state, with three major 'liberation groups' each claiming to be the most legitimate and representative: the FNLA, the MPLA and Unita. The 'People's Movement for the Liberation of Angola' – MPLA – was founded in 1956

around the Angolan Communist Party (PCA). The FNLA had its origin in the Northern Angolan People's Union founded in 1957 while Unita – The National Union for the Total Independence of Angola – was formed by Jonas Savimbi in 1966, after he had broken away from the FNLA two years earlier.

The MPLA had opened its 'military' campaign with several mainly urban attacks in February 1962. These failed miserably, costing the MPLA most of its urban cadres and forcing it to become an organisation in exile. FNLA's ancestor, UPA, began more successfully in the rural areas along the border with Zaire. By the time their campaign of terrorism had been put down in September/October, many thousands had died in what one of their own commanders, Marcos Kassanga, called 'a real fratricidal struggle.' He

added that 'A figure approaching 8000 Angolans were savagely massacred by tribalist elements of UPA.' These revolts then gradually grew into campaigns of insurgency against Portuguese rule, although they never lost the fratricidal element.

By 1974, when the Lisbon coup changed everything, the insurgencies in Angola had been all but defeated by the Portuguese; all three of the major movements were confined to relatively small parts of the territory, largely fragmented and fighting chiefly among themselves. This latter aspect naturally assumed even greater importance after the announcement of decolonisation. One of the MPLA's responses was to despatch a large contingent to the Soviet Union for training in December 1974, capitalising on its PCA background and the early links forged with the USSR. Soviet sponsorship soon proved its value. Not at all enchanted with the possibility of another movement – less devotedly Marxist/socialist – gaining the upper hand, and unconvinced of MPLA military prowess, they took the precaution of mobilising some 'fraternal assistance.'

The first Cuban troops arrived in Angola as advisers to the MPLA from April 1975; they were soon followed by arms shipments – all this while the three 'liberation' groups were ostensibly still preparing to join a united transition government to be followed by elections. By mid-1975 all pretence had ceased, and the three major insurgent groups were back at one another's throats with a vengeance. That August the MPLA Defence Minister travelled to the USSR to seek troops. He was referred to Havana, and Castro was assured that the bills would be settled by

Above: A SAAF C-130 lands at Luso airport on 11 December 1975 immediately after the town had been captured.
Previous page: South African troops leaving Angola are met at the SWA border by Defence Minister Botha.
Main picture, below: The remains of a FAPLA supply column after a South African attack.

the situation and moving to challenge this rather blatant Soviet takeover. When Western help finally did begin to flow to the other two groups, it was in dribs and drabs, never properly planned or co-ordinated. Arguably, the major problem here lay in the very effective work done by Moscow's 'useful idiots' in blocking and delaying such assistance. Then, too, the United States had not yet recovered from the trauma of a lost war – albeit by default – in Vietnam and was not about to rush into another even superficially similar situation.

Concern was not limited to the major Western Powers. South Africa, for instance, was not overjoyed at the prospect of a clearly Marxist group coming to power in Luanda – if only because of the bolstering effect this would have on the insurgency being conducted by SWAPO

Left: South African staff at work amid political graffiti in Angola in early 1976.
Below: Refugees of the Angolan fighting.

Moscow. Two hundred more Cubans arrived in Luanda on 16 August after which their arrivals accelerated, although most were flown or shipped to the Congo (Brazzaville), where they remained in transit until moved into Angola. Much additional equipment was also shipped, both directly to Luanda – by then effectively under MPLA control – and to Pointe Noire in the Congo. This Cuban force finally grew to 15,000 men by early 1976.

By now even the most sanguine Western governments could no longer conceal from themselves what was happening in Angola. There remained, however, a world of difference between recognising

in northern SWA. In fact, it had already become necessary to send troops into southern Angola (9 August 1975) in an effort to protect the Calueque and Ruacana hydro-electric and irrigation schemes; begun in co-operation with the Portuguese, these were now nearing completion. Essential to the development of the region – and particularly northern SWA – they had become a target for PLAN sabotage, and their workers also felt generally threatened by the increasing chaos around them after the departure of Portuguese troops.

Other African states, too, were gravely concerned by the course of events in soon-to-be-independent Angola. Prominent among these were the Ivory Coast, Zambia and Zaire, the latter both neigh-

Below: Unita soldier sporting an unusual line in camouflage uniforms in February 1976. The pictures appearing on his clothes are of Unita's leader, Jonas Savimbi.

bours of Angola with no delusions as to the potential consequences to them of an MPLA victory. As the only regional military power, South Africa soon found herself in the strange position of being approached by a number of normally hostile African Governments with the request that she should shoulder her responsibilities as an African power and intervene in Angola before it was too late. From March 1975 there had also been several approaches by both Jonas Savimbi and Holden Roberto (FNLA), which had been rejected. Finally, South Africa unbent sufficiently in August of that year to supply a quantity of infantry weapons to the FNLA after Roberto had undertaken to bury his differences and to co-operate with Unita. The South African involvement then began to accelerate.

Late in August South African representatives met with the FNLA and Unita in Angola and agreed to provide assistance in the form of training and advisers. Two training camps were set up in southern Angola, partially staffed with SA Army instructors. One, at Calombo south of Silva Porto, trained Unita personnel; another at Mapupa trained FNLA troops loyal to Daniel Chipenda, who had partly broken with Roberto. The FNLA elements in the north had to be content with support from Zaire and – very little – from the United States. Together, the two training camps in southern Angola were to provide a crash training programme for some 6000 troops over a six-week period. Unhappily, these measures proved woefully inadequate to balance out the support in troops and equipment that were going to the MPLA. By mid-September MPLA forces controlled virtually every centre of any importance between Luanda and the SWA border and were holding in the north.

With independence due on 11 November, it was clear that more drastic measures were needed. Accordingly, South African troops in Angola began to take a more active interest in the proceedings, moving from a purely training and advi-

Above left: Soviet-made jeep captured during Operation Savannah and pressed into South African service.
Above: FAPLA prisoners being searched by South African personnel immediately after their capture.

sory role to one of planning, handling heavy weapons and partial command. The immediate priority was to prevent further MPLA penetration of Unita/FNLA territory. Their first clash with a Cuban/MPLA force came on 5 October, when a Unita company with 14 SA advisers moved to block an MPLA advance on Nova Lisboa. Contact with the enemy was made some 7km outside Norton de Matos when the Unita force was ambushed at a bridge. Most of the Unita troops decamped under fire from light artillery, mortars, recoilless rifles and some old T-34 tanks. One of the Panhard AML-90s supplied by Zaire and manned by the advisers managed to destroy a T-34, and another was destroyed by a jeep-mounted 106mm recoilless rifle. A number of anti-tank missiles were then fired at the enemy position, which was promptly abandoned.

The second phase of what had by now become Operation Savannah was to reverse the tide and gain as much ground as possible before independence day. The Unita/FNLA forces were obviously in no position to achieve this. Thus the choice lay between active South African military participation on the one hand and – in effect – acceptance of an MPLA victory on the other. With the Angolans requesting it, several African states urging it, and the United States hinting at passive support at the least, the SA Government decided to bend for once its oft-proclaimed policy of non-interference in the internal affairs of other countries.

Even so, the intervention was to be decidedly low-key, and the force involved actually never grew much beyond 2000 men. The first combat force to be formed after this decision was Task Force Zulu, which was placed under the command of the stoutish, unassuming Colonel Koos van Heerden, who was soon to earn the nickname 'Rommel.' Flown up from Pretoria at short notice on 9 October, he was given the most cursory of briefings and the general mission of gaining as much ground as possible in western Angola before 11 November. He then went on to Cuangar to form his force and plan his operation.

Nothing daunted, van Heerden set to with a will and was ready to move on 14 October with his rather motley force. This consisted of one battalion of mostly Caprivian Bushmen under the command of the irrepressible Cmdt Delville Linford, and another of roughly 1000 FNLA troops under an Angolan, Commandante Basinha, advised by the later Officer Commanding 44 Parachute Brigade, Jan Breytenbach. The training standard of this battalion was anything but likely to inspire confidence – two companies had had one month's training courtesy of the SA Army instructors at Mapupa, the third had enjoyed all of four days of training. This problem was to become serious once the force began to come under artillery fire, as it lacked the cohesion, discipline and experience needed to weather such attention with equanimity. Supporting elements at this stage were few – some 81mm mortars and several elderly Vickers MMGs. Transport consisted mostly of Portuguese vegetable trucks.

From this somewhat shaky start, Task Force Zulu went on to establish a new record for rapid movement:

- 19 October – takes Perreira d'Eca after moving the long way around via Serpa Pinto and Artur de Pavia, having found the direct route impassable;
- 20 October – takes Rocadas in co-operation with armoured cars and a mortar group which are then attached;
- 22 October – takes Joao de Almeida after a brisk fight with MPLA forces protecting this headquarters and communications centre;
- 24 October – takes Sa de Bandeira, the MPLA administrative headquarters; more armoured cars and mortars attached;
- 28 October – takes Mocamedes, threatens to sink a Portuguese corvette if she does not leave by morning – which she does;
- 31 October – stops advance at Catengue and clears eastward to prevent a renewed MPLA attempt to move on Nova Lisboa, destroying the enemy force at Cubal in co-operation with Task Force Foxbat, which had been covering Nova Lisboa;
- 4 November – takes Benguela airport and the outlying MPLA and Cuban training camps and barracks, seizing valuable fuel in the process;

Above: FNLA badge.

- 5 November – takes Benguela;
- 7 November – takes Lobito and is joined by Foxbat, but does not require assistance; further movement is now held up pending a decision whether to withdraw prior to the 11th as originally intended or not;

Below: 5.5-inch gun in action in Angola. These elderly weapons were badly outranged by the opposing BM-21 rocket launchers.

Above: Quadruple 14.5mm anti-aircraft gun system captured by the South African forces in Angola.

- 13 November – takes Novo Redondo after heavy fighting which also brings the first fatal SA casualty of the campaign; part of the force is detached to assist Foxbat in the area of Santa Comba.

Zulu now took up a defensive position to await the outcome of political consideration. Van Heerden made it clear that any further advance would require additional forces, as he was now up against a well-dug-in enemy on the far side of a river and flooded swamps. Finally, Task Force Zulu was ordered to pull back to Novo Redondo, whence it was later ordered to Cela, and there disbanded.

During the 33 days of its advance, Task Force Zulu covered 3159km while fighting 21 skirmishes and launching 16 quick and 14 deliberate attacks. Some 210 enemy troops were killed, 96 wounded and 56 captured for the loss of 5 (1 SA) killed and 41 (20 SA) wounded.

Four other Task Forces, formed at various times during this phase of the operation, also performed well in the face of considerable difficulties. Foxbat was formed in mid-October 1975. Comprising one Unita battalion and a squadron of SA armoured cars, Foxbat moved out on 25 October to block the Cuban/MPLA advance toward Silva Porto; a Cuban general was killed in the ensuing fighting. The bulk of Foxbat then moved west, with detachments sent to Santa Comba and Cela to cover against enemy interference. Foxbat took Quibala on the 27th, co-

operated with Zulu to defeat an enemy force at Cubal on 1 November, took Norton de Matos on the 3rd, deployed east of Lobito on the 6th to block any enemy escape from Zulu's attack, moved to Cela on the 9th to link up with its detachment there, and moved on to Santa Comba on the 11th. Limited action followed in the general Santa Comba-Quibala area over the next three weeks.

North of Santa Comba, near Catofe, Foxbat then fought one of the hardest actions of the campaign around an anonymous bridge marked on the maps as 'Bridge 14.' Now reinforced to include an SA infantry company, a mortar platoon,

some engineers and a mixed battery of eight 140mm (5.5") and 87mm (25pdr) guns, Foxbat came up against a force including a Cuban infantry battalion and liberally supported by artillery elements that included several BM-21 122mm multiple rocket launchers. Fighting around the bridge itself took place between 9 and 12 December before the Cuban/MPLA force conceded the field. Fighting in the general area continued for some ten days in all. Among the equipment captured at the

Below: Despite the lavish Cuban and Soviet aid the MPLA forces also had to improvise. The photo shows an armed and armoured bulldozer knocked out near Luso in December 1975.

bridge were ten 76.2mm field guns, 22 120mm mortars and five BM-21s, one of which was salvageable. It was brought back to South Africa, where it became the pattern from which the Valkiri system was developed.

Task Force Orange was formed on 12 December from a Unita battalion reinforced by an SA armoured car squadron, an SA infantry company and some artillery elements. Its main operations were the seizure of the Salazar Bridge over the Cuanzo River north of Massende and an attack on 15 December toward Quibala to spoil a Cuban attack on Cariango. Task Force X-Ray was formed at the specific request of Jonas Savimbi to protect the Benguela railway line. It opened its operations by taking Luso (11 December) after a three-day fight. Thereafter, X-Ray split into three more or less independent combat teams which conducted clearing operations east of Bucaco – taking the Luchia River bridge, east of Lumege and south of Luso, on 14 December.

In the north, a small South African advisory team had joined Holden Roberto's FNLA force on 6 November after it became clear that he could not cope by himself and that no one else was prepared to help. Their advice – supported by that of the few Americans present – was to concentrate on consolidation and defence of the areas he already controlled. Instead, the FNLA launched an ill-planned and very poorly co-ordinated attack on

MPLA forces north of Luanda. This proved a disaster, but Roberto was not to be deterred and continued in similar vein until he had squandered all his gains and used up the bulk of his forces. From being within 30km of Luanda, the FNLA was quickly pushed back to the Zaire border. The South African advisors were extracted by the frigate SAS *President Steyn* in a tense night operation.

South Africa now found itself facing another major decision. With the northern front stabilised, and the flow of Cuban troops and Soviet weaponry into Angola

Above: Eland-90 armoured cars at Pereira d'Eca in February 1976. Pereira d'Eca was captured in October 1975.

continuing unabated, the forces deployed in Angola would have to be reinforced and provided with heavier weapons if they were to stay in the field. At the same time, the Western nations had essentially given up the cause as lost, and the former limited consensus among the African states had begun to break up, some argu-

Below: Captured Cuban BM-21 122mm rocket launcher.

ing for the retention of SA forces in Angola and others urging their early withdrawal. A measure of embarrassment entered the picture after several SA soldiers were captured and put on public display at the OAU (Organisation for African Unity) conference and elsewhere. What had been a comfortably secret operation had now acquired very unhappy implications. The final straw came when the OAU split neatly down the middle on the issue of whether or not to recognise the MPLA Government.

The South African Government knew that it could not carry the full burden of the Angolan problem alone. If the Western Powers were not willing or able to play their part, South Africa would have to pull out and leave the Angolans to their fate.

Below: One of the most difficult problems in Angola was the poor quality of the roads.

This decision taken, it was still necessary to move elements of the CF into southern Angola and to delay the discharge of National Servicemen to allow a reasonably proper hand-over to Unita and southern FNLA forces and to ensure a controlled withdrawal. The withdrawal began on 22 January 1976, reaching a line just north of the Angola-SWA border by the end of the month. This was held until the end of March, when the remaining forces withdrew into SWA. The advancing Cuban/MPLA forces finally arrived at the border on 1 April, but did not succeed in eliminating Unita, which remains a major thorn in their sides.

For the SADF, Operation Savannah was something of a mixed experience. Certainly its officers and men had performed very well indeed, but the unfinished campaign left a bitter aftertaste, reminding some of the American failure in Viet-

nam. That the failure was political rather than military and that it was, in fact, chiefly a failure on the part of other countries' politicians, was poor consolation. There was also a measure of concern that some future hostile African Government could misinterpret these events and come up with the fond belief that SA forces had been ejected by military means - a misconception that could lead to a fatal decision. Then, too, the obsessive secrecy surrounding the operation even after it had become public knowledge all over the world did serious damage to the standing and credibility of the SADF in the eyes of its nation – damage that has not yet been fully made good.

On the positive side, Savannah did provide the Army with its first taste of warfare since 1945 and the first real experience of mechanised operations in the African bush. As such, it served to highlight some deficiencies in doctrine, logistics and equipment which have since been addressed, by and large successfully. It also gave the Army as a whole the confidence that it would be up to conducting the highly mobile and flexible operations that would become necessary in a serious conflict. Finally, Savannah prevented the early destruction of Unita, which has paid off in that the MPLA Government has demanded the diversion of major PLAN elements to assist it against Unita forays, thereby easing the pressure on northern SWA. In military terms, then, the books for Operation Savannah can be said to balance with, perhaps, a small profit. Had the propaganda aspect been less ineptly handled, Savannah could very easily have been made into at least a partial political success as well.

Above: Bosbok spotter ready to take off from a base in northern SWA.
Right: Badge of the Unita movement.
Below: Soviet-made BRDM-2 APC knocked out during the fighting in the course of Operation Savannah.

ANTI-TERRORIST OPERATIONS

The early hours of 30 January 1981 marked a major change in the South African attitude toward sabotage and terrorism. Whereas previously both reaction and preventative action had been limited to security police work within the Republic, new rules would now apply as they had on the SWA/Angola border since May 1978. If neighbouring countries allowed the ANC's so-called military wing - *Umkhonte we Sizwe*, 'The Spear of the Nation' - to operate from their territory, they would have to accept the fact that the RSA would strike at the ANC establishments on their territory.

Maputo 1 – Raiders in the Suburbs

The first raid went in that morning of 30 January when a small force of specialists struck at three houses in the suburb of Matola, which the ANC was using as its planning and control HQs for operations into the Transvaal. Among other operations, the Silverton bank raid-cum-siege and the various attacks on police stations during 1980 had all been planned and run from there. Matola lies some 16km from the centre of Maputo and some 20km from the major FAM base at Boane on the main road to the RSA. Two of the three houses lay together, while the third was some five kilometers away but still within Matola.

Nothing has been released by the SADF on how the raid was executed, but the Mozambique Government has pieced together one version of how it could have been done. According to their version, a force of about 20 raiders drove from the border to Matola in a number of vehicles similar to those in use with FAM. Once arrived, they put a road block on the main Maputo-Matola road to prevent interference and then attacked the three ANC houses with machine-guns, rocket launchers, mortars and small arms before entering them and seizing what they had come for. Before this could be done, the raiders were engaged by an FAM guard detail protecting the houses, and at least

one raider was killed in the exchange of fire, his body being left on the scene.

Their task completed, the raiders are believed to have driven out of town to a landing zone where they – and their vehicles – were lifted out by helicopter. While this version may contain elements of the truth, it seems unlikely that the SAAF would risk any of its few heavy helicopters to lift out these vehicles, so some other form of extraction may have been used. Certainly suitable vehicles would be available courtesy of PLAN. Exactly how the raid was, in fact, conducted, will have to wait for future history books, although it does seem highly likely that the specialists involved were members of the Reconnaissance Commandos. This thought is strengthened by the fact that the two members of the raiding force who were killed were both PF sergeants.

Whatever the details, the raid apparently brought in a good haul of documents and must have served to disrupt the ANC's operations for some time, leaving it uncertain as to what and who had been compromised. Even more irritating for the ANC is the fact that at least two of its staff were captured in the raid and taken back to the RSA, where they remain in police hands. The SADF estimated that 30 ANC personnel had been killed in the raid, while the Mozambique Government claimed that 11 ANC members and one civilian had died. Whatever the actual figure, the message was clear: terrorist sanctuaries would no longer be tolerated in neighbouring states.

Maseru – Things that go Bump in the Night

Having served notice in January 1981 that terrorist sanctuaries in neighbouring states would no longer be tolerated, South Africa still held back for a considerable time. Finally, intelligence received during November 1982 showed a number of ANC personnel being moved into Lesotho in preparation for a major operation on 16 December. According to the available

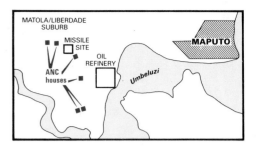

intelligence, this operation was aimed not only at the RSA but also at targets in Ciskei and Transkei. The Lesotho element of the ANC having come under strong PLO influence, the elimination of political leaders and senior officials ranked high among the priorities. When talk clearly failed to have the desired effect on the Lesotho Government, the SADF had to pre-empt *Umkhonte we Sizwe*.

This pre-emption took the form of a brief foray into the Lesotho capital of Maseru, during which no fewer than 12 houses and apartments used by ANC personnel were hit. Both planning and control headquarters and residences were targeted. The raid went in – apparently overland in vehicles – just after one o'clock in the morning, and the last of the raiding force had withdrawn by half past five. More than 30 ANC dead were left behind, and a quantity of documents was seized, along with some weapons and explosives. South African casualties were four wounded who had been evacuated by helicopter in the course of the raid. Ten Lesotho civilians were also killed, according to the Lesotho authorities, although the SADF could only account for seven: five women and two children who became inadvertent casualties of the crossfire between the raiders and those ANC personnel who attempted to make a stand.

A brief clash ensued with the Lesotho Paramilitary Force (LPF) early in the raid when elements of this force rushed to investigate the firing in the suburbs. This unhappy situation was defused by a telephone call to the LPF Operations Room, where the deputy commander,

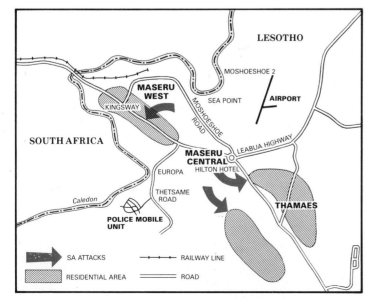

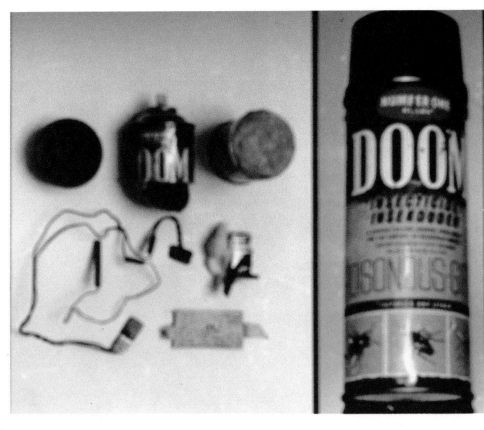

Brigadier Ramotsekana, was monitoring the situation. The nature of the SADF operation was outlined to him with a request to instruct his forces to withdraw and not interfere. After some agonised consideration, he agreed, and the raid was able to proceed unhampered. Some uncalled-for excitement came a little later in the raid when explosives stored in two of the houses under attack blew up. For the rest, the raid went off as planned.

Documents, passports, personal papers and weapons found in the houses confirmed intelligence reports concerning the targets and the personnel inside them. Among the documents was a detailed sketch plan of Bloemfontein railway station, showing possible targets and the location of holes cut in the surrounding fence. Other documents seized included a number of photos of potential targets in various parts of the Republic. A list of demolitions requirements was also found, listing detonators, timers, etc. Finally, there were many documents giving details of the ANC structure, methods and organisation within the Republic and in Transkei. Several of the identified ANC dead were persons long and well known to the security police, and some had previously served prison sentences.

Maputo 2 – Impalas over Matola

TGIF: the thought uppermost in many minds in Pretoria's Church Street just before four o'clock on Friday afternoons. Friday, 20 May 1983, was no different in that respect, as a horde of civilians, civil servants and some soldiers began their weekend routine. The difference on that Friday was that 18 of them would not see another, and many more would never be whole again. At approximately half past four a small car parked outside the Nedbank Building blew up in the best Ulster tradition, scattering pieces of itself and assorted bystanders far and wide. As justice would have it, it also killed both the men who had planted it there.

In due course, the ANC claimed credit for this masterful attack on a 'military installation.' The fact that both the SAAF HQ and the Military Intelligence offices across the street are located in civilian buildings, and that the rush-hour traffic is always largely civilian, were naturally but minor details with which liberation movements do not concern themselves. The brain immediately behind this attack was located in the so-called 'Gobuze

Bottom left: Map of the attack on Maseru.
Below: General view of the Maseru suburbs.

Above: Super Frelon being refuelled at an improvised strip during a counter-insurgency exercise in the northern Cape.

House' in the Maputo suburb, Matola. This headquarters of 'Transvaal Urban Machinery' had long since been identified by South African Intelligence, but sited as it was in the middle of an ordinary residential suburb, it had been considered too difficult a target to hit without unacceptable civilian casualties.

The Church Street bomb changed that. At approximately 0725 hours on Monday, 23 May, the Maputo tower received an ominous call:

Mike Zero One: I have an important message for you. Tell your military HQ that aircraft are conducting operations in your area. Are operating against the ANC. We have no quarrel with the Frelimo government and any interference against these aircraft will result in immediate retaliation.

Maputo Tower. Say again. Say your first call-sign.

This is Mike Zero One.

OK Mike Zero One, say again your message . . .

Some two minutes later Impala Mk IIs of the SAAF swept in over Maputo from the sea and strafed seven targets in Matola with cannon fire and rockets. In less than two minutes the aircraft were gone again; only the smoke rising from the targets remained to indicate to Maputo citizens that times had changed. Apart from a Mozambican SA-3 site which was briefly strafed in order to prevent any interference, the targets hit were:

- Gubuze House – the planning office of 'Transvaal Urban Machinery,' the ANC unit responsible for terrorism and sabotage in the urban areas of the Transvaal;
- September House – planning office of 'Transvaal Rural Machinery';
- The logistics HQ;
- A supply point;
- The command HQ, also used for giving final briefings before missions into the RSA;
- The 'main camp' – a transit camp also used for the training of low-level recruits in weaponry and explosives.

Both the Mozambique Government and the ANC reacted quickly. By the time the press were shown around, all of the targets had become extremely innocent. They now included a jam factory and a creche. Their only slip lay in the ANC statement that the houses hit were not military bases but merely 'ANC residences.' The controversy went on, with the SAAF claiming 41 ANC and 17 FAM fatal casualties and admitting that some six civilians, most of whom had been in a house next to one of the targets, had died in the raid. Maputo countered with a claim that only eight people had died – six civilians, one FAM soldier and one ANC 'refugee.' According to them, the raid was a random reprisal for the Pretoria bomb, intended merely to kill whoever happened to be around in Matola as a warning to the Mozambique Government.

This does not, however, tie in with the few available details, which tend to indicate that the strike was carefully planned, with the specific intention of minimising collateral damage and casualties. The SAAF delayed the strike until the Monday

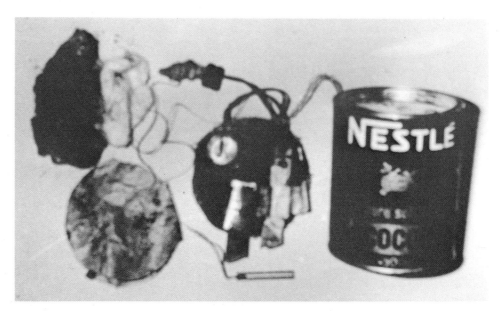

Maputo 3 – Raiders in the City

Above: Impala Mk II of 4 Squadron being readied for a sortie. The Impala squadrons have PF and CF pilots, both trained up to the same basic standard and held to be interchangeable for operations. What the CF pilots may lack in flying time they often make up in enthusiasm.

both because of unfavourable weather conditions that would have reduced its accuracy, and so that most of Matola's ordinary residents would be on their way to work or school and not in the danger area; it restricted the strike to rockets and cannon fire because bombs were felt to be too inaccurate and indiscriminate and, finally, Impalas were used because, being slower, they would be able to deliver the attack with rather greater accuracy than would Mirages. Had the raid been a mere spasmodic reaction, none of these considerations would have applied, and a force of bomb-laden aircraft would have been over Maputo on the Friday evening.

Below: House-to-house work is practiced comparatively seldom by the SA Army but may be important in counter-terrorist operations.
Below left: Captured ANC bomb equipment.

With the ANC continuing to operate out of Maputo, it was only a matter of time before the SADF struck again. The third raid came on 17 October 1983 while President Machel was touring Europe. This raid was even more audacious than the first, the objective being an ANC office suite on the fourth floor and in the penthouse of a building in downtown Maputo – only a few blocks from the FAM Headquarters, around the corner from the officers' club and not far from the official residence of President Machel. As before, the raid followed on to intensive intelligence evaluations. These had identified the offices at 370 Pereira d'Eca Street as one of the ANC's planning offices for a renewed campaign of sabotage and terrorism in the RSA; they also indicated that numerous terrorists had indeed been processed through this address in the weeks before the raid.

As is the case with the other raids, the SADF has not released any details of how the raiding party reached its objective or how it was extracted. What is known is that Maputo residents were awakened at about 3:00 AM by three loud explosions as the raiders blasted their way through the roof of the ANC offices. Four ANC staffers were injured by the blasts, as was a Mozambican civilian in an adjoining flat. The raiders seized whatever documents they had come for and were long gone before there was any effective reaction from either the ANC or the FAM.

The Mozambican/ANC reaction to this raid was the usual outrage at the 'infringement of Mozambique's territorial integrity' and at the 'brutal' attack on un-

armed 'refugees.' In this case, at least the claim was not that refugees had been slaughtered but that an open 'information office' had been the target – a public office with no military connection whatsoever. This claim was reinforced by inviting the press to tour the offices. The preliminary 'clean-up,' however, had not been quite thorough enough – one journalist picking through the mess found an official Mozambique Government document registering the arrival and presence of two ANC 'soldiers.'

The final word on this raid came from the SA Minister of Defence, who spelled out what might happen in future with commendable clarity:

Limpet mines and other bombs which explode inside South Africa do not just fall from the skies – they come here with the knowledge and co-operation of some of our neighbouring states. Let me say this: South Africa is now tired of its people being exposed to and threatened by sabotage and terror, for which the ANC then claims responsibility from some obscure office in some or other Southern African state.... South Africa has conducted this sort of operation clinically, using small task groups. I hope that in the interest of peace and stability, countries like Mozambique will take note and act accordingly. It is in the interests of the whole sub-continent.

This time the warning appears to have had its effect.

OUTLOOK FOR THE FUTURE

By mid-1984 South African defence and foreign policy appeared to be paying dividends. While the insurgency in northern SWA was continuing, and the ANC was still carrying out acts of terrorism, several peace initiatives had been launched and, despite some difficulties, were proceeding.

In the west the disengagement between Angolan and South African forces continued, despite SWAPO's unwillingness to abide by an agreement it had no part in making and despite South African doubts about Angolan willingness and ability to keep PLAN out of the agreed area once the disengagement is completed. Botswana, while not interested in a non-aggression treaty, continued to stress that she would not play host to insurgents.

In the east both Mozambique and Swaziland had signed non-aggression treaties with South Africa and both were taking steps to remove ANC insurgents from their territories. Lesotho, not keen on a formal agreement was, nevertheless, taking similar steps. Only in the north had there been no real improvement in relations, although Zimbabwe continued to deny any intention to allow insurgent operations from her territory and had been making some conciliatory noises in the economic sphere.

The root of much of this new-found willingness to talk with South Africa can be found in the exingencies of economic disaster, worsened by the harshest drought in years. This is not, however, necessarily a bad starting point. At least it

does indicate that the governments concerned have begun to accept economic realities and the economic interdependence of the region – various attempts to do without South Africa notwithstanding. Not least among their considerations is the fact that South Africa – on the spot and well aquainted with regional problems – can offer the most effective aid.

For the rest, they appear finally to have accepted that South Africa will not allow them, in effect, to fight a covert war against her by aiding insurgents. Not only has she struck at insurgent bases on their territory, she has also hinted that supporting insurgency can work both ways. The reality of this situation is simply that South Africa would almost certainly emerge the winner in any such contest. Her support at close range of insurgencies already operating with some success against the ramshackle governments of the region is likely to be rather more effective than that available to insurgents operating against her.

Peace in the region is thus dependent on the realisation that non-aggression and trade are likely to be of mutual benefit – even if they are coupled with a good measure of mutual distaste. Continuing hostility, on the other hand, is something none of the countries of the region can really afford, although South Africa could certainly outlast her neighbours. The other key factor is the willingness and ability of the governments concerned to control the insurgents that have been operating from their territories. Failure will inevitably bring South Africa back to

striking across borders to deal with her attackers and will ruin the chances of economic co-operation. The consequences would be disastrous for much of the region.

Herein may lie the proverbial rub. It is very much open to question just how much control South Africa's neighbours do in fact have over the insurgents. The problem will be particularly complex in Mozambique and Angola, both of which are plagued by insurgencies of their own. As they have not been able to deal effectively with these, the chances of their being able to prevent operations against South Africa or South-West Africa from, or at least across, their territory seem slim. This problem could become almost in-

185

superable should the ANC and SWAPO establish good working relations with Renamo and Unita respectively. Already there have been reports of an initial ANC-Renamo 'understanding,' and it is not impossible that Unita and SWAPO could settle their present differences and return to the co-operation of the days before the Portuguese collapse.

On the other side of the coin, while South Africa may be able severely to restrict the operations of the LLA by

Right: A casualty from the Joint Monitoring Commission is brought in by a joint SAAF/SAMS team after a clash with a SWAPO group.
Below: A G-5 gun, with its barrel fixed in the travelling position, on parade alongside two of the older 5.5-inch weapons.

intensive operations along the border with Lesotho, there is little she can do about the other movements. Both Unita and Renamo appear far too well established simply to fade away should whatever support South Africa may have been giving them cease. For one thing, both countries are virtually awash with weapons and munitions. For another, they also have several open and poorly controlled borders over which South Africa has no control. Finally, both also enjoy government likely to aggravate rather than ameliorate disaffection. The worsening situation in Zimbabwe is not dissimilar. What the reaction will be once it becomes clear that these movements are not merely 'the long arm of the racist regime' remains an open and important question.

Thus while South Africa can certainly hope for a period of peace in which to address her own problems, she cannot yet take it for granted. Even should the present peace efforts be truly successful, Africa has long proved itself a continent where situations can change suddenly and unexpectedly. The continuing interest of the Soviet Union alone will ensure that any potential for trouble will be thoroughly exploited. The various insurgencies, too, will do their best to undo any attempts at peaceful co-operation as nothing could suit them less, thriving as they do on chaos and dissatisfaction.

Internal security problems could arise as extremists of both left and right do their best to interfere with implementation of the new constitutional system and its

Pages 182-183: A bush track is carefully examined for signs of mining.
Below: 32 Battalion soldiers of the Joint Monitoring Commission pass a truckload of FAPLA men in southern Angola.

further development. In general, however, such activities should not be beyond the ability of the SAP to handle without recourse to military support – barring a resumption of insurgent activity across one or more borders. Blocked from infiltrating South Africa, the ANC may, however, choose to exploit its links with other terrorist groups to strike at suitable targets in Europe and elsewhere, much as the PLO did at one time.

For the SADF the situation in mid-1984 held out the prospect of reducing its manpower commitments – particularly if the South-West Africa question is finally settled – and rechanneling funds to areas of major weakness. At the same time, however, it will not be able to relax its vigilance or preparedness: the lesson of

how quickly a military situation can change was too thoroughly learned in 1976. Thus no major reduction in defence spending can be expected. What can be expected is a continuing shift of emphasis from counterinsurgency to conventional capability.

Certainly the continuing success of the Soviets in throwing their weight around the world has done nothing to persuade South Africa to do otherwise. Nor has the growth in Soviet air and sea lift capacity and the increasing numbers of heavy weapons being introduced into the region. Many of these are indeed elderly, but they are familiarising local troops with such equipment and the Soviets with the problems of operating it in this particular theatre. The speedy provision of more

modern equipment and, indeed, the insertion of a proxy force to use it, would not present the Soviets with any real difficulty.

Given that the current peace initiatives produce a workable result, the second half of the 1980s should see the SADF settle down to a period of consolidation and modernisation. The emphasis will lie specifically on enhancing its deterrent effect on those contemplating a major military operation against South Africa. The problems imposed in this regard by the arms embargo will cause South Africa to move increasingly into the international arms market, both as a dealer and as a partner in co-operative projects to develop major systems. Finally, should the difficulties in obtaining or producing the necessary weapons and systems prove

insurmountable, this may leave little choice but to reconsider the tactical nuclear option – despite the political costs which this would incur.

The Nuclear Option

There have been repeated rumours since the mid-1960s about a putative South African nuclear capability. One early argument hinged on the acquisition of Mirage IIIEs which, in French service, had a tactical nuclear capability. The IIIE was, however, also the only Mirage III variant of the period that was optimised for the ground attack and strike roles, both of which were important in the SADF context and for which aircraft were needed.

The first serious discussion of this topic came in 1977, after the Soviets claimed that South Africa was about to detonate a nuclear device at a site in the Kalahari. American satellite photos were then said to have shown a collection of sheds and a tower that looked like a test site. No such site, however, was located by the journalists who thoroughly roamed the area in question for some time thereafter, and South Africa denied that any nuclear test was envisaged. Nevertheless, doubts remained in many minds. These were heightened in 1979 when an American Vela satellite recorded a flash over the South Atlantic that was interpreted as a nuclear detonation. Again, South Africa denied that any test had been carried out, and again there was some doubt as to what had actually been recorded, as the US statements of the period conflicted.

Whatever the truth of these two incidents, there is little doubt that South Africa has the ability to develop and produce nuclear weapons if desired. Also, such weapons could be developed and produced without conducting tests. The only limitations that this would impose lie in the development of low-yield and/or particularly clean or, alternatively, enhanced radiation weapons. 'Simple' nuclear weapons would present little difficulty.

Above: A patrol calls up for orders during a police training exercise in typical bush terrain.
Left: A South African soldier takes a well-earned break at the end of the day.
Below: Policemen dismount from their still-moving vehicle and are ready to go into action immediately.

The question thus becomes one of whether South Africa has a perceived need for nuclear capability. Certainly, such capability would be irrelevant to the insurgency threat. Similarly, it would be tantamount to suicide for South Africa to adopt a strategic targeting policy aimed at the only suitable targets in the region – the capital cities of her neighbours. The only realistic use for nuclear weapons would be in the face of a major conventional assault, which might present lucrative targets for tactical warheads. Even then, however, the political costs are likely to outweigh the advantages under all but the most desperate circumstances.

Ironically, such circumstances seem likely to arise only if the SADF finds itself facing a conventional assault without having been able to obtain replacements for its ageing fleet of fighter and strike aircraft. Given the cardinal importance of air power in the southern African environment, a situation where the South African Air Force was reduced to only a few first-line aircraft could leave South Africa little choice but to take up the tactical nuclear option. The situation would not be dissimilar to that faced by NATO, which is forced to retain a first-use option largely because its conventional forces are outclassed by those of the Warsaw Pact. The difference lies in the fact that NATO has underspent its way into this unhappy situation, whereas South Africa would have been forced into it by an arms embargo initiated by her enemies and supported by her supposed friends. Tragic though such a pass would be, it would be a fitting outcome.

Given this background, what then is the present situation likely to be? The most logical assumption would seem to be that South Africa has done the basic work to allow it to produce nuclear weapons at short notice if needed. In view of the potentially very high political costs of a nuclear weapons programme, and the difficulties of concealing it with absolute certainty, however, it seems unlikely that any weapons have actually been produced. Thus South Africa could conceivably be following a course of using its undoubted ability to produce nuclear weapons, and the doubts as to whether it has done so, as a form of low-key nuclear deterrent. Certainly this would be the option offering the best results for the least cost.

Right: Angolan naval officer and his Soviet instructor.
Opposite, top: 32 Battalion soldiers of the Joint Monitoring Commission board a SAAF Puma.
Opposite, bottom: FAPLA and 32 Bn NCOs of the Monitoring Commission plan their joint movements, a sufficiently unusual event to be filmed by the media.
Below: Soviet and Angolan naval officers during the hand-over of patrol boats to the Angolan Navy.

INDEX

Page numbers in *italics* refer to illustrations

ACKNOWLEDGEMENTS

The publishers would like to thank the following agencies and individuals for supplying the illustrations used in this book.

Author's Collection: pp 6-7, 8 both, 9 bottom, 10-11 all three, 14-15 both, 16 both, 17 top, 18-19 main pic, 19 top right, 23 bottom, 25 top, 44, 61 centre right, 63 centre, 66-67 all three, 101 top, 103 top, 104 left, 107 top, 114-115, 116 bottom, 118, 119, 123 top, 127 bottom, 131 top, 142 both, 144, 146 top, 149 top, 150 bottom, 157 bottom, 159 both, 160-161, 162-163 all three, 164-165 both, 174-175 top centre, 180 top, 181 top, 184-185 centre.
Armed Forces: pp 23 left, 23 top, 39 top, 40-41 all five, 46-47 bottom, 100 top, 101 bottom, 108, 109, 116 top, 126 top, 127 top, 137 top, 169 top, 170 top right, 176-177, 179 top right, 181 bottom, 188 both.
Armscor: pp 18-19 top left, 24 bottom left, 38 bottom, 39 bottom, 42-43, 43 both, 45 both, 46 left, 107 bottom, 120-121, 122 bottom, 124-125 all three, 128, 129 both, 130 both, 131 bottom, 132-133, 133 both.
Imperial War Museum, London: pp 32-33 main pic.
Jutas (via Lt Cdr Bisset): p 77 top
Maps © Richard Natkiel: pp 12, 144, 178 both.
Maritime Museum, Cape Town (with thanks to Lt Cdr Bisset): pp 12, 30 both, 37 both, 50-51, 53 right, 55 top, 56-57 top and bottom, 74-75 all four, 76 top, 76-77, 78-79 all four, 80 both, 81 top, 86-87 bottom, 92-93.
Mediaco: pp 140 top, 140-141, 154 top, 160 top, 161 top.
Military Information bureau, SADF: pp 13 top, 31 bottom, 33 top and

bottom, 34 top, 35 centre right, 51 top, 52-53, 54 top, 55 bottom, 56 left, 94-95, 134-135, 149 bottom, 153 bottom, 155 centre, 156, 166-167, 168 left, 168-169, 169 right, 170 both left, 171 both, 172-173 all four, 174 left, 175 top right and bottom.
Navy News: pp 83 right, 86 left, 87 centre right, 88 top, 91, 92 top
Paratus: pp 17 bottom, 27, 42 left, 46-47 top, 90 both, 98, 104-105 centre, 105 top, 106 bottom, 110, 117, 146 bottom, 148-149, 151, 152 bottom, 179 bottom.
Herman Potgieter: pp 2-3, 20-21, 24 bottom right, 24-25, 28-29, 58 upper left, 59 top right, 62 top, 63 top, 64 upper, 65 top, 70-71 both, 99 both, 102 top, 111, 132 top left.
SAAF: pp 48-49, 57 top right, 60-61, 61 top, 64-65, 68-69 both, 145 bottom.
SADF: pp 1, 4-5, 9 top, 13 bottom, 34-35, 35 top, 36 both, 38 top, 52 top, 53 centre left, 54 bottom, 57 centre right, 58-59, 122 top, 123 bottom, 139, 143 top, 147 both, 182-183, 186-187 all three.
SAN: pp 72-3, 81 bottom, 82-83, 83 left, 84-85 all six, 87 top, 88-89, 89 top, 93 top.
SWAPOL: pp 96 bottom, 102 bottom, 106 top; 112, 158.
SWATF: pp 138 top, 141 top, 152 top.
Sonderling: pp 150 top, 157 top.
Steenkamp Collection: 26, 60 upper, 97, 136-137, 145 top, 154-155, 155 top, 184-185 bottom, 185 top, 189 both.
Terrorism Research Centre: pp 179 top left, 180 bottom.
Gene Travers (Via Mediaco): pp 96 top, 100 bottom, 105 bottom right, 113 bottom.
Wrottesley: pp 103 bottom, 113 top, 153 top.

LIST OF ABBREVIATIONS

ACF   Active Citizen Force
AFU   Area Force Unit
ANC   African National Congress
APC   Armoured Personnel Carrier
Armscor   Armaments Corporation of South Africa
BDF   Bophuthatswana Defence Force
CDF   Ciskei Defence Force
CIO   Central Intelligence Organisation (Rhodesia/Zimbabwe)
COIN   Counterinsurgency
CSS   Ciskei Security Service
FAC   Fast Attack Craft
FAM   Mozambique Armed Forces
FAPLA   Popular Armed Forces for the Liberation of Angola
FNLA   National Liberation Front of Angola
Fremlimo   Front for the Liberation of Mozambique
HMSAS   His Majesty's South African Ship
IFV   Infantry Fighting Vehicle
LLA   Lesotho Liberation Army
MBT   Main Battle Tank
MNR   Mozambique National Resistance
MPLA   Popular Movement for the Liberation of Angola
MRL   Multiple Rocket Launcher
NIS   National Intelligence Service
NSM   National Servicemen
OAU   Organisation of African Unity
OC   Officer Commanding
PAC   Pan-African Congress
PCA   Angolan Communist Party
PF   Permanent Force – regular army, navy, air force
PLAN   Peoples Liberation Army of Namibia
Renamo   Mozabique National Resistance
RLI   Rhodesian Light Infantry

RNVR   Royal Naval Volunteer Reserve
SAAF   South African Air Force
SADF   South African Defence Force
SAN   South African Navy
SANF   South African Naval Forces
SANS   South African Naval Service
SASDF   South African Seaward Defence Force
SAP   South African Police
SAS   South African Ship
SWA   South-West Africa
SWAPO   South-West Africa Peoples' Organisation
SWAPOL   South-West Africa Police
SWASpes   South-west Africa Specialist Unit
SWATF   South-West Africa Territory Force
TDF   Transkei Defence Force
TF   Territorial Force
UDF   Union Defence Force
Unita   Union for the Total Independence of Angola
VDF   Venda Defence Force